Critical Legal Education as a Subversive Activity

In an age when everyone aspires to teach critical thinking skills in the classroom, what does it mean to be a subversive law teacher? Who or what might a subversive law teacher seek to subvert – the authority of the law, the university, their own authority as teachers, perhaps? Are law students ripe for subversion, agents of, or impediments to, subversion? Do they learn to ask critical questions? Responding to the provocation in the classic book *Teaching as a Subversive Activity* by Postman and Weingartner, the idea that teaching could, or even should, be subversive still holds true today, and its premise is particularly relevant in the context of legal education. We therefore draw on this classic book to discuss, in the present volume, the consideration of research into legal education as lifetime learning, as creating meaning, as transformative and as developing world-changing thinking within the legal context. The volume offers research into classroom experiences and theoretical and historical interrogations of what it means to teach law subversively. Primarily aimed at legal educators and doctoral students in law planning careers as academics, its insights speak directly to tensions in higher education more broadly.

Helen Gibbon is a Senior Lecturer in the Faculty of Law & Justice at the University of New South Wales, Australia, where she is Director of the LLB Program.

Ben Golder is a Professor (and a former Associate Dean of Education) in the Faculty of Law & Justice, UNSW, Australia. He teaches subjects on legal theory, law and social theory, public law, and the politics of human rights.

Lucas Lixinski is a Professor in the Faculty of Law & Justice, UNSW, Australia.

Marina Nehme is an Associate Professor in the Faculty of Law & Justice at UNSW, Australia, and a Fellow of the UNSW Scientia Education Academy.

Prue Vines is Professor of Law in the Faculty of Law & Justice, UNSW, Australia, and an Emeritus Fellow of the UNSW Scientia Education Academy.

Emerging Legal Education

Series Editors: Paul Maharg
Osgoode Hall Law School, York University, ON, Canada,
Elizabeth Mertz
University of Wisconsin-Madison/American Bar, USA and
Meera Deo
Thomas Jefferson School of Law, San Diego, CA, USA

Emerging Legal Education is a forum for analysing the discourse of legal education and creating innovative ways of learning the law. The series focuses on research, theory and practice within legal education, drawing attention to historical, interdisciplinary and international characteristics, and is based upon imaginative and sophisticated educational thinking. The series takes a broad view of theory and practice. Series books are written for an international audience and are sensitive to the diversity of contexts in which law is taught, learned and practiced.

Other titles in this series:

Imperatives for Legal Education Research
Then, Now and Tomorrow
Edited by Ben Golder, Marina Nehme, Alex Steel and Prue Vines

Better Law for a Better World
New Approaches to Law Practice and Education
Liz Curran

Public Legal Education
The Role of Law Schools in Building a More Legally Literate Society
Richard Grimes

Clinical Legal Education
Philosophical and Theoretical Perspectives
Omar Madhloom and Hugh McFaul

Critical Legal Education as a Subversive Activity
Edited by Helen Gibbon, Ben Golder, Lucas Lixinski, Marina Nehme, and Prue Vines

For more information about this series, please visit: https://www.routledge.com/Emerging-Legal-Education/book-series/ELE

Critical Legal Education as a Subversive Activity

Edited by Helen Gibbon, Ben Golder, Lucas Lixinski, Marina Nehme, and Prue Vines

Routledge
Taylor & Francis Group
LONDON AND NEW YORK

First published 2023
by Routledge
4 Park Square, Milton Park, Abingdon, Oxon OX14 4RN

and by Routledge
605 Third Avenue, New York, NY 10158

Routledge is an imprint of the Taylor & Francis Group, an informa business

British Library Cataloguing-in-Publication Data
A catalogue record for this book is available from the British Library

ISBN: 978-1-032-00697-0 (hbk)
ISBN: 978-1-032-00698-7 (pbk)
ISBN: 978-1-003-17521-6 (ebk)

DOI: 10.4324/9781003175216

Typeset in Times New Roman
by Apex CoVantage, LLC

Contents

Figures

Tables

1 An Introduction to Subversive Legal Education

Helen Gibbon, Ben Golder, Lucas Lixinski, Marina Nehme, and Prue Vines

The volume you are holding in your hands (or perhaps have mistakenly downloaded to your device) aims to subvert legal education. It is not too late to put it back on the shelf or consign it to the recycle bin on your desktop. But perhaps you are just a little bit curious. Perhaps you think that law and legal education are antithetical to subversion and stand on the side of conservatism, the status quo, and the time-old reproduction of hierarchy. Then again, maybe the juxtaposition of subversion and legal education seems trite or just too convenient. In an age when just about everyone aspires to teach critical thinking skills in the classroom (or, at least, no university teacher would say they want to produce *uncritical* students!), what exactly might it mean today to be a *subversive* law teacher? Who or what might a subversive law teacher seek to subvert – the authority of the law, the university, their own authority as teachers, perhaps? Are law students ripe for subversion, or are they agents of, or impediments to, subversion? Perhaps there is something in this pairing, after all.

This edited volume, *Critical Legal Education as a Subversive Activity*, responds to the provocation in the classic book *Teaching as a Subversive Activity* by Neil Postman and Charles Weingartner.[1] Originally published in 1969, the idea that teaching could, or even should, be subversive still holds true today, and (as our contributors hope to show in the following pages) its premise is particularly relevant in the context of contemporary *legal* education. We therefore use this classic book to discuss, in the present volume, the consideration of research into legal education as lifetime learning, as "crap-detecting", as creating meaning, as transformative and as developing world-changing thinking within the legal context.

Critical Legal Education as a Subversive Activity draws on the proceedings of the second Legal Education Research Conference, organised at the University of New South Wales, Sydney, in late 2019. The first conference resulted in the volume *Imperatives for Legal Education Research: Then, Now and Tomorrow*, edited by Ben Golder, Marina Nehme, Alex Steel, and Prue Vines, which was published by Routledge (2019) in the Emerging Legal Education series. For this second conference, we invited papers ranging from research into classroom experiences to theoretical and historical interrogations of what it means to teach law subversively. The following questions were posed to contributors to frame their papers and undergird the present volume:

DOI: 10.4324/9781003175216-1

What does teaching subversively mean? What is the relation of subversion to transformation, critique, appropriation, and related concepts?
Can we (and should we) teach our students to be subversive? And subversive of what?
Do we aim to subvert the authority of the law, the norms of legal education, the expectations of students (about law, the future, themselves), or the university?
Can we teach black letter law subjects subversively – or is this something you can only do with legal theory or more abstract courses?
Does subversion in legal education take as a point of reference something internal or external to the law? Is subversion about the law itself or its engagement with politics, economics, or culture?
How is the project of subversion linked to existing critiques of legal education in its historical and contemporary guises? How is it linked to existing traditions of critical, radical and subversive pedagogy – and their relation to law, legal education, and critical legal thinking?
What diverse kinds of futures might the subversion (and reimagination) of legal education bring into focus?
Is the subversion of legal education a one-time only or a continuing project?

The aim of this book is not to merely do the opposite of what is currently done but to carefully consider the status quo and determine the extent to which it should be subverted. In some minds, this decision to subvert or not to subvert will amount to a search for justice. In others, it may challenge perspectives and jolt people out of complacency so that they reflect on their practices and consider and even adopt various educational frameworks.

Underlying the responses to these queries are a few key themes and tensions. One of them is the very status of legal education and some of the binaries that do not necessarily constrain legal education but help shed light on some of its basic parameters. Legal education has long been caught in the binary of being a vocational or an academic type of education, for instance. From its origins as only professional training to the need for scholarly work that better contextualises the law in its social, cultural, political, and economic context, legal educators are often left navigating between these two poles.

Likewise, and with a similar origin to the previous binary, legal education is also caught in a dichotomy between theoretical critique and analysis, on the one hand, and professional accreditation, on the other. There is a deep-seated aspiration towards promoting academic freedom to investigate and critique the role of law in shaping society. At the same time, however, legal education is bound by regulatory requirements of minimum content for accreditation of its graduates to practice law. These requirements mandate certain curricula and endorse certain expectations about what "counts as" legal education.

Technically allowing graduates to practice law is only the beginning of the role of legal education, with another theme in the book being the need to provide "graduate outcomes" that nudge graduates towards some version of "job readiness". The focus on "graduate employability" speaks directly to the idea of law as just a professional trade school and legal education as simply the imparting of a set of techniques, both of which are in many ways myopic and miss the wider point of legal education. To use a theatre metaphor, non-subversive legal education trains students to speak and emote the language of power but not to wonder what the other elements on set are doing to the way that dialogue is conveyed to the audience. Subversive education, as many of the contributions suggest, means enabling students to understand and remake the stage management rules that make up the theatre drama of law. Rather than just actors on stage speaking ancient formulas, subverted and subverting students can remake law's *mise en scène*, changing the set design, lighting arrangements and props of law. Even if they cannot change the lines of dialogue, they can transform the overall play.

All of these themes shape, in various ways, what legal education can be and what subversion can look like. Even when accepting that subversion is much-needed, boundaries are usually put in place to frame the discussion. These limits may not be all bad, at least to the extent that they force the educator to exploit, precisely, what lurks in the shadows projected by these imposing frameworks. The truth is that if subversion is taken to an extreme, legal education will stop being able to call itself "legal" education for certain governmental and professional purposes, which would do a disservice to students and educators alike. Consequently, implementing subversion in legal education may create a challenging tightrope on which educators and students need to balance themselves, and this balancing act, especially as part of a theatrical performance, needs careful consideration. It is work done expertly by the contributors to this volume.

Introducing the Chapters

This introductory chapter is followed by Chapter Two, by Prue Vines, which helps set some of the broader themes of the collection. In her chapter, "A Visceral View of Subversion in Legal Education: Teaching and Research in Unusual Domains as a Methodology", Vines challenges the current status quo of legal education on two fronts: students' learning experience and university policies.

She first starts the chapter by reflecting on the concept of subversion, which she defines as "the challenging and undermining of a conventional position, idea or institution" **(p. 12)**. In discussing subversion in the classroom, Vines emphasises the importance of developing learners as critical thinkers by nurturing students' critical thinking capacities and recognising the role that emotions play both in learning and in legal practice. She also highlights the importance of shifting the mindsets of academics to consider moving students from "mechanical learning of techniques to the meta-cognitive" development of judgment **(p. 18)**.

The chapter further discusses subversion beyond the classroom setting and in the broader context of university policy-making. On her account, overregulation currently exists at both a national and a university level, and this has promoted universities' managerialism, which can be harmful to teaching by curtailing innovation and subversion. Accordingly, Vines proposes that legal education research should study this phenomenon so as to propose initiatives that are successful in enhancing learners' experience whilst debunking the many managerialist initiatives that only have a negative impact on teaching. This approach would also help learners to develop a better understanding of legal education and to distinguish it from the hegemonic consumer paradigm currently being promoted by universities.

Vines's chapter is followed by Part I, which is composed of Chapters Three to Six and is entitled "Subverting the Legal Educator's Toolbox". Part I of the collection takes various aspects of the "traditional" repertoire of the legal educator and shows how the mechanics of subversion may be introduced, amplified, and contained in disruptively productive ways. It includes four chapters that illustrate how artwork, politics, and philosophy, "shadow networks" within broader complex systems, and alternative approaches to assessment practices can be used as tools of subversion and innovation in legal education.

In Chapter Three, "Antithesis as Subversive Legal Education: Learning Justice Through Injustice in the Artwork of Sandro Botticelli", Paolo Moro shifts us from the status quo of legal education to the European heritage. He uses the painting *Calumny*, by the Florentine Renaissance painter Sandro Botticelli (1445–1510), to demonstrate how antithesis (usually a speech form) can operate to subvert the rhetorical and reasoning processes that legal educators use. Drawing on the use of "teaching science", or "didactics", he shows how systems of rhetoric, including Socratic dialogue, may be illuminated by a shift to the visual in the form of this painting of a trial as a way of deepening learning. He does this by showing how antithesis can also operate in a visual form. *Calumny*, by showing an unjust trial (its antithesis), illuminates the just trial that is the object of legal education. The use of such material is a powerful way to use subversion for the purposes of justice.

In Chapter Four, "Subversion and Perspectivism in Teaching Property Law", Peter Burdon engages with a perennial question of law teaching: is it better to strive for objectivity and neutrality in the presentation of material to students or to present that material openly and avowedly as political and ideological? By "presenting material", we mean (as does Burdon) everything from the way in which a set of readings is constructed and course learning outcomes and assessments are articulated right through to a teacher's professed beliefs about the world (and her texts) in a classroom setting. In order to answer this question for us again, Burdon first returns to the work of the German sociologist and *inter alia* jurist Max Weber (1864–1920) and the distinctly unlawyerly German philosopher Friedrich Nietzsche (1844–1900). Whereas Weber advocates a strict compartmentalisation of a lecturer's political views from their teaching (decrying the tendency for university lecturers to assume the role of "prophet and demagogue"),[2] Nietzsche suggests the ultimate impossibility of separating politics and (even legal) knowledge, advocating a radical perspectivism. Recalling that the best teaching is performative, Burdon's chapter itself models the kind of careful presentation of both Weber's and Nietzsche's contending viewpoints that his students have doubtless come to expect in an Adelaide Law School property law classroom – before opting unashamedly for the Nietzschean viewpoint. Following Nietzsche's lead, and helpfully for those readers interested to know *how* to best introduce political material politically in a law course, the second half of Burdon's chapter illustrates the different ways in which Burdon pursues a more openly and situated political pedagogy in the context of an Australian property law course.

In Chapter Five, entitled "Valuing our Differences: For the Sake of Adaptive Law Schools", Kylie Fletcher articulates the importance of valuing differences and divergent approaches to learning and teaching law. Itself a subversive move, given the commitment of universities in general and law schools in particular (with one eye on the Priestley 11 and another on university administration) to standardisation, Fletcher presses us to think about the value of difference. The way she does this in her chapter is to make an argument for the importance of complex thinking. Initially developed in the context of the natural sciences and mathematics, Fletcher shows how complexity thinking has increasingly come to be applied to research questions in the social sciences and, in her hands, legal education. Thinking about legal education in the classroom, the university, and indeed the discipline itself as a complex adaptive system means not just valuing, as she puts it, the different inputs into this system but actively designing and leading it in ways that foster "emergence" – opening the way for the new and the innovative to "emerge". How do we design, manage, and reform contemporary law schools so as to reflect and best harness their ruptural, agonistic, and plural energies? Fletcher ultimately counsels an open, dialogic, and consultative process undergirded by principles of academic freedom in law school.

Alex Steel concludes this part's investigation into how the repertoire of the legal educator is being subverted. In Chapter Six, "Re-Thinking Assessment in Law", Steel explores how structural changes to assessment practices could provide long-needed solutions to the increasing challenges faced by legal educators from overcrowded curricula. He argues that the increased complexity of the discipline, the desire of the profession for graduates to possess more skills and capabilities than those traditionally considered necessary, downward pressure placed on law schools by universities to deliver more content in less time, and increasing academic staff workloads as competing demands are placed on teacher's time (not to mention the devastating and enduring impact on staff and students of the pandemic), could potentially be alleviated through the radical transformation of long-held assessment practices. Through his analysis of current approaches to assessment, Steel highlights various dimensions of assessment – design, environment, purpose, grading, structure, for example – that contribute to the burdens on law curricula and provides suggestions for alternative approaches. He concludes the chapter with a proposal to fundamentally disrupt established assessment practices in legal education: to adopt a more genuinely programmatic view of assessment, one that separates assessment from individual courses – the "atomistic" approach to assessment – and introduces larger "stage-based" and capstone assessment. The proposed approach also places greater emphasis on formative assessment to assess competencies and significantly less importance on ranking students against each other – a deeply subversive idea in and of itself in the competitive context of the contemporary law school.

Part II of the collection is entitled "Subverting the Higher Education Sector". This part steps away from the educator and looks at the systemic assumptions and pressures that inevitably affect educators' praxis. It includes two chapters that focus on different aspects of legal education that both have been, and continue to be, sites of resistance: (1) the shift away from face-to-face learning to online modes of learning and teaching as a result of the "massification" and "corporatisation" of the public university sector (latterly intensified under the pressures of the COVID-19 pandemic); and (2) the regulatory framework of legal education, including the "Priestley 11" which is set largely by the legal profession in Australia and determines the basic core curriculum to allow a graduate to be licensed as a practising lawyer, and is mirrored by similar accreditation models in countries all over the world.

In Chapter Seven, "Can Law Schools Provide Students With a Subversive Legal Education in an Online Learning Environment?", K.E. Powell and Nicole Siller look at subversion as a baseline that is challenged by the transformation of the university sector towards scarcer resources and more pressure to treat students as consumers. The subversive baseline is further challenged when teaching is moved to an online environment, a move that predated but was certainly accelerated by the COVID-19 pandemic. In relation to the pressure to educate online, they argue that the "current use of online learning platforms further inhibits law academics from fostering a subversive legal education through active engagement between students and educators" **(p. 169)**. Online learning, somewhat paradoxically, seems to transport (legal) education back to a place where students are passive receptacles of legal knowledge, and the participation that is so important to form critical thinking falls by the wayside in a search for managerial "efficiencies". The fault is not only universities', though, as students commit to more and more extra-curricular and extra-university activities, and their time poverty gets in the way of the breathing room necessary for critical and subversive thinking. Like James and Nakano (in Chapter Thirteen), they discuss the origins of legal education as vocational training, as a platform to query the close regulation of legal education and whether, in the online or physical teaching environments, there is much room left for subversive teaching in the way imagined by Postman and Weingartner.

In Chapter Eight, Kate Galloway, Melissa Castan and Alex Steel report on a project called: "Hacking the Priestleys". The project involved the collective "reimagination" of the core law curriculum as currently mandated by the Priestley 11 through "crowd-sourcing" law academics who were present at the UNSW Legal Education Conference, held on 27–8 November 2019, and who chose to attend the panel session. Through this facilitated workshop, the authors gathered "data" on the interested expert participants' vision of a graduate lawyer, the style of curriculum that would achieve such a graduate, and the core elements of that curriculum. Through analysis of this data, which was categorised as relating to knowledge, skills, dispositions, and pedagogy, the chapter seeks to answer important questions about legal education now and in the future: "What *is* a lawyer in the 21st century? What type of lawyer is the Priestley curriculum serving? What is the ideal law curriculum to develop the graduate lawyer of tomorrow?" The authors seek to answer these questions by subverting the power of and expectations in the model of a universal, regulated curriculum, and imagining law curricula that better serves law graduates in an age of rapid and paradigmatic social, economic, environmental, political, and technological change.

The next part of the book is Part III, entitled "Subverting Through Courses". This part includes four separate chapters demonstrating subversive teaching in practice, including approaching the teaching of law in ways that maintain a focus on the importance of a broad legal education and resist the increasing pressure to merely prepare students for the workforce through a curriculum with a strong vocational orientation. The chapters provide case studies of subversive aspects of the authors' teaching practice, including through the engagement of students as course "co-creators" and the subversion of traditional curriculum and conventional approaches in the teaching of core courses.

In Chapter Nine, "Value and Values in Higher Education: Some Reflections from the UK on the Subversive Dimensions of Historical Approaches in the Study of Law", Sarah Wilson provides reflections on her own teaching experiences in the course "Law and History" – an elective offered to final year undergraduate law students at York Law School, University of York, in the United Kingdom. She describes the nature of the course as subversive in itself since legal education in the UK, she explains, is heavily vocationally oriented and focused on practice-oriented understandings of law and corporate and commercial careers (reflecting the increasingly marketized higher education sector). Her "Law and History" course, in contrast, quite simply, is not. She sees her interdisciplinary approach to teaching law as equally subversive in this vocational environment. Drawing on the discipline of history, she encourages students to think about law in its historical context in order to understand law in the present and law in the future – each located on the same continuum of societal evolution and development. This analytical skill, she reminds us, is an important part of what it means to be a lawyer since identifying the relationship between social change and legal change goes to the heart of law reform.

In Chapter Ten, "Education for Citizenship and Social Justice: Students as Co-Creators", Kelly Toole and Peter Burdon reflect on the contemporary phenomenon of "co-creation, or partnership between students and teaching staff", which represents a "move away from teacher-centred learning toward students taking greater ownership of their learning experience" **(p. 277)**. On their account, the shift towards co-creation or teacher-student partnership can be understood and legitimated according to two quite different rationales. On the one hand, the dominant neoliberal ideology (dominant within universities as it is in wider society) thinks about student-teacher partnerships in terms of credentialism, professionally-oriented learning and consumerism, while on the other, a tradition of democratic and participatory citizenship thinks about the student-teacher partnership as a way of equipping students with a set of skills and an *ethos* that will serve them well as democratic actors in the world. Their chapter reflects on how, in the context of an elective unit on Sentencing and Criminal Justice taught at the Adelaide Law School, the principles of co-creation were embedded in the course design and teaching of the course in a way that subversively supported the goals of democratic citizenship even in the context of a university environment in which students were framed as customers and future employees.

Chapter Eleven takes us from criminal justice to property law. In their chapter, "Unlearning Real Property Law" Nicole Graham and Kate Galloway challenge the existing status quo of teaching real property law. They highlight the tendency of academics to focus on teaching real property law from a very technical aspect without putting it into context. This centring of technique means that learners would not fully appreciate the history of the law and its impact on our daily lives. Consequently, the authors highlight the importance of connecting real property with the broader curriculum and situating it within economic, environmental, political, and legal contexts. Therefore, the chapter proposes to enrich the students' learning experience by contextualising real property law and recognising the impact that colonialism, patriarchy, and anthroparchy have on the development of the law and land distribution.

Continuing the theme of politicising law school subjects, in Chapter Twelve ("The Place of Politics in Teaching International Law"), Dorothea Anthony reflects on subversion in the context of teaching international law and proposes a framework for such an exercise. Consequently, the chapter puts forward three key instances where politics can inform the teaching of international law and shape the students' learning experience. Firstly, this starts with a discussion with students of the influence of everyday politics on international laws. Secondly, the chapter then delves into the impact of imperial structure on international law and provides examples of how to incorporate this discussion in the classroom. Thirdly, the previous discussions would allow the students to delve into the politics of class structures and their impact on international law. Relying on the proposed framework may enrich the pedagogy of international law as students may have a better understanding of the interconnection between law and politics. This may also provide learners with a better understanding of how the current legal structures can entrench "everyday economic inequality and environmental degradation" (**p. 301**).

Part IV of the book, entitled "Subverting Pathways to the Profession", includes one chapter which takes us beyond the classroom and examines law students' career aspirations which, according to the authors, are narrow – a view fostered by the dominant discourses of the legal profession and reinforced by law schools through careers guides and other marketing. The chapter provides strategies for law teachers and law schools to challenge and subvert these dominant discourses and broaden graduates' appreciation of other career opportunities. In Chapter Thirteen, "Challenging BigLaw: Questioning the Dominant Discourse in Law Student Employment Aspirations", Nick James and Kana Nakano discuss the role of legal education in reinforcing power hierarchies in the legal profession. In particular, drawing from their own professional experiences and broader discourse analysis of career paths for law school graduates, they identify a binary that defines success only as being part of what they term "BigLaw", with alternative career paths being conflated under the umbrella of failure. The BigLaw pull not only warps the student experience but also affects legal education and how law schools perceive themselves. A subversive alternative, they suggest, is desperately needed: one that sees success not in the BigLaw pathway but in the pluralism of career choices. Normalizing plural career choices becomes subversive and even, one might say, should be an integral part of legal education's mission, regardless of whether law is treated as a vocational or academic discipline.

And with that, we conclude our brief survey of the chapters of this volume. It remains only for us to thank our contributors, both for their subversive performances at the Legal Education Research Conference at the University of New South Wales and for their subversive words. We hope that you, the readers, enjoy and subvert the reading of these contributions.

Notes

1 *Teaching as a Subversive Activity* (Penguin 1969).
2 Max Weber, 'Science as Vocation' in Hans Gerth and C. Wright Mills (eds), *From Max Weber: Essays in Sociology* (Oxford University Press 1946) 146.

2 A Visceral View of Subversion in Legal Education

Teaching and Research in Unusual Domains as a Methodology

Prue Vines

Subversion is often thought of as upsetting a current status quo. The current status quo in legal education research includes certain patterns of focus on doctrine, relationships with the profession, the idea of professionalism, the idea of the market (as a relatively new one in higher education) etc. The status quo changes, so subversion is a constant necessity, but in this paper, I try to look for the spaces that have not been explored in legal education research. One of these lies in the use of the emotion and the body as learning tools and, indeed, as important in relation to teaching doctrine and to researching in that area. What does it mean to consider this in this context? I argue that both teaching and research are essentially relational and the current status quo, which does not accept relationships beyond that of consumer/provider, fails to grapple with the best evidence about learning. I attempt to consider teaching as subversive activity in relation to developing the student's mind but also to consider how teaching in a university environment which considers teaching as second best to research might also be considered in relation to a university polity.

'Good learners do not need to have an absolute, final, irrevocable resolution to every problem. The sentence "I don't know" does not depress them.' – Neil Postman and Charles Weingartner, *Teaching as a Subversive Activity*.

(Penguin Books 1969) 42

I. Introduction

The theme of this book, one dear to my heart, is *Teaching as a Subversive Activity*, and, of course, it draws on Neil Postman and Charles Weingartner's book,[1] which focuses particularly on education as 'crap-detection'. They begin their book with this statement:

> This book is based on two assumptions of ours. One, it seems to us, is indisputable; the other, highly questionable. We refer to the beliefs that (a) in general, the survival of our society is threatened by an increasing number of unprecedented and, to date, insoluble problems; and (b) that

DOI: 10.4324/9781003175216-2

> something can be done to improve the situation. If you do not know which of these is indisputable and which questionable, you have just finished reading this book.[2]

This quotation shows that Postman and Weingartner did not think of education as solely about the classroom. Education is the bedrock of society, influencing and being influenced by it.

Subversion is often thought of as upsetting a current status quo. This is part of Postman and Weingartner's view of what subversion is. They then move on to give us a methodology – which to my mind, continues to be powerful – about how to do this. They call it 'crap detection'. 'Crap detection' is what they see as the centre of teaching as a subversive activity: 'We have in mind a new education that would set out to cultivate just such people – experts at "crap detecting"'.[3] And indeed, they see it as assisting with the solving of problems such as mental illness, crime, 'damaged' children and misinformation or what they term the 'credibility gap'. In these times of fake news, this latter issue is massive. What really strikes me on the first page of this book, published in 1969, is how very familiar to us the problems they regard as serious are and how little we have managed to solve these issues. They, too, were dealing with a communications revolution – largely brought about by television. Marshall McLuhan's[4] work on media had just come out, and people were thinking about communication in new and different ways.

In their book, Postman and Weingartner emphasise many approaches to education with which we are now familiar – these include student-centred learning, treating the teacher as facilitator, etc. – but we can still learn a great deal by considering their view of education. Re-reading the book is sometimes slightly shocking as when they say 'it is a "good" school, which means, to the people who call it "good", that there are few Negroes in it, that the parents of many of the children want them to go to college'[5] When they ask 'What's worth knowing?' they focus on the questions that need to be asked to find out. So this is what they mean by teaching as a subversive activity – it requires constant consideration of what is worth knowing.

In this chapter, I want to argue that the current status quo in legal education needs to be constantly subverted. What I mean by this statement may be slightly different from what one might think at first glance. I mean that there is always a status quo which is current, and that always needs to be challenged. And that challenge needs to be on two fronts – one of them is the teaching (wherever it is done – classroom, online, whatever), and the other one is the university's view of teaching. Both of these challenges need to be supported by excellence in legal education research.

After defining subversion in section II, the chapter goes on to consider how subversion could be used in the classroom, including the use of critical thinking, using relationships and emotion to subvert the thinking and then how law teachers could learn from poets. Section 4 discusses the regulation of universities and how subversion could operate within the university environment. I conclude that teaching as a subversive activity is a dynamic process which requires constant change and the discipline to see the need for it.

II. Defining Subversion

In my argument, critique is assumed. Subversion is critique in a form which is seeking to do more than check whether material is logical or rational. Part of the entry on 'subversion' in the Oxford English Dictionary[6] states:

> **Origin:** Of multiple origins. Partly a borrowing from French. Partly a borrowing from Latin. **Etymons:** French *subvercion*; Latin *subversion-*, *subversio.*
> **Etymology:** (i) Anglo-Norman *subvercion, subversioun*, Anglo-Norman and Middle French *subversion* . . .
> 1a The overturning or abolition of an established or existing practice, belief, rule, etc., or of a set of these; the transformation of a state of things; an instance of this.
>
> . . . .
>
> d The action or process of undermining the power and authority of an established system or institution, or of attempting to achieve, esp. by covert action, the weakening or removal of a government, political regime, etc. . . .
> 5 The action of turning something upside down or uprooting it from its position; the action of upsetting or overturning a thing. Later: the action of breaking up or turning over ground. Now *rare.*
> 6 orig. *Literary Criticism.* The challenging and undermining of a conventional idea, form, genre, etc., esp. by using or presenting it in a new or unorthodox way. Also: an instance of this. Cf. subvert v. 6.

For our purposes, the first and last of these definitions may be the most useful. The first is 'a. The overturning or abolition of an established or existing practice, belief, rule, etc., or of a set of these; the transformation of a state of things; an instance of this.'

The last is the literary tradition definition (above) about challenging and undermining a conventional idea.

But in the field of law, subversion may also be about the legal system. So, it may also be defined as:

> d. The action or process of undermining the power and authority of an established system or institution, or of attempting to achieve, esp. by covert action, the weakening or removal of a government, political regime, etc.

For the most part, drawing on these definitions, this chapter defines subversion as 'the challenging and undermining of a conventional position, idea or institution'. It further considers the implication of this approach in the context of legal education and legal education research; In doing so, we need to think about our goals. There are two goals I am interested in in this chapter:

1 The goal in relation to educating our students – this covers all forms of teaching, including face-to-face and online (synchronous or asynchronous). This

is, of course, what we all aspire to in developing critical thought, depth and real learning. I call this 'subversion in the classroom'.

2 My second goal is the treatment of teaching in the university environment, that is, how we think about it, how it is valued, etc., outside the classroom itself, by what we now call 'university management'. I call this 'subversion in the university'.

Any discussion of the use of teaching as a subversive activity will need to be considered in the light of these goals.[7] They themselves, of course, may become another status quo which needs to be challenged later.

III. Subversion in the Classroom

In relation to our first goal, in my view, our aim here is to (subversively) teach the ability to subvert. We do this in order to have students/practitioners who always think in a particular critical fashion that is based on a disposition to ask questions about fundamental assumptions. The goal is to support the development of the learner as a critical thinker – the 'crap detector' as Postman and Weingartner would express it.

A. Critical Thinking

Nick James has done some very useful work on this area. He sees the requirements of critical thinking as having six attributes and one disposition.[8] The first requirement is interpretation. One must interpret whatever matter one is thinking about before any further steps can be taken. The next is analysis, which involves finding the hidden aspects of the matter. This will include considering the assumptions on which it is based. Then comes evaluation, in the sense of assessing the matter. Evaluation does refer to value – when we evaluate, we are assigning value to aspects of the matter. After we have interpreted, analysed and evaluated, we come to inference – drawing conclusions about the matter. Additionally, he highlights the importance for learners to communicate these attributes to themselves and others. To this account, he adds the need to apply these skills to one's own thinking, which James calls 'self-regulation'. In his view, to successfully achieve all this, a certain disposition is required. Such a disposition is inquisitive, flexible, alert, fair-minded, diligent, persistent self-confident and so on. There are a range of ways to encourage the development of these characteristics. Some examples are highlighted below with some suggestions about method:

Analysis

Develop students' question techniques: (don't give them answers)

- 'What questions can you ask which will illuminate this item?'
- Classify the questions: Which have certain answers? Which don't? Which could be classed as moral, legal, philosophical, historical, etc., questions? Which have yes/no answers?

- Change perspectives – asking questions from different points of view or different possible persons – this is easy in law because you can start with the parties to a case.
- Using the extended 'why'? Keep asking why until the answer is 'just because'.
- Increasing students' tolerance of uncertainty by keeping them asking questions without giving them answers.

Evaluation

- Ask the student to give a mark to the judgment or the drafting (this is moving the person's perspective from deferential to assessor of the judge).
- Find the point in the case where you can tell what the outcome is going to be.
- Ask evaluator questions – How good is it? Is it valid? Is it true? Is it fair? What values are exhibited?

Encourage Inference – Teach Logic Through

- Inductive logic
- Deductive logic
- Dialectical logic
- Formal logic
- Coming to a conclusion/coming to judgment

Encourage Explanation

- Talking to others in class to explain a concept – peer-to-peer learning in these instances enhances and deepens students learning.
- Think about the audience the information is directed to and ensure that the message is clear for that audience.
- What am I communicating?
- Why am I communicating this information?
- A 3-minute thesis/1-minute debate, etc.

Encourage Playfulness

For example, creating games that students can do in teams while maintaining a playful ambience rather than a very competitive one. Playfulness itself may be surprising to students who are expecting a rigid or a particular model of teaching.

Play, surprise and learning go together. If you break class rules or habits suddenly in some way, the benefit of surprise may be yours. You could establish a pattern: for example, raise a case, ask a student for the facts, then ask a student for the issue, then ask a student for the ratio: establish the pattern over a class and then break it. Suddenly ask a question that is completely different, such as 'Why does this case matter?' The surprise makes the students pay attention and then learn.

There is evidence that the moment of surprise is a critical moment in learning,[9] partly because surprise induces attention. This means creating moments when a student has that moment of sudden insight. For example, in teaching feudal tenures, I might jump on a desk (that's a surprise) and put myself in a position which most students identify as praying. When I tell them this is the position in which the feudal oath was taken, they are surprised and learning follows. Other ways to surprise include telling students a surprising fact about a case; for example, students in torts being told that many people run out of damages (not so surprising) and then are refused access to social security. The lack of access to social security surprises most Australians, and the students never seem to forget this.

We might need to subvert this traditional intellectual space in at least some of our legal education research and law teaching. Most of these ways of developing critical attributes of thought are reasonably accessible to the legal educator, and there is education research about many of these. However, we can go further.

B. Using Relationships and Emotion to Subvert in Teaching

One technique of subversion is based on the recognition that emotion has a place in both law and learning. Descartes'[10] legacy of the split between mind and body needs to be subverted now. That split has fed the notions of objectivity, universality and neutrality, which, in my view, have their place but should not be treated as the only approach to law and reason. The familiar view has been this:

> [The individual] must restrain his emotions, so that they do not cloud his reason, and he must reduce his particularities – as a judge, for example, assumes an institutional role that distances him from personal experiences that might affect his view of the issue before him – so that he can reach a more neutral or universally valid answer.[11]

Law is only newly becoming willing to consider emotion. However, rather than reason in the form of emotionless logic being allowed to control, we are beginning to see richer forms of reason which are enriched by emotion.

Feminist scholarship has been essential in challenging this view of reason as thought-minus-emotion,[12] and it is only more recently that emotion has become (slightly) acceptable in the legal academy.[13]

Related to the increasing acceptance of emotion in law is the recognition of the body as part of teaching. This has, of course, been used by infants' teachers for centuries, but, in universities, phenomenologists have recently begun to develop an approach drawing on the body for learning.[14] We have tended to think of law and legal education as entirely cerebral, simply a matter of thought and that we can divorce this from our bodies. Of course, law operates on bodies – bodies are fundamentally part of how the legal system works, so they certainly are not irrelevant, but it turns out that using the body might alter what we think it means to teach people to 'think like a lawyer' – the danger is that 'thinking like a lawyer' can be thought of as like a pair of sunglasses which exclude many complexities of law and foster 'a subtle but insidious form of legal formalism'.[15] Using a bodily approach to learning using phenomenology includes focusing on how the body feels when thinking about a topic or doing some related activity, learning to draw on the reserves of the body when necessary for intellectual work etc. The focus is on a 'politics of subjectivity' including emotion and may include contemplative techniques to focus the mind.

We need empirical research to help us develop our ideas about how the teacher-student relationship operates to develop a critical mindset and how it can be used even in the digital classroom. Such empirical research might include a comparison of similar classes in which teachers use different techniques and determine whether this affects the level of critical thinking in the students. In recent times, we have been forced to move towards teaching online quite often; this offers another opportunity to record classes and code them for research purposes while different techniques are used.

Some feel that online classes destroy teaching. Tim Parks' mournful view that

> [T]his is the end of a culture in which learning was a collective social experience implying a certain positive hierarchy that invited both teacher and student to grow into the new relationship that every class occasions, the special dynamic that forms with each new group of students.[16]

must be rejected. The dynamic process of teaching critical thinking is not to be confined to the face-to-face classroom. It also has a place in online learning in which emotional connections are forged, albeit in different ways.

That 'special dynamic' of teaching relies on an emotional connection. We need to recognise that teaching is an emotional activity – anyone who has taught for a couple of hours will tell you they feel exhausted well beyond the physical activity involved.[17] Learning can also be tiring. The emotions involved in teaching and learning include the love of the subject matter, the relationship between students and teacher, the eliciting of surprise, which is one of the most effective ways of teaching students, and the use of felt emotions to assist analysis and evaluation. Engagement, that holy grail of education, also involves emotions:

> Consider unpacking engagement – we all talk about the need for engagement, but we usually have quite a simple vision of it – we mean cognitive engagement with the subject matter, but there is also a need for behavioural engagement and for emotional engagement. Indeed, it is likely that emotional engagement is very helpful for the development of the other forms of engagement[18]

This is not just about 'touchy-feely' stuff. This should bring us back to the idea that reason and cognition as processes involve emotion.[19] And that emotion is very often a pointer to morality or norms. Many of what we think of as negative emotions are useful indicators that something in the system is wrong: Anger at unfairness may be a touchstone for justice; fear is also a pointer. Shame is a powerful emotion which has a significant effect and use. It has not been common for law teachers to draw on these emotions, to point them out as markers, but perhaps we need to do that more often. We have tended to consider the positive emotions in the classroom as assisting with learning, e.g. liking and loving classmates/teacher/team; identification as a law student seems to be significant in keeping law students studying, for example, but having an intellectual approach to the recognition of both positive and negative emotions, while allowing them to be felt, may create an extra dimension in teaching.

We might, for example, subversively embrace the reality and truth of emotion as it exists in clients' lives in our teaching.[20] The very fact that the law resisted compensating for psychiatric harm for so long is indicative that bringing emotions into the discourse challenges it.[21] In tort, for example, we can challenge the received wisdom that people who are injured are paid sufficient compensation to make up for what has happened to them.[22] We might also use the idea of real emotions and real lives to challenge the hegemony of appellate courts in our teaching – yes, there is value in that, but the impact of the courts on the mass of people flowing through the lower courts and tribunals touches the lives and emotions of far more people than traditional law school discourse even considers.

C. *Shifting Perspective from Remedial to Preventative*

A further point which might dislocate some of our comfort with traditional law teaching is to shift to preventive law more often. In my view, this actually will arise the more we look at the emotional and physical impact of the law on our clients, particularly the emotional impact of litigation on clients who are not corporations. Most law school curricula might be classed as remedial. They involve looking at what went wrong and the payment of compensation or punishment, etc., to remedy what went wrong – that is, what happened in the courts. But a massive amount of lawyer work is transactional and should be preventive – drafting contracts, drafting trusts, drafting wills – all these are aimed at problem-solving, and it is only when they fail that the courts come into play. As a teacher of succession, I am very much of the view that good succession lawyers' clients don't need to go to court. We don't have to change our teaching completely – we just have to look at the cases we teach and ask a preventive rather than a remedial question, such as how could that contract have been drafted so that this problem would not have happened? Draft a contract that will prevent this person from ending up in court.

D. *The Law Teacher as Poet – Empathic Imagination as an Intellectual Tool*

This might seem a very strange concept. However, I suggest that it is actually an excellent, if unusual, way to think about how we might teach law. Thinking of the law teacher in terms of poetry can create the ability to go deeply into the subject matter and to get students to engage and learn in a way that supports their ability to learn with a critical eye.

I must admit I really chose this heading originally to stir people up, and when I did a lecture on the topic a couple of years ago, a few people were disgruntled about it. It does seem bizarre to talk about legal education in terms of poetry.

But what does this characterisation of the law teacher tell us about teaching as a subversive activity?

Considering the poet as a model can help us recognise the need to move students from mechanical learning of techniques to the meta-cognitive coming to judgment which looks like effortless 'art' (and the fact that they must learn the mechanical first). That is the kind of mastery that is needed. Poets and law students have to hone their craft by paying attention before they can achieve real mastery.

Poetry has many ways of ensuring that attention is paid, one of which links to our consideration of emotion. It is common for poetry to draw on emotion to create its effect, to make insight occur. Poets move beyond the obvious to develop insight or wisdom. They use emotion to help them do this, and they develop our empathic imagination. I would argue that developing an empathic imagination as an intellectual tool is profoundly important for the developing law student. What do I mean by this?[23]

Empathic imagination, in my view, is the ability to imagine the situation of another person in as rich a way as possible. To develop the skill of being able to see what the position of another person is and think through the implications of that position rationally and intellectually is very significant. This is not about feeling sorry for people but about being able to create data which can be tested by a slightly different process. It is valuable to harness the imagination in ways which will help to understand the mental processes of another person (without then making the mistake of assuming that we are them). Teaching students to use empathic imagination not as sheer emotionalism but as an intellectual tool actually requires them to ask themselves such questions as, 'if I were a person in that position, would it be reasonable to require me to do "X"? What implications would that have for my ability to consider various courses of action?'[24]

All these techniques that I am suggesting, many of which I have tried, need to be tested in good, replicable legal education research.

IV. Subversion in the University Environment

I recently had the privilege of spending six weeks at the University of Padua in Italy. This focused me on some of the differences between legal education in Italy and Australia. The history of legal education in common law has, of course, been apprenticeship until relatively recently, but in the civil law world, university study has been the pattern since the Middle Ages. The University of Padua itself is a product of subversive activity. It was set up sometime before 1222 by a group of academics and students who were protesting at the interference with their academic freedom '*libertus scholastica*' at the University of Bologna. 1222 is apparently the date of documents which show the University of Padua as already existing, so it is clearly older. Law and theology were the first subjects. Their preoccupation with academic freedom continued, and the university motto continues to be: '*Universa universis patavina libertas*' (Paduan freedom is freedom for everyone). What I am focusing on here is that it was their freedom to teach how they wanted which was the reason for the move from Bologna.[25]

While the modern university, including the University of Padua, is much more bureaucratic than the mediaeval university, the story shows how precious academic freedom is.

Australian legal education is now highly regulated.[26] There are accreditation authorities – familiar to us in the form of the 'Priestley 11' and its heirs[27] (which, in my opinion, is quite often navigated brilliantly by Australian universities to prevent this from strangling the possibilities of legal education).[28] The Committee of Australian Law Deans (CALD) in particular has navigated this well for us, so that the combination of Law Admissions Consultative Committee's (LACC) view that accreditation requirements should be administered with a light hand and CALD's use of really expert legal education authorities like Sally Kift, means that we have been well served in that respect. There are also political issues created by government in Australia, which appears to think universities are hotbeds of Marxist ideology and are not happy to fund university education. Governmental intervention has tended to focus on 'job readiness' rather than the development of critical thought.[29] Since the 1980s, there has been a proliferation of governmental bodies monitoring higher education – think of the Tertiary Education Quality and Standards Agency (TEQSA), think Higher Education Standards Framework, Education Services for Overseas Students Act 2000 and the National Code of Practice for Providers of Education and Training to Overseas Students 2018, the Australian Learning and Teaching Council etc., not to mention all the bodies monitoring legal education – think the Australian Professional Legal Education Council (APLEC), the LACC and the various accreditation standards.

However, individual universities seem to be doing some strangling all by themselves. Here is where university managerialism is damaging our teaching. As Peter Burdon has pointed out,[30] legal education research has mostly focused on within the classroom and failed to ask questions like 'Why is the student: teacher ratio expanding?' or to ask political questions about the effect of casualisation and the turning of university education into a gig economy on the learning experience of students. The danger for many of us is that the results of this managerialism in education create a level of overwork which we become complicit in and then become unable to critique. One of my favourite books which has considered this is *Whackademia!* by Richard Hil.[31] In *Whackademia*, Hil shows the many bizarre outcomes of the lack of autonomy and excessive bureaucracies existing in many universities, both in Australia and in the United Kingdom. One reaction to this is the 'slow professor' movement. Some are concerned that the 'slow professor' movement is largely the product of literature academics,[32] but their quest for quality rather than quantity, thought rather than soundbites, an emphasis on the need for reflection, seems to me to be exactly what we need.

Many critiques of the neoliberal university have been made,[33] and I am not an expert in this subject. However, I want to argue that one of the problems we have in legal, educational research is that it has not been strong enough to ward off managerialist approaches to education which focus on the student as consumer rather than as learner. I suggest that there are two prongs to this argument:

1 We need to use legal education research to show what works and what doesn't so that universities cannot continue to push what doesn't work; I have already discussed empirical work, and this is very powerful, but we also need to maintain a strong critique of the managerial climate in universities and its effect on academic freedom in teaching. Politicians and the general public, as well as other academics, should be the target of this critique.
2 We need to use legal education to teach students also what legal education is about – that is, not just to educate themselves to be lawyers but to know what legal education is and to understand that the consumer paradigm is far too thin to encompass the process of being a student in a university. The student in a university has their mind enriched, develops a process that ends in life-long learning that goes far beyond 'job readiness' or just getting a 'ticket' and develops habits of critical thought which will continue to be applied to everything that student comes in contact with.

The second of these is a goal which is not always wished for by a neo-liberal university or government. As Cownie observes,[34]

> A state which understands education as merely a commodity, primarily serving the needs of the economy by providing suitably skilled workers, clearly has a vocational focus and is likely to have little sympathy with the idea of a legal education which is primarily designed to produce independently minded critical thinkers.

The current Australian political strategy for higher education fits this picture and adds to it by only being interested in funding commercially applicable research. Acting Minister for Education and Youth (Cth) Stuart Roberts said, on 17 December 2021:

> We need universities and businesses to work together to give students access to practical work experiences and real-world technology so they can develop the skills that industry needs.[35]

Strategising against this view is a longer-term matter which may require at least one generation to achieve. But the first goal is clearly within our grasp. This requires legal education research which is strongly evidence- and theory-based, so that rationales for teaching in particular ways are strongly underpinned. Such legal education research can be used not only to work on the technical issues of what works in teaching. For example, particular forms of groupwork or online projects of a particular form might be used, but such legal education research should include the political critique about *why* we are teaching in large groups or online and not face to face or assessing only by multiple choice; or how the union movement has been so destroyed that a casualised workforce is the norm in Australian universities. These are actually vitally important questions for the future of education and of legal systems. We need to ask questions about the sustainability of systems which are dependent on growth and keep asking those questions and producing evidence about the answers.

To that end, it is worth encouraging the investigation of some of the words we know so well, such as 'efficiency'. There is nothing wrong with efficiency, but it needs to be considered in relation to a goal which may or may not be about money or solely about money. For example, the goal of legal education might be said to be to produce a thoughtful, critically thinking lawyer[36] who understands the legal system and the importance of the rule of law rather than merely to produce a person with an LLB or JD. Efficiency could mean quite different things for both those goals. For example, if we only need to produce a person with an LLB or JD, we may not need to worry at all about whether they can think critically or whether they have learned some theoretical concepts which might, in the future, help them evaluate the legal processes they come across, as the only thing that matters is that they have the form of the LLB or JD. If we wish to produce a thoughtful, critically thinking lawyer who understands the importance of the rule of law, we may insist on other matters such as that they have learned a broader range of content, including more theoretical and critical concepts.

In my view, that process – asking those questions in our legal research, asking whether words like 'efficiency', which we constantly use without interrogating their meaning, really mean what we think they do, teaching students to ask these questions, asking about the political context and so on – will mean that we have created a 'posture' or 'disposition' of critical thinking at the heart of legal education. That is, teaching and legal education (research) as a subversive activity.

V. Conclusion

In this chapter, I have tried to show that the idea of teaching as a subversive activity is a dynamic requirement in legal education which needs constant change. The 'posture' of critical thinking is fundamental to this, but it is vital to aim the critical thought at both of the two goals mentioned – the internal goal within the classroom and the external goal addressed to the general polity within which legal education and legal education research must operate. Only with these twin goals in operation will we achieve the best possible legal education for our students, and only if we base this on rigorous legal education research will we have the confidence that our approach is valid.

Notes

1 Neil Postman and Charles Weingartner, *Teaching as a Subversive Activity* (Penguin Books 1969).
2 ibid 11.

3 Postman and Weingartner (n 1) 16.
4 'The medium is the message' is the famous quote which was used as the title of the first chapter in Marshall McLuhan's book *Understanding Media: The Extensions of Man* (McGraw-Hill 1964).
5 Postman and Weingartner (n 1) 55.
6 OED Third Edition, June 2012 (most recently modified version published online December 2021).
7 Postman and Weingartner (n 1).
8 Nick James, *Critical Legal Thinking* (2nd edn, Pearson 2010) Ch 1.
9 Peter C. Holland and Michela Gallagher, 'Different Roles for Amygdala Central Nucleus and Substantia Innominate in the Surprise-Induced Enhancement of Learning' (2006) 26(14) Journal of Neuroscience 3791.
10 René Descartes translated by Michael Moriarty, *Meditations on First Philosophy: With Selections from the Objections and Replies* (OUP 2008) (first published in Latin, 1641).
11 S.H. Williams, 'Feminist Legal Epistemology' (1993) 8 Berkeley Women's Law Journal 63, 67, quoted in Emma Jones, *Emotions in the Law School* (Routledge 2020) 3.
12 See for example, Louise Antony and Charlotte Witts (eds), *A Mind of One's Own: Feminist Essays on Reason and Objectivity* (Westview Press 1993) and Sandra Harding and Merrill Hintikka (eds), *Discovering Reality: Feminist Perspectives on Epistemology, Metaphysics, Methodology and Philosophy of Science* (Reidel Publishing 1983).
13 Susan Bandes (ed), *The Passions of Law* (NYU Press 2000); Heather Conway and John Stannard, *The Emotional Dynamics of Law and Legal Discourse* (Hart Publishing 2016); Martha Nussbaum, *Upheavals of Thought: The Intelligence of Emotions* (CUP 2001). Note a 'law and emotion' stream was launched at the Socio-Legal Studies Association's 2017 conference; and see also Emma Jones, *Emotions in the Law School* (Routledge 2020).
14 See P. Morgan and D. Abrahamson, 'Cultivating the Ineffable: The Role of Contemplative Practice in Enactivist Learning' (2016) 36(3) For the Learning of Mathematics 31; C. Petitmengin, 'Towards the Source of Thoughts: The Gestural and Transmodal Dimension of Lived Experience' (2007) 14(3) Journal of Consciousness Studies 54; 'Patricia Morgan' (*Academia*) <https://unsw.academia.edu/Morgan>; see also, Prue Vines and Patricia Morgan, 'Contemplative Practice in the Law School: Breaking Barriers to Learning and Resilience' in R. Field and others (eds), *Promoting Law Student and Lawyer Wellbeing in Australia and Beyond* (Routledge 2016).
15 T. Foley and S. Tang, 'Being, Not Just Thinking Like, A Lawyer' in R Field and others (eds), *Promoting Law Student and Lawyer Wellbeing in Australia and Beyond* (Routledge 2016) 134.
16 Tim Parks, 'The Dying Art of Instruction in the Digital Classroom' *New York Review of Books* (31 July 2019).
17 I will not mention the emotions involved in marking here!
18 Vathsala Sagayadevan and Senthu Jeyaraj, 'The Role of Emotional Engagement in Lecturer-student Interaction and the Impact on Academic Outcomes of Student Achievement and Learning' (2012) 12(3) Journal of the Scholarship of Teaching and Learning 1.
19 Nussbaum (n 13).
20 Prue Vines and Arno Akkermans (eds), *Unexpected Consequences of Compensation Law* (Hart Publishing 2020).
21 P. Handford, *Tort Liability for Mental Harm* (3rd edn, Thomson Reuters 2017); D. Butler, 'Identifying the Compensable Damage in "Nervous Shock"' (1997) 5(1) Torts Law Journal 67.
22 Prue Vines, Matthew Butt and Genevieve Grant, 'When Lump Sum Compensation Runs Out: Personal Responsibility or Legal System Failure?' (2017) 39 Sydney Law Review 365.

23 Here I draw on an article on including Indigenous Issues in the Curriculum: Prue Vines, 'Putting Indigenous Issues into the Curriculum – Succession and Equity' (2012) 4 Ngiya Talk the Law 46, 52 ff.

24 'For example, consider the argument that the government owes a fiduciary duty to Aboriginal children who were removed from their parents. In *Cubillo v Commonwealth (No 2)* (2001) 112 FCR 455, it was argued that the government owed such a duty to Cubillo and Gunner. However O'Loughlin J rejected the argument that the duty of a guardian to a child should be seen as fiduciary on the basis that such a duty had traditionally been considered only to exist in relation to economic interests. But what were the interests of these children which had been impacted by the states' behaviour. If we step into the shoes of the children we find that they have suffered the loss of their connection with their families, and their connection with their land. We further find that they have lost their ability to bring actions for native title land for this reason. If we consider this logically and intellectually, we come to the conclusion that clearly economic interests of the plaintiffs have been affected. One of the interests of a ward which a guardian should protect is their economic interest. Taking students through this process teaches them the intellectual value of empathic imagination as a reasoning process. It requires real care, though, to think this through in order to avoid a form of appropriation occurring. There is a danger that the stereotypical white, middle class, law student may simply project themselves in a limited way into the position of the people concerned and fail to comprehend the whole scope of the issue for that person. This is the reason I emphasise the word 'empathy' with its element of comprehension, as opposed to 'sympathy' which is more about an emotional response. It is also the reason I emphasise that it is an intellectual tool which must be practised.': Vines, 'Putting Indigenous Issues into the Curriculum (n 23) 53.

25 'Our History' (*Università di* Padova) <http://800anniunipd.it/en/history/>.

26 Tertiary Education Quality and Standards Act 2011; Higher Education Standards Framework (Threshold Standards) 2015 (HES Framework), which requires learning outcomes be consistent with the classification in the Australian Qualifications Framework; Education Services for Overseas Students Act 2000; National Code of Practice for Providers of Education and Training to Overseas Students 2018.

27 LACC Model Admission Rules 2015; LACC Practical Legal Training: Competency Standards for Entry Level Lawyers 2015; LACC Accreditation Standards for Australian Law courses 2018; Legal Services Council Uniform Standards for PLT Courses and Providers 2015. CALD (Committee of Australian Law Deans) has also developed its own standards: *Threshold Learning Outcomes for Law* (Amended 2013).

28 See Sally Kift, 'A Virtuous Journey through the Regulation Minefield: Reflections on Two Decades of Australian Legal Education Scholarship' in B. Golder, M. Nehme, A. Steel and P. Vines (eds), *Imperatives for Legal Education Research: Then, Now and Tomorrow* (Routledge 2020).

29 Tim Moore and Janne Morton, 'The Myth of Job Readiness in Higher Education' (2017) 42(3) Studies in Higher Education 591.

30 Peter D. Burdon, 'Neoliberalism in Legal Education Research' in Golder and others (n 28).

31 Richard Hil, *Whackademia: An Insider's Account of the Troubled University* (UNSW Press 2012).

32 Maggie Berg and Barbara K Seeber, *The Slow Professor: Challenging the Culture of Speed in the Academy* (University of Toronto Press 2016). Berg and Seeber are professors of English language and literature respectively at Queen's University and Brock University (Canada).

33 See, inter alia, Margaret Thornton, *Privatising the Public University: The Case of Law* (Routledge 2011) and a range of articles by her on this topic; Jane Kelsey 'Privatizing the Universities' (1998) 25 Journal of Law and Society 51; Nickolas James,

'Power-Knowledge in Australian Legal Education: Corporatism's Reign' (2004) 126(4) Sydney Law Review 587; Raewyn Connell, *The Good University: What Universities Actually Do and Why It's Time for Radical Change* (Zed 2019).

34 F. Cownie, 'Conceptualising Stakeholders in the Law School' in F Cownie (ed), *Stakeholders in the Law School* (Hart Publishing 2010) 13.

35 The Hon Stuart Robert MP (Acting Minister for Education and Youth), 'Bringing Together Universities and Industry' (Media Release, 7 December 2021) <https://ministers.dese.gov.au/robert/bringing-together-universities-and-industry>

36 A. Bradney, *Conversations, Choices and Chances: the Liberal Law School in the 21st Century* (Hart 2003); R Brownsword, 'Law Schools for Lawyers, Citizens and People' in F. Cownie (ed), *The Law School: Global Issues, Local Questions* (Ashgate Publishing 1999).

Part I

Subverting the Legal Educator's Toolbox

3 Antithesis as Subversive Legal Education

Learning Justice Through Injustice in the Artwork of Sandro Botticelli

Paolo Moro

I. Introduction

In the contemporary era, the primary goal of legal education is to achieve a mediation between theory and practice, strengthening the relationship between knowledge and skills in order to create dynamic and active learning.

This chapter argues that the most appropriate form for developing problem-based learning in legal education is competitive dialogue, and we can probably find the origin of this way of teaching in the Socratic method or, more widely, in ancient Legal Rhetoric.

In didactics (the science of teaching), the performative use of figurative art is a part of visual Rhetoric, and it can explain a legal issue because it can subvert monologic legal education and develop an understanding of right from wrong on a different plane from the original. Antithesis represents one of the most common figures of speech used in Legal Rhetoric. It allows people to change their point of view, as is the case in trials.

In European culture, an interesting example of the rhetorical use of antithesis is *The Calumny*, in which Sandro Botticelli determines the legal value of justice through injustice, describing the structure of an unfair trial in a mythological and rhetorical perspective. The use of antithesis and other figures of speech by the Florentine painter is a founding trace of ancient visual thinking and of the contemporary legal design, which shows a subversive and critical way of thinking about law. This approach to legal education is explored in this chapter.

II. Legal Education and Legal Rhetoric

The function of didactics in law is to strengthen the relationship between knowledge and skills and increasingly to support the development of professional capabilities, enabling a student to transition to further vocational training or directly into a wide range of legal jobs.[1]

Nowadays, everyone agrees that legal education must create dynamic and active learning and cannot be limited to a simple transfer of knowledge to the learner. Teaching law means the student must be involved in the experience of problem-solving. Therefore, an informative methodology is not enough. Instead,

DOI: 10.4324/9781003175216-4

we require performative teaching, that is, an action which does things with words or manipulates them.[2]

In legal studies in particular, didactics, or the science of teaching, is not a simple communication of information. This is because taught information is not merely knowledge but an active and interactive process which extends issues, analyses questions, makes decisions, and solves problems.[3]

Performative teaching presupposes subverting the professor's monologue through the dialogic involvement of the learner. Here, the learner can resolve the controversial issue and consider it worthy of learning not only if it is understood correctly but, above all, if the learner plays an active role in determining the process of its resolution.[4]

The most appropriate form for developing problem-based learning in legal education is competitive or Socratic dialogue. The educational program of such dialogue is coherent with the development of critical thinking and the teaching of soft skills. Reflection and debates about hard cases are aimed at expanding the knowledge of the learner and improving their complex thinking.[5] Competitive dialogue and critical thinking allows the student to orient consciously as a legal professional in the different contexts of Bauman's liquid society.[6]

We can probably find the origin of this way of teaching in the Socratic version of common law methodology, whose focus is the debate of a controversial case. However, this approach is not only an empirical technique but a philosophical method; its cultural origin is in the ancient dialectic of Socrates, who applied it with legal proficiency during his trial in Athens in 399 B.C.[7]

Nevertheless, the Socratic method is the most interesting approach to globalising legal education. In fact, we can apply the philosophical standard of dialectic and its development when we use Legal Rhetoric, whose cultural heritage, at least in the Roman tradition, is in the origins of lawyers' argumentation.[8] Rhetoric is the synthesis of soft skills and is an effective way to involve law students in cooperative research and discussion communities, aided by information technologies, in order to achieve real learning by doing.

The Socratic method helps develop social interaction and builds an active learning environment in a student-centred approach, ensuring positive learning outcomes and facilitating the development of professional capabilities.[9] Rhetorical action, based on the dialectical method of Socrates, therefore becomes a critical model of globalising legal education, with the purpose of making the learners authentic world citizens of democracy.[10]

The study of liberal arts (such as Grammar, Dialectic, and Rhetoric) is typical of jurists. It was theorised by the Carthaginian lawyer Felix Martianus Capella, who, in 410 AD, published his allegorical treatise *De Nuptiis Mercurii et Philologiae* [On the Marriage of Philology and Mercury], which directed the whole of school teaching of the Middle Ages. The renaissance of Rhetoric in contemporary argumentation theory allows us to denote legal reasoning not as a normative logic but rather as a litigation methodology.[11]

Therefore, the Socratic method becomes performative didactics and moves from 'law in books' to 'law in action' when it pursues three goals: (1) the cross-disciplinary nature of every legal case; (2) the osmosis of legal theory and practice, which lets students experience controversial issues; and (3) the rhetorical study of legal reasoning and the dialectical exercise of problem-solving.

The most appropriate legal phenomenon to mediate theoretical teaching and practical training is the trial, which is both the theory and practice of dispute resolution. It is this unity which is the essence of law.

The lawyers' activities and the judges' decision-making are at the centre of every question of common and civil law systems. The adversarial model of the trial organizes the solution of the controversial case in a rhetorical way through norms, facts, and arguments, and it is formative when transmitting critical knowledge and challenging skills.

Legal clinics, moot courts, role-playing, or flipped classrooms offer clear examples of the legal procedure of dispute resolution, which is a highly formative interactive experience for every learner. Of course, these best practices promote a global student's experience, but these good tools of performative teaching in law are surely found in the background of Rhetoric. Philosophy, literature, art, music, or other humanities help law because they build the cultural fitness of a law graduate when they search for a job.

III. Legal Rhetoric, Figures of Speech, and the Visual

The cultural tradition, particularly in Italy, has handed down the idea that rhetorical style is shown mainly in the figures (which are expressive shapes) used in elocution (in Greek *léxis* and in Latin *elocutio*) to distinguish and improve the persuasiveness of speech.

These logical schemes come from the common use of natural language and are frequently found in everyday experience, but in legal discourse, they exhibit particular forms which are less seen in literary, philosophical, or historical work. In legal discourse, rhetorical figures assume specific functions in explaining the persuasive activity of lawyers who elaborate their defensive thesis in the adversarial system of trial.

Indeed, rhetorical figures constitute the thoughtful product of visual logic, which develops with specific characteristics in Legal Rhetoric. This use of images to represent concepts is aimed at increasing the persuasiveness of an argument that, having to be supported in the judicial opposition, must prove its aesthetic structure because it must be resistant to confutation in a trial hearing.[12]

In didactics, the performative use of figurative art is a part of visual Rhetoric, and it can explain a legal issue. Visualizing the experience of law is the most widely used method of representation of mental content in Eastern and Western cultures. It is (mistakenly) said that Confucius had stated: 'I hear and I forget; I see and I remember; I do and I understand'. Aristotle specifies that the orator can create brilliant expressions and 'set things before the eyes', whose meaning is 'words in action'.[13]

In Rhetoric, the term 'Topics' indicates the art of finding a repertoire of arguments, such as legal norms or judicial precedents, which lawyers and judges are called to use as premises of their discourse.[14] The etymological meaning of Topics is traceable in the spatial metaphor of 'places' (*tópoi* in Greek or *loci* in Latin), supposedly for the ease of remembering it.[15]

In Topics, we can see the symbolic representation of a concept through an image constituting the result of a discovery that aims to accentuate the persuasive force of an existing argument and is the combination of natural elements of speech.[16] Figures of speech constitute the paradigm of visual thinking, which presents a purpose that is not only meaningful but also, above all, effective because it produces quickly and intuitively a useful result, such as the persuasion of the reader or the listener.[17]

The communicative power of speech acts is an essential part of the human mind which expands into the interactive way and is certainly possible in law.[18] This form of visual Rhetoric emerges nowadays in some legal design.[19]

Through the adoption of argumentative maps and graphic analysis of texts, legal design intends to propose digital images and normative depictions of legal text based on visual language, generally with the aim of making the legislation more understandable and attractive to the recipients, as happens in Europe with the privacy protection established by the General Data Protection Regulation.[20] By extending this perspective of visual law to legal professionals, drafting of legal documents supported by digital images becomes an evident aspect of the argumentative technique of lawyers as, for example, in the composition of graphic contracts.[21]

IV. Antithesis as Subversion

Antithesis represents one of the most common figures of speech that is useful to highlight the contradictions of counterparty statements. The term *antithesis* derives from the Greek word *antíthesis*, whose meaning is 'opposite position'. It consists in the opposition of two sentences so that the thesis we want to support stands out better in their contrast. In the logical meaning, antithesis is the proposition which contradicts the thesis in an antinomy.

As opposed to the adversarial sentence, in a legal proceeding, antithesis (*contrarium* in Latin) is the juxtaposition of contrasting ideas and the manifestation of confutation. In legal style, this rhetorical figure concerns not so much the expressive form as the order (*dispositio*) of the arguments in the context and, therefore, the dialectical opposition.

Indeed, the critique subverts the thesis attacked and validates the opposite one. In fact, changing the point of view, as happens in a dialectical procedure (like a trial), by antithesis, we can subvert monologic legal education and better understand right from wrong.

In classical oratory, the usefulness of the antithesis is mainly due to the success of objections expressed in the lawsuit. According to Cicero, evidence is what brings trust (*faciat fidem*) in judicial argumentation, and it is not only the fact-checking that confirms the correctness of defence (*confirmatio*) but also and mainly the demolition of the opponent's allegations (*reprehensio* or *refutatio*).[22]

Antithesis appears in the legal discourse also as a drafting figure, and it is frequently found in the Latin *brocards*, as it happens in the expression *cuius commoda eius et incommoda* (who benefits from the advantages also has the disadvantages).

Since controversy is the root of legal experience, the real possibility of understanding the rule of law is its violation. Learning about justice means knowing about injustice, and this is the didactic reason for why students have to engage in practical training during the course of a law degree.

If 'speaking well' is 'behaving well', then the morality of Rhetoric concerns the aim of a fair trial, which imposes cooperation in the discussion of controversy. It compels all the participants to find a common point of view in the dispute through persuasive reasoning and good argumentation.

The diligence of the legal professional is not a conceptual measure, but it is in daily legal practice, where lawyers run the organised method of risk management or dispute settlement. Here, Rhetoric is an adversarial logic by which every lawyer builds a well-argued solution of the case in defence of his client.[23]

'Rhetoric has not to persuade, but to identify the means of persuasion'. It is an interesting sentence of Aristotle, who adds that Rhetoric is like medicine, whose function is not simply to make a man healthy but to put him on the road to health as much as possible. Therefore, he concludes that Rhetoric is not an exact science but a faculty to provide arguments.[24]

Based on its dialectical foundation, Rhetoric manages objections and, therefore, enables lawyers to distinguish the oppositions which arise every day in dealing with judges, clients, colleagues, and third parties. In fact, the discovery of Rhetoric appears in Greek philosophy as the most suitable form of dispute settlement because of Dialectic, which constitutes the conceptual foundation of law in action.

Dialectic has been widely rediscovered in the contemporary theory of argumentation.[25] It is an art of antilogy (or contradiction in terms) and mediation in a public debate, like a trial, and it confirms that justice is conflict[26] and, at the same time, appeasement.[27] Thus, Rhetoric is a method that allows one not only to persuade others but also to make a choice among alternative behaviours with an assumption of responsibility.

In the dialectical perspective, Rhetoric is founded on confutation; Plato says that confutation is a 'purification'[28] because the logical division (which is a difference created by the opposition) has an ethical value when it educates through debate by dropping in contradiction one who believes to know the truth.

Therefore, the most important image of law in dialectic action is the adversarial opposition between parties in the trial, saying in a rhetorical word, 'antithesis'. When we consider that law is a social practice whose nature is in the trial, we can say that the rhetorical figure of antithesis symbolises the continued subversion of law and the permanent attempt to restore an unstable balance. Consequently, it is right to state that the current *status quo* in legal education needs to be constantly subverted, challenged, and overhauled but also assessed and judged because objection and mediation are the essence of law.[29]

Antithesis is the logical form of the subversion of an established order because it shows in words the action of uprooting something or someone from its position. This overturning is very important in legal education, which includes not only the ability to interpret positive norms or to use legal precedents but, above all, the capability of disobedience, refutation, and objection. Every legal system is valid when it contains within itself the possibility of its own overcoming, as it happens in the trial when a lawyer raises a rebuttal and generates an opposition, that is, an antithesis.

A couple of persuasive applications of antithesis in legal education include the use of the case method in the mock appeal or the challenge of lawsuit debate in the flipped classroom. In this perspective, which draws on the cultural foundations of Legal Rhetoric, the argumentation of an opposite thesis necessarily takes place within the framework of a dialogue between two interlocutors: it is not a simple conversation but akin to a trial, an open and fair discussion of contrasting positions.[30]

V. The *Calumny* of Sandro Botticelli

An interesting example of rhetorical use of antithesis in European culture is Sandro Botticelli's painting dedicated to the *Calumny*, an artwork which can explain law not only textually but also visually.

Recovering the classical interpretation of the fair trial in the Renaissance, Botticelli determines the legal value of justice through injustice, describing the structure of an unfair trial in a mythological and rhetorical perspective.[31]

The *Calumny*, preserved at the Uffizi Gallery in Florence, is a tempera on panel executed between 1494 and 1497 by the famous painter Sandro Botticelli, whose real name was Alessandro Filipepi. It reproduces the lost allegorical painting of the Greek artist, Apelles of Kos (fourth century BC), previously defined in the era of the Second Sophistry (second century AD) by the ancient Greek poet, Lucian of Samosata, in a short essay about calumny, in which he explains how to defend oneself from slander.

The works of Lucian were edited in 1503 in Venice by Aldo Manuzio, the first publisher in the modern era. We can see the illustrated essay of Lucian about calumny, printed in ancient Greek. Since Apelles was unfairly convicted of a false accusation, perhaps Botticelli intended to vindicate his innocence against slander or even refer to friar Girolamo Savonarola, considered unjustly persecuted by the political and ecclesiastical powers in Florence.

Taking into account Lucian, who describes Apelle's scene from right to left, the work of Botticelli can be divided into three distinct sections:[32]

a In the first part of the picture, on the right, King Midas is the judge, sitting on the throne and considering the decision, whilst two girls (embodying Suspicion and Ignorance) whisper false words in his donkey ears. King Midas has lowered eyes and is neglecting the scene in front of him, relying on his bad counsellors. The judge tends his right arm to a man (covered with a hood) who personifies Rage and represents the prosecutor.

b An agitated group occupies the central part of the painting. The angry prosecutor squeezes the wrist of a female figure representing Calumny which, in turn, drags the slandered one by the hair. Meanwhile, two girls, who are allegories of Conspiracy and Fraud, are adorning Calumny's hair with roses and a white ribbon, images of purity and innocence. Calumny is depicted as a woman of extraordinary beauty, holding a burning torch in her left hand, whilst with her right hand, she drags the naked, slandered man before the judge.

c In the third part of the picture, on the left, an elderly woman with a black hood symbolises Repentance and averts her eyes from the scene. She turns to look at Truth, naked and motionless. The presence of Truth outside of the trial concludes the description of the main features of the judgment and it is at the same time forgotten but necessary.

Botticelli uses an ekphrastic technique, typical of the Greek culture, and rewords mythology in a modern style. The Greek word *ékphrasis* (description) is an allusion to the verbal description of the artistic image, arousing a visual experience with words.

The writer tells a story until it becomes almost visible through words. Since the end of the fifteenth century, when the ancient texts become more available, Renaissance artists have tried their hand at a sort of adaptation of the *ékphrasis* to painting. The ekphrastic reconversion, by extension, is also achieved when the artist faithfully reproduces a description from an ancient work, reconstructing the details and the compositional order on the basis of the description of the text.[33]

The great humanist Leon Battista Alberti says that also the painters must imitate the work of the ancient authors, as Botticelli indeed does in the *Calumny of Apelles*. The call of the ancient world thus becomes the typical work model of the Renaissance artist who, like Botticelli, imitates the forms of classicism to reinvent an archetype that provokes new interpretations rather than copying a prototype that imposes aseptic repetitions. The *Calumny* thus appears as the reconstruction of a lost ancient masterpiece that the Florentine painter performed for various reasons, but also, and above all, to demonstrate the excellence and modernity of the classical model.[34]

The main scene represents an unfair trial, and it allows us to understand justice through injustice in the evident figure of antithesis. The accused cannot defend himself and is dragged by the Calumny in front of a judge who looks and listens only to the accuser, who is the personification of Rage and a supporter of false accusation.

Finally, differentiating himself from the Lucian description of the Apelles painting, Botticelli draws the scenographical space of the artwork, highlighting the contrasting and dialectical relationship between the agitation of the characters who move seamlessly on the one hand and the serenity of the landscape on the other.

Like Apelles, perhaps Botticelli intended to claim his innocence in the face of a false accusation[35] or to defend the banker Antonio Segni, who was unjustly slandered and to whom the painter had donated the painting.[36] Botticelli, as mentioned above, could have even referred to Girolamo Savonarola, who was considered to be unfairly persecuted by the political and ecclesiastical powers in Florence.

Botticelli was struck by Savonarola's references to an authentic religiosity, and in the last years of the fifteenth century, he managed to modify his own expressive language. He rejected the rules of the Renaissance perspective, abandoning profane themes and precious decorations, which were in turn replaced by the creation of restless figures with broken lines and livid colours.[37]

The critical fortune of the *Calumny of Apelles* in Renaissance artistic culture is closely linked to its interpretation and reception in Italian Humanism as a scene of judgment, which originates in the similarity between the donkey ears of the man sitting on the left of the composition and the ears of King Midas. In fact, the mythical king of Phrygia, a corrupt arbiter in the contest between Apollo and Marsyas, is the prototype of the bad judge, who is opposed to the biblical King Solomon, the wise judge *par excellence*.

By this expressive and not casual choice, the painter accentuates the properly judicial value of the allegory and underlines the personification of Truth, which appears in the painting naked and isolated from all the other protagonists of the scene, turning his gaze upwards and pointing to the sky.

VI. Conclusion

The use of antithesis by Botticelli is a founding trace of ancient visual thinking and of contemporary legal design. Teaching visual law with the rhetorical figure of antithesis, Botticelli can be considered a skilled communicator and an extraordinary jurist who clarifies what the fair trial is by way of its opposition.

Therefore, the picture can be considered a frantic scene of an unfair trial, whose participants include the judge and the other two disputing parties: the accuser, who personifies Rage, and the accused, who is naked like Truth. The looming presence of various allegorical figures demonstrates the characters of judicial dispute, all of whom are female (Suspicion and Ignorance, Envy and Fraud, Slander and Repentance, and Truth). There is an unstable space in which everyone moves with intense agitation in a quiet setting.

The *Calumny* of Botticelli can be more effectively interpreted from the perspective of iconology. With this term, used by Cesare Ripa in his code of allegorical images of 1593, we intend to recall the method introduced by Erwin Panofsky in his analysis of art. According to Panofsky, the history of art is not only the history of style or technique, but it is, above all, the history of the images and symbols transmitted by the work, which is also the manifestation of a cultural context and tradition which is employed in the best teaching of law.[38]

The allegories of Botticelli's painting have a rhetorical frame, alluding to psychological causes (Suspicion, Ignorance, Rage, Envy, Fraud) of every unjust judgment (Calumny) and the reasons to remedy them (Repentance and Truth). With this rhetorical frame, an observer of the painting can discern injustice and understand justice in the due process of law.

In order to understand the implied subversive meaning of Botticelli's masterpiece, it is interesting to notice that the accused has no defender because a lawyer in the king's court is not permitted. Hence, the visual use of antithesis by Botticelli is a subversion of injustice which makes possible the achievement of the dual task of every lawyer. It suggests the importance of protection of freedom from the arbitrariness of power and opens the ethical way for the appearance of truth as fairness in the trial.

Notes

1 Rebecca Geoghegan Gladwin and Christina Thompson, 'Responding to the Pandemic: Technological and Ethical Implications of Covid-19 on Legal Education' (2021) 3(1) *JELT* 1.
2 J. L. Austin, *How to Do Things with Words* (Clarendon Press 1962).
3 Molly T. O' Brien, 'An Active Learning Smorgasbord for Teaching Evidence' (2011) 4(1/2) JALTA 31.
4 Neil Postman and Charles Weingartner, *Teaching as a Subversive Activity* (Penguin Books 1969).
5 Edgar Morin, *Introduction à la pensée complexe* [Introduction to Complex Thinking] (Le Seuil 1990).
6 Zygmunt Bauman, *Liquid Modernity* (Polity Press 2000).
7 Paolo Moro, *Socrate avvocato. Introduzione all'«Apologia di Socrate» di Platone* [Socrates's Lawyer: Introduction to Plato's 'Apology of Socrates'] (Libreria Al Segno Editrice 2018).
8 Michael H. Frost, *Introduction to Classical Legal Rhetoric: A Lost Heritage* (Ashgate 2005).
9 Myunghee Kang and Tami Im, 'Factors of Learner–Instructor Interaction Which Predict Perceived Learning Outcomes in Online Learning Environment' (2013) 29(3) JCAL 292.
10 Martha Nussbaum, *Not for Profit: Why Democracy Needs the Humanities* (Princeton University Press 2010).
11 Chaïm Perelman and Lucie Olbrechts-Tyteca, *Traité de l'argumentation. La Nouvelle Rhétorique* [The New Rhetoric: A Treatise on Argumentation] (Presses Universitaires de France 1958).

12 Paolo Moro, 'Figures of Speech and Legal Style. The Visual Shape of Law' (2020) 1 TCRS 131.
13 Aristotle, *Ars Rhetorica* (W. D. Ross ed, Clarendon Press 1959) 1411b.
14 J. M. Balkin, 'A Night in the Topics: The Reason of Legal Rhetoric and the Rhetoric of Legal Reason' in Peter Brooks and Paul Gewirtz (eds), *Law's Stories: Narrative and Rhetoric in the Law* (Yale University Press 1996).
15 Frances Yates, *The Art of Memory* (Routledge & Kegan Paul 1966).
16 Roland Barthes, 'L'ancienne rhétorique' [Ancient Rhetoric] (1970) 16 Communications 172.
17 Rudolf Arnheim, *Visual Thinking* (University of California Press 1969).
18 Patrick Maynard, *Drawing Distinctions: The Varieties of Graphic Expression* (Cornell University Press 2005).
19 Margaret Hagan, 'Participatory Design for Innovation in Access to Justice' (2019) 148 Daedalus 120.
20 Monica Palmirani, Arianna Rossi, Michele Martoni and Margaret Hagan, 'A Methodological Framework to Design a Machine-Readable Privacy Icon Set' in Erich Schweighofer (ed), *Data Protection/LegalTech Proceedings of the 21st International Legal Informatics Symposium IRIS* (Editions Weblaw 2018).
21 Stefania Passera and Helena Haapio, 'Transforming Contracts from Legal Rules to User-Centered Communication Tool: A Human-Information Interaction Challenge' [2013] CDQ 38.
22 Cicero, *Partitiones oratoriae* [Oratorical Partitions] in *Qual e il miglior oratore; Le suddivisioni dell'arte oratoria; I topici* [The Best Kind of Orator; The Subdivisions of the Oratory Art; Topics] (G. Galeazzo Tissoni ed, Mondadori 1973) 90ss.
23 Paolo Moro, *L'arte della scrittura giuridica. Retorica e testo difensivo* [The Art of Legal Writing: Rhetoric and Defensive Text] (Libreria Al Segno Editrice 2016).
24 Aristotle, *The Works of Aristotle: Ars Rhetorica* (W. D. Ross ed, Oxford University Press 1912) 1356a.
25 Stephen E. Toulmin, *The Uses of Argument* (Cambridge University Press 1958); H. P. Grice, 'Logic and Conversation' in Donald Davidson and Gilbert Harman (eds), *The Logic of Grammar* (Dickenson 1975); Robert Alexy, *Theorie der juristischen Argumentation* [Theory of Legal Argumentation] (Suhrkamp Verlag 1978); Paul Lorenzen, *Dialogische Logik* [Dialogical Logic] (Wissenschaftliche Buchgesellschaft 1978); Frans H. van Eemeren and Rob Grootendorst, *Argumentation, Communication, and Fallacies: A Pragma-Dialectical Perspective* (Erlbaum 1992); Douglas N. Walton and Erik C. W. Krabbe, *Commitment in Dialogue: Basic Concepts of Interpersonal Reasoning* (State University of New York Press 1995); Henry Prakken, *Logical Tools for Modelling Legal Arguments* (Kluwer 1997).
26 Stuart Hampshire, *Justice is Conflict* (Duckworth 1999).
27 Paolo Moro, 'Il diritto come processo. Una prospettiva critica per il giurista contemporaneo' [Law as Process: A Critical Perspective for the Contemporary Jurist] in Paolo Moro (ed), *Il diritto come processo. Princìpi, regole e brocardi per la formazione critica del giurista* [Law as Process: Principles, Rules, and Brocard for the Critical Training of the Jurist] (FrancoAngeli 2012).
28 Plato, 'Sophist' in John Burnet (ed), *Platonis Opera* (Oxford University Press 1903).
29 Prue Vines, 'A Visceral View of Subversion in Legal Education – Teaching and Research in Unusual Domains as a Methodology' (Legal Education Research Conference, Sydney, November 2019).
30 Paolo Moro, 'Rhetoric and Fair Play: The Cultural Background of Legal Ethics' (2017) 2(14) US-China Law Review 72.
31 Paolo Moro, 'Forme del processo e figure della verità. Interpretazione retorica del dipinto *La Calunnia* di Sandro Botticelli' [Forms of Process and Figures of Truth: Rhetorical Interpretation of Sandro Botticelli's Painting *La Calunnia*] (2014) 7 ISLL <https://

www.lawandliterature.org/area/papers/Moro%20Vol.%207%202014.pdf> accessed 10 October 2021.

32 Guido Cornini, 'Botticelli' in *Art e Dossier* [Art and Dossier] (Giunti 1990) 49.

33 Jean-Michel Massing, *Du texte à l'image. La Calomnie d'Apelle et son iconographie* [From Text to Image: The Calumny of Apelles and Its Iconography] (Presses Universitaires 1990).

34 Andre Chastel, *Botticelli* (Plon 1957).

35 Ronald Lightbown, *Botticelli: Life and Work* (□Abbeville Press 1989).

36 Giorgio Vasari, *Vite de'più eccellenti architetti, pittori, et scultori italiani* [The Lives of the Most Excellent Painters, Sculptors, and Architects] (first published 1550, Lorenzo Torrentino 1568).

37 Giulio Carlo Argan, *Botticelli. Étude biographique et critique* [Botticelli: Biographical and Critical Study] (Skira 1957).

38 Erwin Panofsky, *Studies in Iconology: Humanistic Themes in the Art of the Renaissance* (Oxford University Press 1939).

4 Subversion and Perspectivism in Teaching Property Law

Peter D. Burdon

When I first became a university teacher, a good friend of mine handed me a small pile of books. The bundle contained *Teaching Community* by bell hooks,[1] *Becoming a Critically Reflective Teacher* by Stephen Brookfield[2] and *Teaching as a Subversive Activity* by Neil Postman and Charles Weingartner.[3] Each of these books was formative to my development as a teacher, but I was particularly struck by the way Postman and Weingartner presented teachers as having an active role in improving society and contributing to the common good. The ambition of the book leapt from the page – it was written because the authors shared a belief 'in the improvability of the human condition through education (1971, 2).'[4]

Not everything about *Teaching as a Subversive Activity* has aged well. Most notably, the authors reinforce outdated gender stereotypes,[5] and their analysis lacks a coherent theory of change. The project is idealistic in that it assumes that the power of their progressive ideas will be sufficient to bring about the change they desire. And yet, even with these flaws, the book felt like a revelation in comparison to the legal education that I had received as a student. With some notable exceptions, the dominant model of legal education sought to divide the law into discrete units and treat each topic through the lens of legal science.[6] In striving for objectivity, my teachers removed themselves (their biography and beliefs) from the classroom. We did not explore the ideological or theoretical underpinnings of the subject, and the law was handed down fully formed, like Athena emerging from the head of Zeus.[7]

Postman and Weingartner would describe this as 'information delivery' rather than teaching.[8] They argue that the latter ought to be bent towards inquiry and empower students to take ownership over their learning.[9] A pedagogy grounded in these principles requires something of a teacher – they must place themselves into the production of knowledge and model critical inquiry for students.[10] As the authors note: 'teaching is what a teacher does.'[11] And the primary skill that teachers must model for students is to develop an 'anthropological perspective.'[12] As the authors explain:

> This perspective allows one to be part of his own culture and, at the same time, to be out of it. One views the activities of his own group as would an

DOI: 10.4324/9781003175216-5

anthropologist, observing its tribal rituals its fears, its conceits, its ethnocentrism. In this way, one is able to recognize when reality begins to drift too far away from the grasp of the tribe.[13]

Connected to the anthropological perspective is the idea of 'crap detecting.' In my reading, crap detecting shares similarities to critical thinking, but it also has a constructive element. It is the ability to identify the values or ideology that underpin a fact and the constructive mindset to correct the record or call out falsehoods. For Postman and Weingartner, teachers have a responsibility to model this kind of behaviour and cultivate it in their students. This is indispensable for the production of knowledge and also connects to the role of universities as sites of training for democratic citizenship.[14] As the authors note, democratic societies can only be renewed if citizens have the 'motivation and courage to sound alarms.'[15]

Because of their direct connection to politics, I think it is relatively simple for law academics to engage Postman and Weingartner. While some colleagues hold onto the ideal of objectivity, I don't think it is controversial to say that 'law is politics,' and many of us promote critical thinking (or crap detecting) in our classrooms. However, reasonable people will disagree about where to draw the line on questions such as: *Is it appropriate for the teacher to share their values and political analysis in the classroom? Should politics, values and ideology be discussed in the law curriculum? And should a classroom be a site for knowledge production and meaning-making?*

In response to these questions, Postman and Weingartner give us conclusions but not the reasoning that supports their argument. For this reason, I put their text into conversation with two different scholars who addressed similar problems in the 19th and 20th centuries.[16] The sociologist, Max Weber, stands for the proposition that politics and the perspective of the teacher have no place in the classroom. In fact, the introduction of either of these forces does violence to the production of knowledge. Against this reading, I position Friedrich Nietzsche as the first critical exponent of perspectivism. Consistent with Postman and Weingartner, Nietzsche argued against the pretence of objectivity and argued that attempts to remove the subjectivity of the knower was a different kind of violence – what he calls the 'castration of the intellect.'[17]

Ultimately, I conclude that Nietzsche has the better argument. In the final part of the chapter, I describe how I use Nietzsche's epistemology in teaching property law. While it is possible to cover the Priestley 11 material in property law through the doctrinal method, that approach would miss an opportunity to explore topics such as the meaning and content of property, First Nations land law, justifications for private property, the relationship between the Torrens System and the market, the ethics of charging interest in a mortgage, and much more. Including these topics and aligning the content with assessment and course learning outcomes[18] provides clear opportunities for teachers and students to engage in a set of meaning-making practices which aim to understand the contingent nature of law and what its future might look like.

I. Objectivity in the Classroom

The conversation about objectivity and knowledge dates back to the ancient Greeks. For our purpose, there is no need to provide a historical sketch. Instead, I focus on two influential thinkers who explicitly addressed the issue of objectivity– Max Weber and Friedrich Nietzsche. Before presenting their opinions, I will first provide a very brief biographical sketch of each thinker. The primary reason for this is so that I am consistent with my ultimate argument – that the production of knowledge is not pure but situated and embodied. A person's biography, in other words, is relevant to how they apprehended the world and the kinds of knowledge they produced.[19]

Max Weber was born in Germany in 1864. His father was a politician, his mother a religious liberal who ministered to the poor. At the time when Weber studied law, the degree had a very strong sociological emphasis that included history and economics. These were the topics that sustained him, and he only practised briefly as a lawyer. After leaving the profession, he studied on his own before becoming a professor of economics in 1894. Weber had a hard time holding down a teaching job and was forced to leave his post at the University of Heidelberg in 1899 after a nervous breakdown.[20] However, this did not stop him from cultivating a different part of his character which he described to friends as a 'secret love' for politics.[21] To this end, Weber made frequent attempts to 'stand for office, form a party, negotiate a treaty, and write a constitution.'[22]

Weber put these identities – the professor and the politician – into tension during his final two lectures delivered in 1917. The date, of course, is important. Weber was writing against the backdrop of Germany's defeat in the First World War and a political class which he derided for their inability to think critically:[23] 'The familiar structure of bureaucratic paternalism' he wrote, had shaped the German people to act 'as objects, not agents.'[24] Weber lay the blame for this directly at the feet of German higher education and outlined a litany of problems that he believed gave rise to thoughtlessness: Using numbers as a 'measure of success' while ignoring 'unquantifiable' standards such as quality and the 'mediocrities in leading university positions.'[25]

This all sounds oddly contemporary but what interests me here is Weber's response. Rather than upholding Wilhelm von Humboldt's description of the university as the 'pinnacle' of moral culture, Weber offered no program for reform. Instead, he affirmed the value of specialised research over moral instruction and criticised professors who posed as prophets.[26] Weber's justification for this approach is complex and distinct from contemporary debates about this topic. To appreciate his meaning, we first need to draw a distinction between the realm of politics and the realm of knowledge (or science).[27]

For Weber, politics and knowledge are two ideal forms whose essences are fundamentally distinct. He recognises that knowledge can contribute to politics (power). In fact, his strongest argument on behalf of science is that it can enhance political power by helping an individual achieve a particular goal – think Machiavelli's book *The Prince*.[28] Weber's point is rather that power has no place whatever in inquiry or knowledge production. Power, for Weber, contaminates science and diminishes the pursuit of truth. Weber makes this point as follows:

> When speaking in a political meeting about democracy, one does not hide one's personal standpoint; indeed, to come out clearly and take a stand is one's damned duty. The words one uses in such a meeting are not means of scientific analysis but means of canvassing votes and winning over others. They are not plowshares to loosen the soil of contemplative thought; they are swords against the enemies such words are weapons.[29]

In these sentences, Weber draws a distinction between words that are power-free[30] ('ploughshares to contemplative thought') and words that have political effect ('swords against the enemies' words'). In this formation, knowledge and science are value-free and detached from power. The search for truth requires this separation because power anywhere near the domain of knowledge will kill objectivity. Politics, by contrast, is value-laden and bent on the forge of power. It makes no pretence to objectivity and is instrumental to the core. This analysis tracks closely to Weber's broader conception of 'instrumentally rational action.'[31] This is behaviour that is shaped by the most efficient way to achieve a goal. Today we might think about this as being purely calculating and without fixed values.

With this distinction in mind, Weber argues that it would be an 'outrage' to bring politics into the classroom.[32] This is for two reasons. First, when professors inject their own politics into the classroom, they exploit the vulnerability of students who are less capable of mounting a counter-argument and who are dependent on the teacher for their grades. Weber notes: 'I deem it irresponsible to exploit the circumstance that for the sake of their career the students have to attend a teacher's course while there is nobody present to oppose him with criticism.'[33] He goes further and suggests that politics in the classroom is violent. It literally violates the classroom with the weapons of politics. As he puts it: 'The prophet and the demagogue do not belong on the academic platform.'[34]

Thus, for Weber, politics must be excised absolutely from the classroom. Teachers need the 'intellectual integrity' to limit themselves to facts, theories, and texts that will, on the one hand, bring the world to students and, on the other, loosen students' attachments and convictions by giving them some alternative perspectives and texts. Today we might express this ideal in terms of teaching critical thinking. Weber notes:

> The primary task of a useful teacher is to teach his students to recognize 'inconvenient' facts – I mean facts that are inconvenient for their party opinions . . . I believe the teacher accomplishes more than a mere intellectual task if he compels his audience to accustom itself to the existence of such facts.[35]

I think there is something really compelling about this view. Weber is insisting on a space of knowledge and thought that is independent from coercion and bids for power. He is calling for a space of inquiry, a domain for thoughtfulness and discovery that is the opposite of organising, polemicizing and mobilizing people – which is what you do in political life. In this, Weber is trying to protect not only science but the pedagogic field from a certain kind of denigration and exploitation. He is also trying to make the classroom a space where students can clarify and test their values, where they can greet what he calls 'inconvenient facts'.[36] He wants students to see the implications of the positions they hold and get a hold of the meaning of their conduct.

In one sense, this argument is consistent with that put forward by Postman and Weingartner. In fact, while I doubt Weber would appreciate the language, their insistence on crap detecting is serving a similar purpose. But there is also an important difference – Weber's insistence on the purity of knowledge-generation excludes the possibility that the classroom can be a space for meaning-making or generating values. It can only be a space for producing and acquiring an objective sense of things. This is contrary to Postman and Weingartner, who insist that meaning and values are in short supply in the modern world and should be actively cultivated in the classroom.[37] Moreover, while Weber views objectivity as inherent to knowledge production, Postman and Weingartner are at pains to situate teachers in a time, place, and body. From this perspective, there is no such thing as pure knowledge production, only communication between embodied subjects. To understand this perspective, I now turn to Nietzsche's writing on perspectivism and his critique of pure objectivity.

II. Perspectivism

Nietzsche's tortured and creative life has been well documented.[38] In my view, Nietzsche prized more creativity from his personal suffering than any other writer in modernity. He studied theology intensively as a student and, at 19, won a prestigious scholarship to a university prep school. This is where he began to acquire the enormous erudition with which his writing is peppered. His mother hoped he would become a minister, but his studies took him to philology, and, at the age of 24, he was recommended for a professorship at the University of Basel. However, after being confirmed as a Professor, Nietzsche began to struggle with mental health and physical ailments which forced him to travel frequently in search of good climate and remedies. It was during these travels that Nietzsche wrote *The Genealogy of Morality* which contains his clearest statement on the production of knowledge.

In Part III of the Genealogy, Nietzsche argued that all worthwhile human achievements – from art to philosophy – have required some kind of ascetic suffering. His final aphorism is explicit: 'Apart from the ascetic ideal, man, the human animal, had no meaning so far.'[39] What kind of asceticism does Nietzsche have in mind? A fully embodied and physical search for truth. Contra Weber, Nietzsche argued that knowledge cannot be produced in a pure way, and in aphorism 12, he railed against Vedanta philosophy and other attempts to attain knowledge through bodily transcendence.[40] For Nietzsche, the production of knowledge cannot be done in a dispassionate or disinterested way – he regarded 'contemplation without interest' as a 'nonsensical absurdity.'[41] Knowledge requires active participation, the weighing of pros and cons, and active interpretation. I quote at some length:

> Henceforth, my dear philosophers, let us be on guard against the dangerous old conceptual fiction that posited a 'pure, will-less, painless, timeless knowing subject'; let us guard against the snares of such contradictory concepts as 'pure reason,' 'absolute spirituality,' 'knowledge-in-itself': these always demand that we should think of an eye that is completely unthinkable, an eye turned in no particular direction, in which the active and interpreting forces, through which alone seeing becomes seeing something, are supposed to be lacking; these always demand of the eye an absurdity and a nonsense. There is only a perspective seeing, only a perspective 'knowing'; and the more affects we allow to speak about one thing, the more eyes, different eyes, we can use to observe one thing, the more complete will our 'concept' of this thing, our 'objectivity,' be. But to eliminate the will altogether, to suspend each and every affect, supposing we were capable of this—what would that mean but to castrate the intellect?[42]

At this juncture, it is tempting to digress into psychoanalysis and castration anxiety.[43] In the interest of space, I will put this to the side and unpack this passage. Some interpretations limit Nietzsche's comments to a banal endorsement of Kantian epistemology[44]– the simplicity of that reading should itself tell us that Nietzsche had something else in mind. Indeed, Christoph Cox notes that Nietzsche is really weaving together two ideas: perspective and interpretation.[45] With regard to the first point, Nietzsche is alerting us to the fact that seeing and knowing always take place from somewhere: from an embodied, situated existence. We don't just take in the world in a pure way. All knowledge is first apprehended through the senses – our eyes, ears, nose, sense of touch, and smell. Knowledge is also conducted through the body, and the body is always somewhere geographically and in time and space. Hence, the knower is embodied, situated, and brings a frame or an interpretation to that knowledge. We never just 'take in the world.' We take in the world through a unique and situated being.

Nietzsche's second point is also crucial. To know is always to interpret. There is no fact and then interpretation. Facts may be out there, but we never encounter them in a pure way. Rather, interpretation occurs at the moment that a sensory fact is perceived by the senses, and it stretches across 'all events in the organic world.'[46] While the authors do not cite Nietzsche, this is the explicit position adopted by Postman and Weingartner. Their entire analysis of meaning-making is predicated on the idea that students are fully embodied and not disembodied minds that we encounter in the classroom: 'You have never met anyone who was "thinking", who was not at the same time also "emoting", "spiritualizing", and for that matter, "livering."'[47] During their discussion of crap detecting, the authors also explicitly endorse the way knowledge is filtered through the body:

> [W]e do not get our perceptions from the 'things' around us. Our perceptions come from us. This does not mean that there is nothing outside of our skins.

> It does mean that whatever is 'out there' can never be known except as it is filtered through a human nervous system.[48]

There are high stakes in this analysis for Nietzsche. He argues, for example, that 'interpretation' is the 'essence of life, its will to power . . . the essential priority of the spontaneous, aggressive, expansive, form-giving forces that give new interpretations and directions.'[49] Perception and interpretation are, in other words, part of the constitution of persons, objects, and events. Moreover, as noted in the long quotation above, Nietzsche argues that to attempt to ignore or eliminate this fact is the greatest assault yet on the human being. It involves an attempt to eliminate ourselves completely and reconstruct ourselves as a non-willing, non-interpreting subject who apprehends the world in a disembodied way. This is why he introduces provocative language such as the 'castration of the intellect.'

What about truth? Weber, it will be recalled, regarded the classroom as a space where knowledge and truth could be produced in an objective way. For Nietzsche, the attempt to eliminate the human subject from the project of knowing in the valorisation of objectivity is also an act which aims to put truth outside of us/above us. It is to say that truth is there, and we are simply its servants. To be its servants, we have to eliminate all the faculties with which we actually see or know something, such as our mind and body. As I have noted, Nietzsche regards this as a denigration of the human and a terrible error about truth. Truth – he is saying – is never really out there. Truth is always a human production. It is not 'out there' waiting to be discovered. It is always going to be perspectival, developed and posited.

III. Perspectivism in Practice

All of the thinkers canvassed above have something important to teach us about education and the responsibility of teachers in the classroom. On the question of objectivity, it seems to me that perspectivism is the stronger position. As Nietzsche, Postman and Weingartner have all noted, there is no such thing as an objective presentation of a social phenomenon, a concept, or a legal subject. We always see the world from a particular angle, from a particular interpretation, and with a particular lens – even if that is not perceptible to us. Thus, I don't think that Weber's commitment to objectivity holds even though we might affirm his advocacy of presenting inconvenient facts and the importance of challenging our values. One can even affirm the importance of avoiding explicitly political stands in the classroom, but these things don't keep politics out of knowledge or out of pedagogy (including, importantly, Weber's).

Certain things flow from this recognition. Most basically, I contend that we ought to convey to our students that we do not teach law in a purely objective way. We offer interpretations and encounters with a subject, and they would get different inflexions, readings, and emphases from different teachers.[50] That does not mean that what happens in the classroom is purely ideological or merely opinion. But any teacher worth the name would struggle to give students anything more than their own reading of a subject. Further, I contend that one of the worst pedagogical crimes a teacher could commit is to tell their students that there is an objective way to learn law and that they are delivering it. Or, more commonly, to present our subjects as though that were the case.

So how might this play out in practice? To conclude this chapter, I offer three examples of how I incorporate perspectivism and crap detecting into Property Law at the Adelaide Law School. My comments relate primarily to course content, but I will also touch on assessment and the alignment of course learning outcomes with graduate attributes at my school. In taking this approach, I also acknowledge that perspectivism cannot be confined to textual analysis or curriculum design. It is also located in teaching techniques, power negotiations[51] and the spatial configuration of the classroom itself.

A. The Idea of Property

The simplest way to introduce perspectivism in property law is to use the introductory class to unpack the *idea* of property.[52] Most property law textbooks tend to skip over this analysis or position economic analysis as the dominant framework.[53] The most common statement is that property concerns the use, distribution, and allocation of scarce resources.[54] For individuals, property is shaped in such a way as to maximise 'use, exclusivity and alienability.'[55] This is a useful starting point, but if the discussion is left at this point, it disguises the influence of liberalism (and neoliberalism) on our conception of property. As Babie reminds us, liberalism has structured our thinking to emphasise the importance of 'choice' in property law.[56] But a different political philosophy would highlight the performativity of property,[57] highlight alternative values such as obligation/stewardship[58] or give greater prominence to common ownership arrangements.[59]

Once the idea of property is introduced and its relationship to liberalism is laid bare, the entire subject opens up. Property can be seen as a dynamic social construct that is shaped by economic, legal, religious, and philosophical factors. As C Edwin Baker observes: 'Property rights are a cultural creation and a legal conclusion.'[60] The meaning of property is not fixed and determined by and through scientific inquiry. If you want to know what property means, then one must engage with the messy ferment of social relations. And all insights will be partial and subject to change.[61]

Within property law, there is one school of thought that neatly captures this understanding – social relations theory (SRT). SRT makes no pretence of neutrality – it has an explicit objective to shift our thinking about property from 'habits of individualistic thought' to 'habits of relational thought.'[62] To support this analysis, advocates of SRT present an alternative to the liberal conception of individual autonomy. 'What makes autonomy possible,' argues Nedelsky, 'is not separation, but relationship.'[63] From this perspective, the individualism that pertains to the liberal concept of private property is misconceived. People are not 'islands unto themselves' and best function to achieve their own goals in the context of 'social relations that support their own abilities to flourish.'[64] Individuals achieve autonomy through a mixture of dependence and independence.[65] Ngaire Naffine summarises this point and its consequence for law:

> Within relations we become what we are as persons; here, we must make sense of our lives, which in turn must be understood by scholars who wish to explain us. There is never a full separation between persons, and indeed, human beings draw their very identity from their relations. When they work well, relations are not only formative (but unavoidable) but also conducive to human autonomy and to the flourishing of the individual. It follows that the role of law is to regulate relations rather than to ward them off. Law's job is to ensure that they run smoothly and that they neither oppress nor harm us.[66]

At their best, property rights represent enforceable rules that give shape to human relationships. If the community deems the rules to be fair and the rules contain an appropriate acknowledgement of the social aspect of property, then they can assist in structuring a framework for the allocation and distribution of resources that serves the collective good. In this way, property law can be understood as part of the 'patterns of relationship' that sustain our society and create the conditions for individual autonomy.[67] Property rights are not natural and absolute. They are socially situated and contingent on their impact on others and the environment.

In sum, introducing students to SRT (or any other theory of property) serves a vital pedagogical function. Primarily it empowers students to see that property law has ideological content – it is not natural, neutral or objective. Moreover, once the influence of liberalism and economic rationalism have been named, they need to be justified.[68] And if our working idea of property cannot be justified, then it needs to be remade in a way that matches social expectations and need. From this perspective, property law is not a closed system that students need to learn – it is a dynamic institution that we can all play a role in shaping.

B. Whose Property?

Another way of teaching perspectivism in property law is to introduce alternative and marginalised voices into the curriculum. Of particular importance here are the voices of First Nation people whose land our entire system of real property occupies. As Nicole Graham has observed, most real property courses exclude First Nations' land laws and sometimes don't make space to teach native title.[69]

Despite this practice, it is desirable to teach native title in a way that is integrated into existing topics such as the idea of property, tenure, estates,[70] and leases.[71] The benefit of this approach is twofold – students learn the substantive law without 'disingenuous classificatory segregation,' and it also creates space to discuss the relationship between politics and law.[72] In this sense, the classroom becomes a space for meaning-making and testing values. I could list dozens of examples of how this could be done,[73] but one of my favourites is to ask students to engage Dawson J's advocacy for judicial restraint in *Mabo (no 2)*:

> The policy which lay behind the legal regime was determined politically and, however insensitive the politics may now seem to have been, a change in view does not of itself mean a change in the law. It requires the implementation of a new policy to do that and that is a matter for government rather than the courts.[74]

Even the most liberally-minded law student needs a response to Dawson J's challenge. Did the High Court engage in judicial activism? A liberal interpretation of the common law? And on the other side of the political spectrum, what about Michael Mansel's contention that the High Court

> did not overturn anything of substance, but merely propounded white domination and superiority over Aborigines by recognising such a meagre Aboriginal form of rights over land?[75]

Irene Watson strengthens this reading by highlighting the power of extinguishment that was also created in *Mabo (No. 2)*:

> *Mabo (No.2)* created an illusion of doing justice, while also justifying and expanding the muldarbi, into a new form – and life – in its power of extinguishment. A colonising theory, is not only renewed by the High Court, but also sanctioned, and purified; once more made good, as an act of god – an act of the British state in establishing a colony that formed into the Australian state and its constituted sovereignty.[76]

As teachers, it is not our role to tell students what to think about these debates – it is not violence in the sense that Weber feared. But nor do we need to pretend to be neutral about these issues and remove ourselves from the knowledge that is produced in the classroom. If we are honest about our position and create a safe space for disagreement, students can make an informed choice about whether they accept or reject our reading. And that is far better, in my opinion, than attempting to disguise our politics or presenting our reading as objective fact.

Alongside native title, I also think it is important to create space for First Nations land law. This topic ought to be treated separately from traditional property laws and western political ideas such as communitarian property.[77] To do otherwise inhibits the intellectual development of our students. Moreover, Graham argues, it 'misses the opportunity that Indigenous Australian land laws offer to the development of a distinctively Australian property law – one that has confidently departed from its colonial origins and is well-adapted and responsive to the reality of real property, the country itself.'[78]

The contents of First Nations' laws are complex and diverse. It is impossible to make generalisations across the over 400 Indigenous nations that occupied and possessed Australia prior to colonisations. However, possible topics include discussion of First Nations farming[79] and fire management practices[80] as a counter-narrative to the traditional Lockean labour theory of property which was used to justify the doctrine of *terra nullius* and colonisation. First Nations' expressions of stewardship offer an important counter-narrative to the liberal theory of property which focuses on individual preference maximisation.[81] Notions of inalienability of title and inclusion[82] contrast sharply to the Torrens System's focus on exclusion and priority disputes.[83] And contemporary First Nations scholars write about the continuation of first law and the responsibilities it brings into the present day.[84]

For non-indigenous students, these topics act to decentre their perspective and help them to see objects of property law through a different lens and in a different light. Moreover, because of the injustices suffered by First Nations people, this content also provides an opportunity to talk about the role of emotion in the production of knowledge.[85] In another blow to pure objectivity, we understand very clearly today that emotions are central to thinking.[86] And in my own experience, I have seen a kaleidoscope of responses. Some students feel fear as they grapple with alternative ways of thinking or guilt as they learn about Australia's colonial and legal history. Other students feel joy and even exhilaration as they break through into new ways of seeing the world. As teachers, we ignore these experiences and the constitutive role of emotions in producing legal knowledge at our own peril – and our students' loss.[87]

C. Constructive Alignment

As well as introducing these topics into our teaching, it is also important that we think about the architecture of our course and how perspectivism relates to course objectives and assessment. This simple point was neatly captured by Thomas Shuell: 'If students are to learn the desired outcomes in a reasonably effective manner, then the teacher's fundamental task is to get students to engage in learning activities that are likely to result in their achieving those outcomes.'[88] Without this broader planning, the introduction of alternative voices and meaning-making practices will be seen by students as tokenistic and less important than legal doctrine. For this reason, I have adopted the following practices in my own course.

First, two of my six course learning outcomes express the kinds of behaviour I wish students to develop.[89] They are: 'Analyse, evaluate and synthesise information from a wide variety of sources and experiences to answer complex legal questions in a principled manner' and 'Identify and analyse cultural, theoretical and social factors impacting on property law.' These learning outcomes are then specifically addressed in each seminar and in every piece of assessment.

For seminars, we provide students with a 'perspectives' reading each week for discussion. In addition to those issues already discussed, we examine a range of justifications for private property: feminist theory when discussing the presumption of advancement; Islamic finance and the ethics of usury for mortgages; and the relationship between law and the market when looking at protections that the Torrens System gives to a bona fide purchaser.[90] The perspectives readings are all integrated into the substantive legal issue under discussion. For example, students might be asked to examine a fact pattern where a mortgagor exercises the power of sale. In response, students are asked to formulate the best arguments for and against charging interest and whether principles derived from Islamic finance offer a more ethical alternative.

As noted above, perspective questions also feature prominently in assessment. Our mid-term assignment and the exam have the same structure – a fact pattern followed by three questions. The first two questions have a combined weight of 50%, and they examine doctrinal areas of law. The third question draws directly on a prescribed perspectives reading and requires students to think from multiple perspectives before giving their own opinion about an issue.[91] Here is an example from our 2020 primary exam:

> In response to COVID-19, several jurisdictions in Australia are looking to end 'no cause' evictions and requiring landlords to prove they have a genuine reason for ending the lease. Provide (a) the strongest argument for; and (b) the strongest argument against this idea. Do you think the government in South Australia should introduce a similar amendment?

A question like this encourages students to adopt the 'anthropological perspective'[92] by requiring them to think from the perspective of someone else and articulate a position they do not hold. Even if they don't ultimately accept the argument, we are giving them the opportunity to cultivate respect for others and to see the world through a different lens.[93] The final part of the question engages students as active participants in the future of law. It is not uncommon for students to struggle with this question or to report that they are not used to being asked for their own opinion. But the marking rubric is specifically designed to reward students that articulate a position and make compelling original arguments.

The final piece of assessment students undertake is a group exercise that involves constructing a case log. For this exercise, groups select one case from the weekly readings and provide a basic case summary: material facts, legal issue and ratio. The final part of the assessment is structured around a series of critical questions that preclude any clear resolution or answer.[94] At the start of the exercise, students are given the following protocol which contains the essence of perspectivism:

> Critical reading happens when readers (1) make explicit the assumptions authors hold about what constitutes legitimate knowledge and how such knowledge comes to be known, (2) take alternative perspectives on the knowledge being offered so that this knowledge comes to be seen as culturally constructed, (3) undertake positive and negative appraisals of the grounds for and expression of this knowledge, and (4) analyse commonly held ideas for the extent to which they support or oppose various political ideologies.[95]

Following this, students are asked to pick three questions from the following list and provide a critical analysis.[96]

- Was the judge influenced by political or cultural bias, or did they introduce their own values or assumptions into the judgment? For example, does the judge reference a particular idea of justice or morality?
- Whose voices are heard in the judgment? Are there any perspectives that cannot be heard, i.e. traditional owners or members of the public?
- What individuals' or groups' interests were taken into account in the judgment? Were any interests excluded?
- To what extent is the majority approach consistent with the previous authority in the area? If it is not consistent, how does the judge justify their approach?
- If there is a dissenting judgment, what different views were paramount in that dissent? Do you prefer the dissenting judgment to the majority view?
- Did the practical consequences of the outcome inform the judgment? If so, how?

This list is deliberately structured to contain questions related to epistemology, experience, communication and politics. Others can be added, but we have found that asking students to engage with these questions on a weekly basis dramatically improves class discussion, prepares them for other assessment tasks and opens their eyes to new ways of thinking about property law and the role of judges in the production of legal knowledge.

IV. Conclusion

This chapter has sought to expand on Postman and Weingartner's argument that the classroom should be a space for meaning-making, instruction in crap detecting, and the development of an anthropological perspective. Underlying this advocacy is an old tension relating to the appropriateness of incorporating politics into teaching. Because Postman and Weingartner do not defend their position, I engaged in a close reading of two proponents of each view. On the one hand, Max Weber argued that the classroom should be a space that is liberated from politics, and teachers should present material in an objective way. On the other, Friedrich Nietzsche argued that knowledge is always perspectival and that any attempt to remove the self from knowledge does harm to the intellect. Ultimately, I concluded that Nietzsche had the better argument but that teachers might also retain Weber's insistence that teachers not use the classroom for political violence.

In the second part of the chapter, I described how I apply Nietzsche's argument for perspectivism to teaching Property Law. Specifically, I discussed how we integrated alternative perspectives relating to the idea of property and First Nations voices into our curriculum. Further introducing new material, I also described how we align perspectivism with course learning outcomes and assessment. In arguing for perspectivism in property law, I acknowledge that colleagues are constrained by the Priestley 11 and that we increasingly teach property law in a single semester. We are forced to make hard choices about content, and there will inevitably be topics that cannot be taught. However, in making these choices and exercising our discretion, there is great value in teaching perspectivism and empowering students to co-create knowledge. In this way, we might work towards Postman and Weingartner's ideal that education can address social ills and create active citizens with the tools for responding to future problems.

Notes

1 bell hooks, *Teaching Community: A Pedagogy of Hope* (Routledge 2003).
2 Stephen Brookfield, *Becoming a Critically Reflective Teacher* (Jossey-Bass 1995).
3 Neil Postman and Charles Weingartner, *Teaching as a Subversive Activity* (Delta 1971).
4 ibid 2.
5 ibid 84–85.
6 With respect to property law see Nicole Graham, *Lawscape: Property, Environment, Law* (Routledge 2011) and Lynden Griggs and Rick Snell, 'The Curriculum and Teaching of Property Law in Australian Law Schools' (1997) 5 *Australian Property Law Journal* 213.
7 This is an ancient analogy but my immediate inspiration is from Joseph William Singer, *Entitlement: The Paradoxes of Property* (Yale University Press 2000) 13.
8 Postman and Weingartner (n 3) 3.
9 ibid 37.
10 These ideas have been more fully developed in Brookfield (n 2).
11 Postman and Weingartner (n 3) 37.
12 There are clear limits on the extent to which we can abstract from our own culture. See for example Mari Matsuda's classic critique of Rawls's theory of justice: 'Liberal Jurisprudence and Abstracted Visions of Human Nature: A Feminist Critique of Rawls' Theory of Justice' (1986) 16(3) *New Mexico Law Review* 613.
13 ibid 4.
14 Postman and Weingartner were heavily influenced by John Dewey for this vision of higher education. See John Dewey, *Democracy and Education* (Free Press 1966).
15 I also like Graham's (2009, 294) idea of using the Wik decision to talk about the power of lobby groups such as the minerals council and the farmers' federation in Australian law. Such as discussion is vital when teaching the 1998 amendments to the *Native Title Act 1993* (Cth).
16 I also acknowledge that law academics have addressed this topic in a different way. See for example Robert W. Gordon, 'Critical Legal Studies as a Teaching Method, Against the Background of the Intellectual Politics of Modern Legal Education in the United States' (1989) 1(1) *Legal Education Review* 59 and Kim Rubenstein, 'Citizenship and Gender in the Public Law Curriculum' (1995) 6(2) *Legal Education Review* 241.
17 Friedrich Nietzsche, *On the Geneology of Morals* (Knopf 1967) 119.
18 John Biggs and Catherine Tang, *Teaching for Quality Learning at University* (Open University Press 2011).
19 Wendy Brown, *Manhood and Politics: A Feminist Reading in Political Theory* (Rowman & Littlefield 1988) xi.
20 Paul Reitter and Chad Wellmon, 'Introduction' in *Max Weber, Charisma and Disenchantment: The Vocation Lectures* (New York Review of Books 2020) vii.
21 Eduard Baumgarten, *Max Weber: Werk und Person* (Work and Person) (Mohr 1967) 671. Quoted in Reitter and Wellmon (n 20).
22 Corey Robin, 'The Professor and the Politician' *The New Yorker* (12 November 2020) <https://www.newyorker.com/books/under-review/max-weber-the-professor-and-the-politician>
23 Hannah Arendt brought a similar charge in the aftermath of the Second World War. Her phrase 'the banality of evil' referred specifically to 'the heedless recklessness or hopeless confusion or complacent repetition of "truths" which have become trivial and empty' See Hannah Arendt, *The Human Condition* (University of Chicago Press 1958) 5.

24 Max Weber cited in Reitter and Wellmon (n 20) ix–x.
25 Reitter and Wellmon (n 20) 7.
26 ibid. A contemporary reader may imply from this that Weber was attacking liberal or progressive professors. His critique cuts both ways but the immediate issue before him was a hiring issue at the University of Berlin where Friedrich Althoff, the Prussian Minister of Education, appointed the economist Ludwig Bernhard because, in Weber's view, Bernhard's research agenda matched the political interest of the state. In a phrase that we will see again with Nietzsche, Weber argued that political hirings would "castrate" intellectual development, Reitter and Wellmon (n 20) vii & ix.
27 Weber's understanding of 'science' is much broader than how we use the term today. He reserved it specifically for knowledge gained through causal analysis and the analysis of human actions. See further Fritz Ringer, *Max Weber: An Intellectual Biography* (University of Chicago Press 2004) 231.
28 Niccolo Machiavelli, *The Prince* (Penguin 2009).
29 Max Weber, 'Science as Vocation' in Gerth and Mills (eds), *From Max Weber: Essays in Sociology* (Oxford University Press 1946) 145.
30 That is the conceit here – that you can have power-free words. I return to this in the next section.
31 Max Weber, *Economy and Society* (University of California Press 1978) 24–25.
32 ibid 145.
33 ibid 146.
34 ibid.
35 ibid 147.
36 ibid.
37 Postman and Weingartner (n 3) 3, 82–87.
38 Walter Kaufmann, *Nietzsche: Philosopher, Psychologist, Antichrist* (Princeton University Press 1974).
39 Nietzsche (n 17) 162.
40 ibid 118.
41 ibid 119.
42 ibid.
43 Irving Sarnoff and Seth Corwin, 'Castration Anxiety and the Fear of Death' 27(3) (1959) Journal of Personality 374. Weber also references castration (n 25).
44 Brian Leiter, 'Perspectivism in Nietzsche's Genealogy of Morals' in Richard Schacht (ed), *Nietzsche, Genealogy, Morality: Essays on Nietzsche's Genealogy of Morals* (University of California Press 1994) 351.
45 Christoph Cox, 'The "Subject" of Nietzsche's Perspectivism' (1997) 35(2) Journal of the History of Philosophy 269, 271.
46 Friedrich Nietzsche, *The Will to Power* (Penguin 2017) 643.
47 Postman and Weingartner (n 3) 85.
48 ibid 90.
49 Nietzsche (n 46) 643.
50 Here I follow Robin DG Kelley who argues that teachers and scholars should 'make no pretence about some kind of dispassionate, detached objectivity.... Objectivity is a false stance. I'm not neutral. I've never been neutral. I write about struggles and social movements because I actually don't think the world is right and something needs to change.' Vinson Cunningham, 'The Future of L.A. Is Here. Robin D.G. Kelley's Radical Imagination Shows Us the Way' *The LA Times* (17 March 2021) <https://www.latimes.com/lifestyle/image/story/2021-03-17/robin-dg-kelley-black-marxism-protests-la-politics>
51 On the relationship between objectivity and authority see the contribution by Toole and Burdon in this volume.
52 Professor Paul Babie introduced this topic at my school. Arguably the best example of this in a property law textbook is Bruce Ziff, *Principles of Property Law* (Carswell

1996) 1–48. See also Peter Burdon, 'Property: Concept, Rationale, Contexts' in H. Esmaeili and B. Grigg (eds), *The Boundaries of Australian Property Law* (Cambridge University Press 2016a) 6–21 & David Kairys, *The Politics of Law: A Progressive Critique* (Basic Books 1998) 240–258.

53 See for example Moore, Griggs and Grattan (2020 19–20).

54 Anthony M. Honoré, 'Ownership' in Anthony G. Guest (ed), *Oxford Essays in Jurisprudence: A Collaborative Work* (Oxford University Press 1961) 107.

55 Margaret Jane Radin, 'The Liberal Conception of Property: Cross Currents in the Jurisprudence of Takings' (1988) 88(8) Columbia Law Review 1667.

56 Paul Babie, 'Choices that Matter: Three Propositions on the Individual, Private Property, and Anthropogenic Climate Change' (2011) 22 Colorado Journal of International Environmental Law and Policy 323.

57 Nicholas Blomley, 'Performing Property: Making the World' (2013) 26(1) The Canadian Journal of Law and Jurisprudence 23–48.

58 See Eric T. Freyfogle, *The Land We Share: Private Property and the Common Good* (Shearwater Books 2003) and Irene Watson, *Aboriginal Peoples, Colonialism and International Law: Raw Law* (Routledge 2014).

59 Elinor Ostrom, *Governing the Commons* (Cambridge University Press 1990).

60 C. Edwin Baker, 'Property and Its Relation to Constitutionally Protected Liberty' (1986) 134 University of Pennsylvania Law Review 741, 744.

61 Laura Underkuffler-Freund, 'Property: A Special Right' (1996) 1 Notre Dame Law Review 1033, 1046.

62 Jennifer Nedelsky, *Law's Relations: A Relational Theory of Self, Autonomy, and Law* (Oxford University Press 2013) 25.

63 Jennifer Nedelsky, 'Reconcieving Rights as Relationship' (1993) 1 Review of Constitutional Studies 1.

64 Singer (n 7) 131.

65 Jennifer Nedelsky, 'Reconceiving Autonomy: Sources, Thoughts and Possibilities' (1989) 1 Yale Journal of Law and Feminism 7.

66 Ngaire Naffine, 'The Liberal Legal Individual Accused: The Relational Case' (2013) Canadian Journal of Law and Society 1.

67 Nedelsky (n 62) 8.

68 Ziff (n 49) 1–48.

69 Nicole Graham, 'Indigenous Property Matters: Embedding Indigenous Content and Perspectives in Real Property' (2009) 19(2) Legal Education Review 289. The norm is to teach native title – see Melissa Castan and Jenny Schultz, 'Teaching Native Title' (1997) 8(1) Legal Education Review 75, 78.

70 In teaching tenure and estates we require students to contrast the judgments of Brennan J. in *Mabo (No. 2)* and Gummow J in *Wik.*

71 Castan and Schultz (n 69) 78.

72 Graham (n 69) 292.

73 I also like Graham's idea of using the *Wik* decision to talk about the power of lobby groups such as the minerals council and the farmers' federation in Australian law. Such as discussion is vital when teaching the 1998 amendments to the *Native Title Act* (Cth) 1993. See further Graham (n 69) 294.

74 *Mabo v Queensland (No 2)* (1992) 175 CLR 1at 145.

75 Michael Mansel, 'The Court Gives an Inch But Takes Another Mile' (1992) 2(57) Aboriginal Law Bulletin 4, 6.

76 Irene Watson, 'Buried Alive' (2002) 13 (3) Law and Critique 253, 259–260. Muldarbi means demon spirit.

77 JW Harris conflates native title with communitarian property. See James Harris, *Property and Justice* (Oxford University Press 1996) 104.

78 Graham (n 68) 290.

79 Bruce Pascoe, *Dark Emu* (Magabala Books 2018).
80 Bill Gammage, *The Biggest Estate on Earth: How Aborigines Made Australia* (Allen & Unwin 2012).
81 For an excellent overview of this topic see chapters 2 & 4 of Heather McRae and Garth Nettheim, *Indigenous Legal Issues: Commentary & Materials* (4th edn, Thomson Reuters 2009). See also Peter Burdon, 'Native Title' in H. Esmaeili and B. Grigg (eds), *The Boundaries of Australian Property Law* (Cambridge University Press 2016b). Graham (n 68) 298–304 also argues that this material invites students to engage with different language and expressions of value.
82 Peter Sutton, *Native Title in Australia: An Ethnographic Perspective* (Cambridge University Press 2003) 21–22.
83 On this point, Graham (n 69) notes:

> process of solving priorities between competing interests enables them to grasp the inherently individualistic structure of private property interests in Anglo-Australian law and, further, allows them to contrast these interests with the communal structure of property interests in Indigenous-Australian laws.
>
> 295

84 Watson (n 58).
85 Postman and Weingartner (n 3) 52.
86 Jonathan Haidt, *The Righteous Mind: Why Good People Are Divided by Politics and Religion* (Penguin 2013).
87 Stephen Brookfield, *Developing Critical Thinkers* (Jossey-Bass 1987) 7.
88 Thomas Shuell, 'Cognitive Conceptions of Learning' (1986) 56 Review of Educational Research 411, 429.
89 John Biggs, 'Constructive Alignment in University Teaching' (2014) 1 HERDSA Review of Higher Education 115.
90 In South Australia the proviso says: "nothing included in this subsection shall affect the title of a registered proprietor who has taken bona fide for valuable consideration, or any person bona fide claiming through or under him". See for example, section 69(a) of the Real Property Act 1886 (SA).
91 Brookfield (n 89) 8–9.
92 Postman and Weingartner (n 3) 4.
93 Brookfield (n 89) 8–9.
94 Stephen Brookfield and Stephen Preskill, *Discussion as a Way of Teaching* (Jossey-Bass 2005) 56.
95 ibid 57.
96 These questions have been adapted from ibid 57–59.

5 Valuing our Differences

For the Sake of Adaptive Law Schools

*Kylie Fletcher**

I. Introduction

Education can be understood as a complex system. Our law schools, law programs and law classrooms may be conceptualised as complex systems nested within the broader complex system of legal education. Complexity thinking offers insights into how these systems function and evolve. Through complex systems theories, we gain unique perspectives that assist us in better understanding our academic environment.

As a community of law teachers, we have much in common. We tend to hold comparable qualifications and have a shared interest in teaching law. We also adopt similar teaching practices. We generally aim to achieve a shared purpose, and we strive to teach in accordance with mutually understood expectations. We are well aware of the professional admission requirements and academic standards that are embedded within our qualifying law degrees. We teach, at least in part, to a set curriculum, and we aim to see our students achieve designated learning outcomes. We generally adhere to coordinated plans and adopt signature and recognised pedagogies. We also draw on accepted legal education norms, practices and habits.

Despite our similarities, we are also very different from one another in many respects. We hail from a variety of backgrounds, have distinct professional and personal experience, and have diverse views and perspectives. While facilitating learning, we also tend to demonstrate some diversity and variation in what we do. Among other things, we incorporate additional topics, adopt a variety of methods and approaches and develop unique responses to expected and impromptu challenges. It is fair to say that, at times, we deviate from the status quo.

In recent years, law schools have tended to adopt a standardised view towards valuing the individual attributes and skills of legal educators. We have also seen an increasing emphasis on standardising our approaches to learning and teaching. The position taken by this chapter is that, given this trend towards standardisation, we ought to move to emphasise the value that we place on the differences that exist among individual legal educators and their approaches to teaching law. In exploring this issue and making this argument, this chapter draws on the complexity sciences scholarship.

DOI: 10.4324/9781003175216-6

The chapter begins by providing a brief description of complex systems and identifies that both legal education and law schools operate in a manner consistent with this description. The chapter then introduces the scholarship that highlights the value of difference in complex systems. Rather than addressing the pedagogical benefits of allowing flexibility and surprise in designing curriculum with complexity in mind, this chapter focuses on law schools as adaptable organisations and the potential importance of difference in that context. In doing so, it draws on insights offered by complexity researchers who emphasise that organisational innovation is supported within adaptive spaces where differences exist.

In particular, the chapter canvasses the proposals made by several scholars writing within the complexity leadership space. These authors propose that there is value to be gained by cultivating and making use of differences within complex systems. In order to further demonstrate the value of difference, the chapter canvasses the concept of 'positive deviance', which occurs when detours from the status quo lead to improved outcomes. To emphasize the point, the chapter explores the concept in the context of the introduction of the case method, a well-known historical innovation in legal education.

This chapter does not advocate for subversion as it is classically understood. It does not propose that legal educators work towards overthrowing the system. Instead, this chapter makes the case that when legal educators express or enact difference, they are edging towards or engaging in a type of micro subversion at an operational, and sometimes higher, level. If our ability to do so is overly stifled, law schools risk settling into what might eventually become a stale and outdated status quo.

The chapter then draws again on complexity leadership to explain how leaders might encourage and support difference within legal education. It identifies that these insights might be particularly important in a system with inherent traits, such as the need to comply with 'academic knowledge' requirements (commonly known as the 'Priestley 11'), that tend to pull law schools towards a homogenised status quo. The chapter goes on to identify that academic freedom operates to complement the proposals made within the complexity leadership scholarship. Taken at face value, academic freedom, which protects scholarly inquiry and opinion, offers space for the interaction of difference. To ensure that this important space survives, the chapter prompts leaders to be mindful of certain increasing trends that may exert pressure on and erode the traditional freedom. As a tool for enriching the interaction of difference, this chapter recognises and supports the continuing conversations that value this freedom.

II. Legal Education as a Complex System

The education system can be viewed as a complex system.[1] This generally accepted understanding presents us with a starting point from which to explore legal education. Complexity theory assists us in understanding how complex systems adapt to changes and evolve. It also helps us to appreciate how we may prime the system so that it is better able to respond to its ever-evolving environment.

It is common for authors writing in this space to commence discussions by describing a complex system. A basic opening explanation is usually offered in order to initiate the reader. In doing so, individual complexity scholars typically embrace a description or set of shared traits presented by founding scholars. However, there is no single source or conventional standard adopted to begin discussions.[2] This means that there is a wide range of potential starting points.

Cilliers describes a complex system as comprising 'a large number of elements' whose 'interactions are rich, dynamic, fed back, and above all, non-linear' and emphasises that these characteristics result in 'emergence'.[3] He also makes the point that complex systems are dependent on history, engage with their environments and adapt independently of extrinsic control.[4] The morning traffic,[5] the economy and the earth's climate are each an example of a complex system.[6] Complexity scholars frequently refer to Cilliers's 'elements' as system 'agents'.[7] In a system of people, the agents regularly include individuals and collectives or organisational groups of individuals.[8]

While not exclusive to complexity theory, the idea of emergence is considered one of its most critical mainstays.[9] Johnson explains emergence as:

> [The system's] agents residing on the one scale start producing behaviour that lies one scale above them: ants create colonies; urbanities create neighbourhoods; simple pattern-recognition software learns how to recommend new books. The movement from low-level rules to higher-level sophistication is what we call emergence.[10]

Lichtenstein observes that emergence is a 'process' that produces 'an emergent'.[11] On this view, an emergent is an identified creation that has emerged.[12] Lichtenstein emphasises that an emergent is not merely a shift or growth but rather the creation of something entirely new.[13] Examples of emergents include a brand-new market product and a new organisational strategic plan.[14]

Given that complex systems display emergence, they are often said to be 'more than the sum of [their] parts'.[15] Due to the number of alternative theories that shape our understanding and expression of complexity concepts, there are various views on what leads to emergence.[16] Lichtenstein explains that emergence is viewed in a number of different ways; sometimes as the spontaneous result of agent interaction; and other times as being created through the intentional effort of agents.[17]

The original scholars of complexity worked principally on phenomena and theories arising in the natural sciences and mathematics.[18] Scholars in the social sciences identified the potential in the various theories and developed them in order to contribute to their own discipline.[19] Numerous scholars have identified social systems as complex systems.[20] As a type of social system, organisations are also described by many as complex systems.[21] Complex systems theories have been adopted by scholars to inform the organisational sciences.[22] While much of the work is theoretical, research testing, modelling and utilising the complexity sciences in this field is increasing.[23]

Complex systems thinking has also been adopted by educationalists. Those who write about the complexity of education systems often cite the work of their counterparts in the organisational sciences.[24] In doing so, these scholars recognise the obvious analogies between educational systems and organisations. Educational scholars adopt complexity thinking to study certain challenges and opportunities that arise within education. Some of these scholars focus on the complexity of the systems in which education is provided.[25] According to Fenwick, Edwards and Sawchuk, 'the focus here is on the broader systems of education – policies, governance, conventions, formal curriculum, collective practices, and education as organizations – to understand how they change and what interventions promote productive change'.[26] These scholars recognise that we gain new understanding when we view national and area education systems, schools, universities and individual degree programs through a complex systems lens.[27] The smaller of these systems are sub-systems nested within the larger systems.[28] There are other scholars who adopt the theory to contribute to the scholarship addressing learning and teaching within collectives.[29] They adopt complexity principles, such as emergence, to inform research on, and practices adopted in engaging with, learning collectives such as classrooms.

As Webb explains, legal education is a complex system.[30] This system involves complex networks of, among others, law-school curriculum and law-school learning and teaching. Drawing on Cilliers' traits of a complex system, we can identify that the legal education system is complex, in part because there are a multitude of agents – universities, law schools, managers, academics and students, for example – all interacting in nonlinear ways.[31] These interactions permeate the system in that the behaviours of some agents affect those outside of the immediate agent relationship.[32] The agents adapt in response to the behaviours, and, in some cases, this results in organisation and a metamorphosis that can be observed at a higher level.[33] These behaviours and their outcomes are also influenced by the history of the legal education system and exchanges occurring between it and its external environment.[34] The system's history includes the early days of apprenticeship-style legal training, the shift to academic law programs and the formal reviews of legal education. Its external environment includes the legal profession, the legal system and the economy. Like the legal education system, individual law schools are also complex systems.

We can identify emergence occurring within the legal education system. At the highest system levels, we might recognise emergence when we look to the establishment of the Committee of Deans (now, the Council of Australian Law Deans (CALD)),[35] which, among other things, acts in the 'furtherance of legal education' and to foster cooperation between the various law schools.[36] In more recent times, emergence can be seen in the adoption of new values within the sector influenced, in part, by the standards and best practice guides implemented by CALD.[37] At a law-school level, examples of emergence include the innovations introduced at the various law schools, such as the offering of novel law programs and subjects. At a classroom level, we might recognise emergence, for instance, as the new learning that arises among a collective of students engaged in collaborative peer learning.[38] While not exclusive to legal education, the advent of student note-sharing websites is a classic example of emergence.

This paper focuses on law schools as complex systems rather than the legal education system as a whole. Having said that, the same principles apply to the wider collective, and so sensible abstractions are possible.

III. Why We Should Value Our Differences

Given that law schools can be identified as complex systems, it is worthwhile considering the role that difference plays in their operation. This chapter concentrates on what Page calls 'cognitive and behavioural differences – differences in how people solve problems, make predictions, and behave in strategic settings'.[39] Following Page's lead, it is important to note that this emphasis is not intended to discount the influence and important role played by other types of diversity and difference.[40]

Law schools must adapt and evolve in order to successfully endure. Representative groups within the legal profession have commissioned various high-profile reports that consider the future of the profession in light of ever-increasing challenges confronting the sector.[41] These challenges include shifting societal needs, technological advancements and the demand for new client service models.[42] In addition, aspects of society and the other professions are experiencing rapid change.[43] Theorists propose that in order to keep pace with their environments, entities such as law schools ought to be working to respond appropriately to the complexity of their environments.[44] To assist them in doing so, some propose that they value the benefits that may be gained from the differences that exist within their ranks.[45] The impetus to do so may increase in importance as their environments become more complex.[46]

In his book, *The Difference*, Page famously emphasises the critical role that difference plays in group problem solving and innovation.[47] He dedicates an entire subsequent publication to exploring, including through the use of models and data, difference in complex systems.[48] In a more recent publication, he discusses the manner in which diversity can add significant value to a business.[49] Without some level of internal difference, organisations risk remaining stationary while society, markets and other forces move around them. While uniformity provides 'order', a level of difference assists in pushing a system ideally towards, but not into, a state of 'randomness or chaos'.[50] The complexity sciences recognise that organisations are better able to adapt and innovate in this state.[51]

Internal differences can arm a complex system to better respond to challenges.[52] When a system is confronted by change, it is its differences and combinations of differences that, in part, dictate the steps available to the system.[53] This is akin to the idea that 'two (or more) minds are better than one'. Importantly, scholars in the field emphasise that these two minds produce more than two diverse responses, as together, their differences mean that they have the potential to produce blended or brand-new ideas that neither held before.[54] As such, a system comprised of those who approach things differently is arguably better at addressing challenges and, as a consequence, is more resilient.[55]

A number of organisational complexity scholars propose that the differences within a system play a role in the processes of emergence that occur within the system.[56] Some identify that leadership should be geared towards, among other things, establishing the conditions that promote emergence.[57] Others support certain actions because they have identified a connection between those actions and particular 'phases of emergence'.[58] Lichtenstein refers to these 'frameworks' as those that relate to 'enacting emergence'.[59] This chapter discusses selected parts of these frameworks in order to demonstrate the value of difference.

Hazy, Goldstein and Lichtenstein are the editors of a collection of scholarly works written by various authors who present 'complexity leadership theory', and, in their introductory chapter, they adopt complex systems concepts to explain the fact that leadership is an 'emergent phenomenon' that occurs through interactions at all echelons of an organisation.[60] Generally speaking, complexity leadership theory contends that leadership arises or evolves through agent interaction at various levels.[61] The authors in the field draw on complexity theory principles. Hazy, Goldstein and Lichtenstein describe such a principle when they refer us to agents and their 'local rules of interaction'.[62] Local rules generally develop over time, for example, through established norms, practices and habits.[63] In this work, these scholars describe 'leadership' as the interactions that lead to some kind of variation in these local rules.[64] The interactions that initiate these variations are not necessarily managerial in nature.[65] The expression and enacting of difference or, to adopt language inspired by the theme of this book, the 'micro subversion' of local rules, can be viewed as leadership when it results in changes to those local rules. Such changes have the potential to ripple through the system producing new prospects.[66] In this way, our differences have the ability to shape future local rules and even the wider system. Notwithstanding the value that difference offers, scholars in the field emphasise the ongoing need for complexity-informed managerial control because, without it, internal differences have the potential to exhaust the system.[67]

Expanding on many of the principles introduced in their earlier and concurrent scholarship, including the work published in the collection described above, Uhl-Bien, Marion and McKelvey detail their framework of 'complexity leadership'.[68] They identify three 'leadership functions' that support an adaptive organisation.[69] In a later work, Uhl-Bien and Arena reorder and partially relabel these leadership functions as – 'entrepreneurial leadership', 'enabling leadership' and 'operational leadership'.[70] The multilevel enabling leadership function involves 'creating, engaging and protecting "adaptive space" needed to nurture and sustain the adaptability process in organizations'.[71] Enabling leadership is leadership that creates the appropriate conditions for this adaptive space.[72] Uhl-Bien, Marion and McKelvey identify that ensuring agent heterogeneity is an important objective of this leadership function.[73] Agent heterogeneity is part of a wider recipe that prompts 'internal tension' and 'conflicting' between agents that propel problem-solving behaviours leading to innovation.[74]

Goldstein, Hazy and Lichtenstein propose their 'ecologies of innovation' framework.[75] They focus on organisational emergence and identify the four 'phases of emergence' as being 'disequilibrium conditions, amplifying actions, recombinations, and stabilizing feedback'.[76] Once exposed to disequilibrium conditions, or, in other words, internal or external pressure to change, the system relies on experimentation, including at a local level.[77] These experiments, which are described as 'micro-level diversity' or differences, have the potential to lead to solutions that can be drawn on in responding to the abovementioned pressure.[78]

The frameworks outlined above propose that difference is a feature of collective problem solving, or what Uhl-Bien and Arena call the 'adaptive space'. Ultimately, the expression of difference may, in some cases, result in emergence. In order to explain the value of difference to the process of emergence, it might assist us to consider emergence in the classroom context. As legal educators, we are likely to instinctively understand the concept of emergence in this context even if we are not acquainted with complex systems theories. This is because the ever-so-familiar concept of collective learning can be expressed in terms of emergence.[79] Emergence in this context occurs when the collective transitions to a higher-order or new understanding.[80] While we might not presently frame it in the context of emergence, we likely already value diversity as being critical to this process. Davis and Simmt and Davis and Sumara identify the various conditions that facilitate this type of classroom emergence as including 'internal diversity'.[81] As legal educators, we appreciate that it is the back-and-forth between, merging among and generation from internal differences that, along with other things, lead to this type of collective learning.[82] We are encouraged to ensure that the diversity in our classrooms is seen and valued.[83] We understand that the group benefits from the new understanding that results, in part, from its own internal diversity. Much like classes, organisations can also evolve and create as a result of their internal differences.[84]

IV. Difference Leading to Positive Outcomes in Law Schools

In order to demonstrate the potential benefit of difference within complex systems, and as a suggested tool for identifying and embracing it, Goldstein, Hazy and Lichtenstein discuss, in some detail, the relevance of 'positive deviance'.[85] There are various definitions of positive deviance in circulation, and its parameters and inclusions are debated by some.[86] As this chapter uses positive deviance simply to discuss the benefits of difference rather than as a method of inquiry, it does not engage in the debate. This chapter adopts the understanding of positive deviance employed and developed by Zeitlin and others, and further developed by Jerry and Monique Sternin, as it is referred to in complex systems scholarship.[87]

Generally speaking, positive deviance occurs when variations in behaviour result in ameliorated or superior outcomes.[88] It has been developed into a community-centred problem-solving approach used to address challenges, such as malnutrition.[89] The positive deviance approach has been developed from the insight that there are 'individuals whose uncommon behaviours or practices enable them to outperform or find better solutions to pervasive problems than their neighbours with whom they share the same resource base'.[90]

The story behind the advancement of the concept into this approach is quite an incredible one. The approach was developed by the Sternins. Jerry Sternin describes the evolution of the approach in a co-authored book.[91] It is worthwhile recounting some of the key details relayed by him. This will assist us in understanding the concept. Sternin explains that, on behalf of the US NGO, Save the Children, he responded to an invitation from the Vietnamese Government to establish a program aimed at resolving the difficult challenge of childhood malnutrition in the country's poorer villages. He recounts that the eventual solution was grounded in the existing, but rarer, practices adopted by some of the residents of these villages. Sternin explains that, in order to identify these, they explored the 'common' and 'uncommon practices' among the families of malnourished and well-nourished children. The latter of these two groups are the 'positive deviants'. Interestingly, Sternin goes on to describe the behaviours that this group shared. These included the fact that the families of the well-nourished children were incorporating additional unpopular foods, such as small rice-field shrimps and crabs, into their children's diet. Sternin then explains in detail how they worked with the residents in collectively embracing these behaviours. The program was extremely effective, and the approach has been adopted in implementing similar programs.[92] Sternin and others suggest that businesses seeking to address certain types of challenges consider a similar approach.[93]

Goldstein, Hazy and Lichtenstein explain that important innovations often result from differences.[94] They contend that these are instances of positive deviance.[95] In doing so, they provide several industry examples of differences leading to meaningful advances.[96] Likewise, we can look, admittedly in a somewhat speculative way, to similar examples within the legal education system to demonstrate the value of adopting different approaches.

There are, no doubt, a litany of differences that have emerged as recognisable successes within the system. The illustration that most readily comes to mind is the evolution of the case method. It is appreciated that the case method is probably one of the more debated aspects of our legal education system,[97] so this example is not provided in defence of the pedagogy. Rather, this discussion is offered to demonstrate the benefit of difference by reference to a revolution that is well understood by legal educators.

We are all familiar with the case method, devised by Christopher Columbus Langdell as a method to teach law in the late 1800s.[98] Educators who use this method, in pure or hybrid form, ask students to study primary sources of law such as cases. After studying the cases, students are asked to participate in concentrated class discussions. Students are expected to, among other things, articulate the reasoning adopted in the cases. While not necessarily considered part of the pedagogy, some educators use the Socratic method in facilitating these discussions. Other educators guide a more voluntary form of discussion. Many case method teachers provide students with hypothetical problems to solve. Some believe that this is a component of the case method, while others consider this an adaption.[99] It is reported that Langdell himself presented students with both case extracts and hypotheticals,[100] and in a contemporary context, we seldom see one without the other.

At the time of its inception, the case method replaced a pedagogy that was dependent on traditional lectures and textbooks.[101] While students participated, this pedagogy relied more heavily on the teacher, or the author of a textbook, to explain the cases to the students.[102] In introducing the case method, one of Langdell's aims was to ensure that students were involved in developing and expressing their own understanding of the subject cases.[103]

When it was first developed, the case method was used exclusively by Langdell.[104] At that time, the pedagogy was rejected by others, including his peers at Harvard, and Langdell's efforts initially resulted in lower enrolments.[105] Eventually, the case method was recognised as successful for a variety of reasons, including due to the accomplishment of Langdell's students in gaining employment and prospering once they had done so.[106] The method was eventually embraced by others, in part perhaps for ideological reasons,[107] and is now recognised as a signature pedagogy of legal education.[108] Even if we debate the case method's status as a signature pedagogy in Australian legal education, we cannot deny its significant influence.

Langdell's detour might be considered a positive departure from the status quo that existed at the time. No matter how we view the pedagogy these days, we can all appreciate that Langdell was an innovator. As part of its continuing evolution, today, the pedagogy is often adopted in an adapted or supplemented form. In some cases, the pedagogy has been replaced by other situationally more suitable pedagogies. These variations have emerged from the initial steps taken by other legal educators who also departed from standard practice. Even if not recognised at the time of their inception, some of these variations may have led or may lead to positive change.

There are many other examples of small-scale changes to standard practice in legal education that have been or are becoming more widely adopted for the benefit of all. To name a few, these include the development of clinical legal education in Australia,[109] the wellness movement,[110] and the addition of new subjects and opportunities addressing legal technologies.[111]

There are those who point to the potential benefits of using the approach adopted by the Sternins to solve problems, including, in certain cases, those occurring within complex organisations.[112] Those adopting the approach follow a number of guiding steps.[113] It is suggested that law schools, and in fact, other educational systems, already engage in a highly unconscious and informalized version of this approach on a regular basis. This was particularly evident when, in response to the COVID-19 pandemic and the related restrictions, Australian law schools hastily converted to remote and multi-modal learning and teaching. In the initial stages of this transformation, legal educators were encouraged, more than ever before, to share their approaches, in part, so that conforming successes and, indeed, positive variations could be identified and emulated by those confronting similar challenges. As this occurred in the midst of fast-paced disruption, it was conducted through, in some cases, informal communities of practice established in faculty meetings and via social media (through blogs and the like).

We can extract the following points from the scholarship outlined above and apply them to law schools. In a law school context, our differences have the potential to produce friction leading to creative problem-solving.[114] Our different approaches serve as a possibly valuable form of experimentation.[115] Some of us, without even knowing it, may be in the process of addressing a number of the challenges faced by a number of other legal educators and, perhaps, law schools as entities.[116] These differences may inform more-widely adopted future solutions. Some of these differences may contribute to change and development, while others might lead to emergence in that they may lead to the creation of something entirely new. Failing that, it is recognised that value, in the form of organisational learning, may also be derived from our mistakes.[117]

V. Encouraging Difference in Law Schools

If we were all the same and all approached things in an identical way, law schools may find it difficult to adapt to their increasingly complex environments. This is especially the case in the context of the higher education system, where most formal changes are implemented through slow-to-respond curriculum and other review processes. The frameworks discussed above provide good reason to believe that leaders should look to ensure that law schools are readied for adaption and emergence by, among other things, cultivating differences and identifying and making use of them when appropriate. In a university context, this approach should not be limited to responding to the commercial market. Our differences may also, and likely most importantly, assist us in responding to the shifting needs of society and the common good.

As discussed above, Uhl-Bien, Marion and McKelvey's framework highlights three leadership functions. Those involved in enabling leadership at higher levels appreciate the value of diversity and encourage the agents in the system to engage with each other, explore differences and work to settle them.[118] This process provides adaptive space for the growth of solutions and innovations.[119] This is encouraged in a number of ways, including by ensuring that spaces for divergence, where difference can drive creativity, are provided.[120] This can be done, in part, by making interactive physical and virtual spaces available, instilling an agenda of creativity and ensuring that employees have the motivation and time to work towards that agenda.[121]

While most leaders understand that managing performance is important, several scholars make the point that an adaptive space also requires an environment of mutual confidence.[122] In order to achieve this, some propose that a certain level of autonomy or distributed control ought to be permitted and that, within certain boundaries, experimentation and the consequential mistakes that follow should be accepted.[123] It is also suggested that in order to properly further the adaptive space, leaders should be mindful of ensuring a working environment that is free from demeaning or punitive responses to, among other things, differences.[124] De Zilwa, whose scholarship considers adaptive academic departments, adopts complexity principles to make a number of recommendations, including that such departments provide academics with greater autonomy by decentralising some control and enabling 'self-organising teams' that provide academics with 'greater freedom and control over their teaching and research work'.[125]

Goldstein, Hazy and Lichtenstein's 'ecologies of innovation' involves an evolving multilevel interactive leadership endeavour that facilitates the phases of emergence.[126] In order to realise such an endeavour, these authors encourage us to embrace differences.[127] In each case, these differences are a form of experimentation, often occurring at an operational level, that will endure, for the most part, unintentionally concealed from management.[128] When pressure arises, some of these experiments may be drawn upon and used as foundations for wider testing and application.[129] On this understanding, at least some of the challenges faced by law schools were and are being solved by different legal educators through day-to-day experiments, even if they are not yet identified as positive. Similarly, Siemens, Dawson and Eshleman, who write on education leadership, recommend, among other things, that leaders provide experimental spaces for educators.[130]

While difference is important, Page cautions that a complex system also needs to maintain a certain level of conformity.[131] This prevents the systems from becoming 'random' and 'chaotic'.[132] Too many novel ideas can engulf an organisation.[133] Page also reminds us that some agents will employ differences for their own benefit rather than for the benefit of the system.[134] For these and other reasons, certain limitations, including those that might be imposed through coordination efforts, are appropriate to support adaptive spaces.[135] Fullan, who is a prominent scholar of change in education systems, points to the value of difference and autonomy but notes that these are not akin to isolation.[136] He emphasizes the importance of difference and autonomy taking place within the context of ongoing collaboration.[137] He also stresses the need for leaders to, among other things, ensure 'direction' and 'accountability'.[138] Permitting adaptive space is not the same as suggesting that the space be free from goals, direction, limitations, or accountability. Further, enabling difference in approaches in the form of experimentation is not the same as suggesting that learning and teaching should be unplanned or haphazard; nor does it discount the need to adhere to academic standards, evidence-based practice and cooperation in ensuring constructive alignment.

Of course, difference does not ensure positive innovation. Further, it will not, by itself, result in change or emergence. The frameworks outlined above do not focus on difference alone. The scholars proposing these frameworks also support other conditions or behaviours. Page also emphasises that not all combinations of difference offer the same problem-solving dynamics and that desired outcomes may not be achieved (or may even be hindered) due to insufficient, or perhaps, too much conflict existing within the adaptive space.[139] However, complexivists would urge law schools to avoid instinctively rejecting difference as such a view may result in a rigid and less responsive system.[140]

In a recent article on adaption to COVID-19 and the related restrictions, Uhl-Bien refers specifically to the utilisation of the adaptive space that occurred within, among others, the education sector.[141] She states that:

> [U]niversity and educational leaders work[ed] with faculty, students, and parents to agree upon how to teach online. . . . In these cases, innovation was already present in the form of tech solutions – adaptive space occurred

mostly on the operational side to loosen up formal systems and administration to accommodate the change.[142]

Universities and law schools in Australia responded quickly in shifting to an online learning and teaching environment due, in part, to the adaptive space enacted within the operational, including academic, spaces. Uhl-Bien encourages research into the organisational and systemic responses to COVID-19.[143] There is, no doubt, much to learn from the likely empirical research to follow. The scholarship in the field of complexity leadership suggests that the ability to harness difference within the relevant systems when needed was likely a contributing factor.[144] Howden, Beresford and Martindale have already published research employing complexity leadership theory to reflect on the conversion to remote and multi-modal learning within university schools during COVID-19. Among other things, they note the importance of creating an adaptive space in which heterogeneous agents were provided with the opportunity to interact and propose creative solutions.[145] At the levels of enabling and entrepreneurial leadership, they supported and harvested that adaptive space in order to implement timely responses to changing needs.[146] In order to see universities, including law schools, continuing to adapt and innovate at the appropriate time, it is incumbent upon us to ensure that the appropriate conditions exist. At this stage, it appears that providing space that encourages the interaction and enabling of difference is an important feature.

VI. Characteristics That Limit Difference Within Law Schools

In attempting to ensure that the appropriate conditions, including difference, are present within our law schools, we find ourselves confronted by certain challenges. Most prominently, Australian law schools sensibly offer programs that comply with the external regulation of admission to practice.

The Model Admission Rules, which have been adopted by the relevant regulators and decision-makers in the various Australian jurisdictions, specify, among other things, the 'academic areas of knowledge' required for admission to the practice of law.[147] These areas of knowledge are also known as the 'Priestley 11' subjects. The Priestley 11 subjects are Criminal Law and Procedure, Torts, Contracts, Property, Equity, Company Law, Administrative Law, Constitutional Law, Civil Procedure, Evidence and Ethics and Professional Responsibility.[148] The Priestley 11 subject requirements include lists of topics that are to be included in qualifying law programs.[149] Although, it is accepted that there will be some variation between law schools, and broader descriptive content requirements are also provided for use in place of the prescribed lists of topics.[150]

There is some debate regarding the Priestley 11's influence on difference. Thornton views the requirements as 'homogen[ising]' the law school curriculum.[151] On the other hand, Adams contends that there is still some marked variation among Australian law programs and observes that each of the Australian law schools has maintained or developed its own unique identity.[152] Those familiar with legal education in Australia would recognise that some law school curriculum is orientated more towards social justice, while other curriculum focuses on the commercial areas of practice. Some law schools are known as doctrinal schools, and others boast a practical skills focus. It is clear that law schools have been able to adapt despite the limitations imposed by the Priestley 11, and, in this regard, they are perhaps semi-autonomous. There is, however, little doubt that the Priestley 11 has had a significant influence on Australian law school curriculum and does limit the differences that are expressed and enacted.

The influence of the Priestley 11 is perhaps exacerbated when new generations of legal educators adopt the practices of the past generation. All who teach within the system were students, and while students, they observed school teachers and other educators, including legal educators, use certain techniques.[153] When those students come to teach, one might say that they are already, at least in part, influenced by these observations through, what Lortie calls, an 'apprenticeship of observation'.[154] Moss and Curtis identify this as being a 'significant challenge to bring all faculty to a reform-minded perspective'.[155] This is potentially intensified within institutions that engage in 'academic inbreeding', which occurs when academic departments hire their former students.[156] Melville, Barrow and Morgan studied this phenomenon and identified that it occurs, to a certain extent, within Australian law schools.[157] They argue that this practice creates a form of cultural and intellectual replication that, among other things, inhibits diversity.[158]

Complexity theorists adopt various theories to explain these behaviours.[159] Without delving into this detail, the examples demonstrate the influence that pulls law schools towards a certain collective homogenised status quo. This insight might incentivise legal educators to, at the very least, critically examine any efforts to further homogenise who we are and what we do. Such conversations will likely see legal educators reminiscing the loss of a sector that was historically more open and flexible, particularly in its management of learning and teaching, and perhaps more open to difference. Within the legal education sector and, in fact, the wider academy, this discussion often arises in the context of debates about academic freedom.

VII. Academic Freedom as a Space for the Interaction of Difference

The 2005 Global Colloquium of University Presidents defined academic freedom as 'the freedom to conduct research, teach, speak, and publish, subject to the norms and standards of scholarly inquiry, without interference or penalty, wherever the search for truth and understanding may lead'.[160] Most accepted versions of academic freedom acknowledge that it only protects lawful expression.[161] However, there is ongoing deliberation about the exact limits.

In Australia, the debate has gathered momentum in recent times leading to independent reviews and legal challenges.[162] This chapter does not speak to the relevant Australian regulatory and policy framework dealing with academic freedom,[163] nor does it discuss the independent reviews or recent legal challenges involving academic freedom.[164] The reason for this is that scholars of complexity leadership do not suggest that adaptive spaces should be free of limitations. In fact, most of these scholars recognise that certain constraints are appropriate.[165] Consequently, this chapter will leave the discussion of the finer details of the limitations on academic freedom to those who are more qualified to remark. Instead, this chapter draws on the insights presented by the scholars of complexity leadership to emphasize the value of academic freedom to academic organisations and suggests that they present us with additional impetus to carefully examine encroachments.

It is suggested that, within the context of legal education, and indeed the wider academy, academic freedom operates to complement the proposals provided by the scholars of complexity leadership. Taken at face value, academic freedom offers space for the interaction of difference. It also offers a level of comfort that difference will not be penalised, thus encouraging, as scholars urge complexity leaders to do, the types of tension and experimentation referred to above. As such, academic freedom has the potential to serve not only its wider often-stated objectives but also the interests of the individual organisations involved.

Academic freedom covers certain specific freedoms, including an academic's freedom to research, publish and teach, an academic's freedom to participate in the governance of academic matters, a student's freedom to learn and an institution's right to a certain level of autonomy.[166] In relation to learning and teaching, Evans and Stone state that academics 'have a degree of autonomy in determining what and how they teach'.[167] Of course, they do not suggest that this right is unlimited. They consider requirements to adhere to certain standards, which may influence the method adopted and materials taught, to be appropriate.[168]

There are several justifications provided in support of academic freedom. The High Court of Australia acknowledges 'the search for truth in the contested marketplace of ideas' as being 'instrumental'.[169] Another, perhaps overlapping or intersecting, justification that receives a great deal of attention among scholars of academic freedom is the university's role in serving the common good by 'advanc[ing] and dissemin[ating] knowledge'.[170] With these, and other, justifications in mind, scholars regularly opine on how we might ensure academic freedom. Some of these observations align quite neatly with the proposals advanced by those who advocate for complexity leadership within organisations. For example, in discussing the institution's role in serving academic freedom, Abdel-Motaal says that 'the fundamental purpose of Academic Freedom . . . is to instill and to maintain those conditions within the university that are conducive to fostering and advancing creativity, social development and to sustaining the advancement of knowledge'.[171] In addition, scholars often highlight the expression of difference as being critical in meeting the objectives of academic freedom.[172]

While they do not often use the terminology of complex systems, advocates for academic freedom understand the potential that occurs where difference is encouraged. As such, it is not surprising to see that some of the arguments in favour of academic freedom are akin to acknowledging the value that might be derived from differences within a complex system. The search for truth and advancement of knowledge that is said to be generated in environments of academic freedom may be described by the scholars of complexity leadership as a process of emergence, or, in some cases, as an emergent, and the interaction of difference as being a condition of emergence. Of course, in serving the common good by advancing knowledge, much of this process and any resulting emergence is occurring at levels beyond individual academic organisations.[173] However, it seems possible that, if harnessed properly, academic freedom has the potential to also nourish adaptive space and change within, and for the benefit of, individual academic organisations. Law schools, as organisations, may very well derive benefits from the adaptive space that academic freedom likely cultivates. Although, it is acknowledged that academic freedom produces challenges not seen within organisations operating in other sectors[174] and may create some hurdles in implementing several of the other proposals made by the scholars of complexity leadership. These challenges are perhaps observed, for example, when academic freedom is cited by those resisting necessary innovations. Additionally, academic freedom and difference will not, by themselves, result in change and innovation. Notwithstanding academic freedom, the academy is observed as being slow to respond, and prominent change scholars provide several recommendations targeted at promoting change within the sector.[175]

The proposals made by the scholars of complexity leadership appear to provide additional reasons for being wary of the increasing influences that promote absolute conformity and erode the freedom. These influences may include the decrease in academic job security[176] and the over 'corporatization' and 'consumerism' of tertiary education,[177] to name a few. When we consider the implementation of some of the proposals made by complexity scholars, it appears that law schools, as organisations, may enjoy certain benefits that come with the systemic entrenchment of the principles of academic freedom. It would be a shame to see the system suffer the loss of that benefit by adopting measures that unnecessarily erode the freedom.

VIII. Conclusion

As complex systems, law schools need to work to ensure that they are responding to society, the profession and their other environments. The scholars of complexity leadership propose that leadership should be designed to cultivate conditions that support adaption and emergence. These scholars highlight the value of allowing for difference within complex systems and propose that leaders make space for and utilise this difference.

In seeking to be more adaptable, law schools might consider adopting the principles of complexity leadership. In doing so, law schools should welcome different ideas and approaches to learning and teaching as an investment in future adaptation. These differences may very well provide a benefit as the demand to evolve increases. Law schools might take the opportunity to view differences as providing capacity for change.

In seeking to encourage and make use of difference, law schools are already the beneficiaries of the principles of academic freedom. The benefits afforded by academic freedom align with some of the proposals made by the scholars of complexity leadership. As such, there is good reason to believe that academic freedom is or could be utilised to advance the adaptive space and innovation within law schools. There are numerous articles describing the reasons to be wary of threats to academic freedom, and it is argued that the scholars of complexity leadership provide us with yet another.

Notes

* This research was supported by an Australian Government Research Training Program (RTP) Scholarship.

1 Navid Ghaffarzadegan, Richard Larson and Joshua Hawley, 'Education as a Complex System' (2017) 34(3) Systems Research and Behavioural Science 211, 212–213.

2 Julian Webb, 'Law, Ethics and Complexity: Complexity Theory and The Normative Reconstruction of Law' (2004) 52(1) Cleveland State Law Review 227, 228.

3 Paul Cilliers, 'Knowing Complex Systems' in Kurt A. Richardson (ed), *Managing Organizational Complexity* (IAP 2005) 8–9.

4 ibid 9.

5 Neil F. Johnson, *Simply Complexity: A Clear Guide to Complexity Theory* (Oneworld 2012) 19.

6 Complex Systems Society, 'What Are Complex Systems' (Complex Systems Society) <https://cssociety.org/about-us/what-are-cs> accessed 20 September 2021.

7 Johnson (n 5) 13.

8 J. B. Ruhl and Daniel M. Katz, 'Mapping Law's Complexity with "Legal Maps"' in Jamie Murray, Thomas E. Webb and Steven Wheatley (eds), *Complexity Theory and Law: Mapping and Emergent Jurisprudence* (Routledge 2018) 31–32.

9 Mark Mason, 'What Is Complexity Theory and What Are Its Implications for Educational Change?' (2008) 40(1) Educational Philosophy and Theory 35, 37.

10 Steven Johnson, *Emergence: The Connected Lives of Ants, Brains, Cities and Software* (Penguin 2001) 18.

11 Benyamin Lichtenstein, 'Emergence and Emergents in Entrepreneurship: Complexity Science Insights into New Venture Creation' (2016) 6(1) Entrepreneurship Research Journal 43, 44–45.

12 ibid 45.

13 Benyamin Lichtenstein, *Generative Emergence: A New Discipline of Organizational, Entrepreneurial, and Social Innovation* (Oxford University Press 2014) 5.

14 Benyamin B. Lichtenstein, 'Complexity Science at a Crossroads: Exploring a Science of Emergence' (2016) 1 Academy of Management Proceedings 542, 544.

15 The quote 'the whole is more than the sum of its parts' is attributed to Aristotle. See Complex Systems Society (n 6).

16 Lichtenstein, 'Complexity Science at a Crossroads' (n 14) 544–546.

17 ibid 546.

18 Brent Davis and Dennis Sumara, *Complexity and Education: Inquiries Into Learning, Teaching and Research* (Lawrence Erlbaum Associates 2006) 8.

19 For an introduction to complexity theory and the social sciences, see David Byrne, *Complexity Theory and the Social Sciences: An Introduction* (Routledge 1998).

20 See, for eg, John H. Miller and Scott E. Page, *Complex Adaptive Systems: An Introduction to Computational Models of Social Life* (Princeton University Press 2007) 10.

21 See, for eg, Cilliers (n 3).

22 See, for eg, Ralph D. Stacey, *Strategic Management and Organisational Dynamics* (2nd edn, Pitman Publishing 1996) and Ralph D. Stacey, *Complexity and Creativity in Organizations* (Berrett-Koehler 1996). Stacey has moved away from the approach taken in his earlier works and now focuses on complex responsive processes. See, for

eg, Ralph D. Stacey, Douglas Griffin and Patricia Shaw, *Complexity and Management: Fad or Radical Challenge to System's Thinking* (Routledge 2000) and Ralph D. Stacey and Chris Mowles, *Strategic Management and Organizational Dynamics* (7th edn, Pearson 2016).

23 An explanation of the methods used and references to examples are provided at pages 533–537 in Benyamin Lichtenstein, 'Applying the 15 Complexity Sciences: Methods for Studying Emergence in Organizations' in Eve Mitleton-Kelly, Alexandros Paraskevas and Christopher Day (eds), *Handbook of Research Methods in Complexity Science: Theory and Applications* (Edward Elgar Publishing 2018).

24 Tara Fenwick, Richard Edwards and Peter Sawchuk, *Emerging Approaches to Educational Research: Tracing the Sociomaterial* (Routledge 2011) 40.

25 See, for eg, the collective works published in Tracey Burns and Florian Köster (eds), *Governing Education in a Complex World* (OECD Publishing 2016).

26 Fenwick, Edwards and Sawchuk (n 24) 40.

27 In relation to national and area education systems, refer to Tracy Burns and Florian Köster, 'Modern Governance Challenges in Education' in Burns and Köster (eds) (n 25) 22. In relation to schools, refer to Keith Morrison, *School Leadership and Complexity Theory* (Routledge 2002) 26, Eileen S. Johnson, 'Ecological Systems and Complexity Theory: Toward an Alternative Model of Accountability in Education' (2008) 5(1) Complicity: An International Journal of Complexity and Education 1, 6, and Nastaran Keshavarz and others, 'Schools as Social Complex Adaptive Systems: A New Way to Understand the Challenges of Introducing the Health Promoting Schools Concept' (2010) 70 Social Science & Medicine 1467, 1472–1473. In relation to Universities, refer to Rómulo Pinheiro and Mitchell Young, 'The University as an Adaptive Resilient Organization: A Complex Systems Perspective' in Jeroen Huisman and Malcolm Tight (eds), *Theory and Method in Higher Education Research* (Volume 3, Emerald Publishing Limited 2017) 122. In relation to degree programs, refer to Elly Govers, 'Embracing Complexity of Educational Programs' (2016) 3 Cogent Education 1, 3.

28 Keshavarz and others (n 27) 1468.

29 See, for eg, Davis and Sumara (n 18) 129–152.

30 Julian Webb, 'Why Learning is a Complex Business' (Conference Paper, The Higher Education Academy, UK Centre for Legal Education 2004) <http://ials.sas.ac.uk/ukcle/78.158.56.101/archive/law/learning-inlaw-annual-conference/2004/papers/webb/index.html> accessed 8 February 2018.

31 Cilliers (n 3) 8.

32 ibid.

33 ibid 9–10.

34 ibid 9.

35 David Barker, *A History of Australian Legal Education* (The Federation Press 2017) 147.

36 'Council of Australian Law Deans (CALD) Is the Peak Body of Australian Law Schools' (CALD) <https://cald.asn.au/> accessed 20 September 2021.

37 See, for eg, Council of Australian Law Deans (CALD), CALD Standards for Australian Law Schools (CALD 2009) <https://cald.asn.au/wp-content/uploads/2017/11/CALD-Standards-Final-Version-as-adopted-17-November-2009-Booklet1.pdf> accessed 31 October 2021. See also CALD's various Best Practice Guidelines available at <https://cald.asn.au/resources/> accessed 16 April 2021.

38 A. Reva Ramiah, 'Complexity Thinking in ALL Practice' (2014) 8(3) Journal of Academic Language and Learning 62, 65.

39 Scott E. Page, 'Where Diversity Comes from and Why It Matters?' (2014) 44(4) European Journal of Social Psychology 267, 268.

40 This reflects the approach taken by Page 'Where Diversity Comes from and Why It Matters?' (n 39) 268, 269.

41 See, for eg, The Canadian Bar Association, *Futures: Transforming the Delivery of Legal Services in Canada* (The Canadian Bar Association 2014), Law Institute of Victoria, *Disruption, Innovation and Change: The Future of the Legal Profession* (Law Institute of Victoria 2015), The Law Society of England and Wales, *The Future of Legal Services* (The Law Society of England and Wales 2016), American Bar Association, *Commission on the Future of Legal Services, Report on the Future of Legal Services in the United States* (American Bar Association 2016), The Law Society of New South Wales, *The Future of Law and Innovation in the Profession Report* (Commission of Inquiry, The Law Society of New South Wales 2017), and The Law Society of England and Wales, *Capturing Technological Innovation in Legal Services* (The Law Society of England and Wales 2017).
42 The Law Society of New South Wales (n 41) 12, 15–26, 31–43, 57–63.
43 For a discussion of several of the changes occurring within society, refer to Alina Narcisa Crişan, 'Higher Education and the Challenges of Postmodern Society' (2019) IX(LXXI) (2) Journal of Educational Sciences & Psychology 10–14. For a discussion of the changes impacting the professions, refer to Richard Susskind and Daniel Susskind, *The Future of the Professions: How Technology Will Transform the Work of Human Experts* (Oxford University Press 2015) 101–142.
44 Max Boisot and Bill McKelvey, 'Complexity and Organization – Environment Relations: Revisiting Ashby's Law of Requite Varity' in Peter Allen, Steve Maguire and Bill McKelvey (eds), *The Sage Handbook of Complexity and Management* (Sage 2011) 279–298.
45 Page, 'Where Diversity Comes from and Why It Matters?' (n 39) 268, 277.
46 ibid 268.
47 Scott E. Page, *The Difference: How the Power of Diversity Creates Better Groups, Firms, Schools, and Societies* (ProQuest edn, Princeton University Press 2007).
48 Scott E. Page, *Diversity and Complexity* (ProQuest edn, Princeton University Press 2011).
49 Scott E. Page, *The Diversity Bonus: How Great Teams Pay Off in the Knowledge Economy* (2nd edn, ProQuest edn, Princeton University Press 2019).
50 Page, *Diversity and Complexity* (n 48) 26, 146.
51 Buck Lawrimore, 'From Excellence to Emergence: The Evolution of Management Thinking and the Influence of Complexity' in Kurt A. Richardson (ed), *Managing Organizational Complexity* (IAP 2005) 130.
52 Page, 'Where Diversity Comes from and Why It Matters?' (n 39) 276–277; Page, *Diversity and Complexity* (n 48) 89.
53 Page, 'Where Diversity Comes from and Why It Matters?' (n 39) 276–277.
54 ibid 276; Mary Uhl-Bien, Russ Marion and Bill McKelvey, 'Complexity Leadership Theory: Shifting Leadership from the Industrial Age to the Knowledge Era' (2007) 18(4) The Leadership Quarterly 298, 307.
55 Page, 'Where Diversity Comes from and Why It Matters?' (n 39) 276–277.
56 Uhl-Bien, Marion and McKelvey (n 54) 311; Jeffrey Goldstein, James K. Hazy and Benyamin B. Lichtenstein, *Complexity and the Nexus of Leadership* (Palgrave Macmillan 2010) 28.
57 Russ Marion, 'Complexity Theory for Organizations and Organizational Leadership' in Mary Uhl-Bien and Russ Marion (eds), *Complexity Leadership* (Information Age Publishing, Incorporated 2007) 1, 11; Uhl-Bien, Marion and McKelvey (n 54) 309. See also, Lichtenstein, *Generative Emergence* (n 13) 395.
58 Goldstein, Hazy and Lichtenstein (n 56) 79–100; Benyamin B. Lichtenstein and Donde Ashmos Plowman, 'The Leadership of Emergence: A Complex Systems Leadership Theory of Emergence at Successive Organizational Levels' (2009) 20(4) The Leadership Quarterly 617, 620–621. See also, Lichtenstein, *Generative Emergence* (n 13) 396.
59 Lichtenstein, *Generative Emergence* (n 13) 395.

60 James K. Hazy, Jeffrey A. Goldstein and Benyamin B. Lichtenstein, 'Complex Systems Leadership Theory: An Introduction' in James K. Hazy, Jeffrey A. Goldstein and Benyamin B. Lichtenstein (eds), *Complex Systems Leadership Theory* (ISCE Publishing 2007) 2. There are a number of contributing authors including Russ Marion, Mary Uhl-Bien and Bill McKelvey.
61 Benyamin B. Lichtenstein and others, 'Complexity Leadership Theory: An Interactive Perspective on Leading in Complex Adaptive Systems' in James K. Hazy, Jeffrey A. Goldstein and Benyamin B. Lichtenstein (eds), *Complex Systems Leadership Theory* (ISCE Publishing 2007) 133.
62 Hazy, Goldstein and Lichtenstein (n 60) 5.
63 Stacey, *Complexity and Creativity in Organizations* (n 22) 25–26.
64 Hazy, Goldstein and Lichtenstein (n 60) 7.
65 ibid 2.
66 ibid 7.
67 ibid 10.
68 Uhl-Bien, Marion and McKelvey (n 54).
69 ibid 198–199.
70 Mary Uhl-Bien and Michael Arena, 'Leadership for Organizational Adaptability: A Theoretical Synthesis and Integrative Framework' (2018) 29(1) The Leadership Quarterly 89, 98.
71 ibid.
72 ibid.
73 Uhl-Bien, Marion and McKelvey (n 54) 311.
74 ibid.
75 Goldstein, Hazy and Lichtenstein (n 56).
76 ibid 82.
77 ibid 82–88, 102–103.
78 ibid 11, 29, 86–88, 104–105.
79 Brent Davis and Elaine Simmt, 'Understanding Learning Systems: Mathematics Education and Complexity Science' (2003) 34(2) Journal for Research in Mathematics Education 137, 144; Davis and Sumara (n 18) 135–151; Craig Newell, 'The Class as a Learning Entity (Complex Adaptive System): An Idea from Complexity Science and Educational Research' (2008) 2 Simon Fraser University Educational Review 5, 13.
80 Davis and Simmt (n 79) 144; Newell (n 79) 11, 13.
81 Davis and Simmt (n 79) 147–150, 159–160; Davis and Sumara (n 18) 137–140; Newell (n 79) 9–10.
82 Davis and Simmt (n 79) 147–157, 159–163; Davis and Sumara (n 18) 137–149.
83 Denis J. Sumara and Brent A. Davis, 'Correspondence, Coherence, Complexity: Theories of Learning and Their Influences on Processes of Literary Composition' (2006) 5(2) English Teaching: Practice and Critique 34, 46.
84 Page, *The Difference* (n 47) 323.
85 Goldstein, Hazy and Lichtenstein (n 56) 125–146.
86 Gretchen M. Spreitzer and Scott Sonenshein, 'Toward the Construct Definition of Positive Deviance' (2004) 47(6) American Behavioural Scientist 828; Matthew J. Herington and Elske van de Fliert, 'Positive Deviance in Theory and Practice: A Conceptual Review' (2018) 39(5) Deviant Behaviour 664.
87 See, for eg, Goldstein, Hazy and Lichtenstein (n 56) 125–146, and Thomas R. Clancy, 'Diamonds in the Rough: Positive Deviance and Complexity' (2010) 40(2) Journal of Nursing Administrations 53.
88 David Marsh and others, 'The Power of Positive Deviance' (2004) 329 British Medical Journal 1177, 1177.
89 Jerry Sternin and Robert Choo, 'The Power of Positive Deviancy' (2000) 78(1) Harvard Business Review 14, 14–15.

90 Jerry Sternin, 'Positive Deviance: A New Paradigm for Addressing Today's Problems Today' (2002) 5 The Journal of Corporate Citizenship 57, 58.
91 Richard T. Pascale, Jerry Sternin and Monique Sternin, *The Power of Positive Deviance: How Unlikely Innovators Solve the World's Toughest Problems* (Harvard Business Review Press 2010) 20–46.
92 Sternin and Choo (n 89) 15. Examples and case studies of positive deviance in action can be found at <https://positivedeviance.org/>.
93 Sternin and Choo (n 89) 15.
94 Goldstein, Hazy and Lichtenstein (n 56) 11.
95 ibid.
96 ibid 137–142.
97 For a discission of the pros and cons of the case method, see David D. Garner, 'The Continuing Vitality of the Case Method in the Twenty-First Century' (2000) 2 Brigham Young University Education and Law Journal 307 and Upinder Dhar and Santosh Dhar, 'The Case Method in Legal Education' (2018) 5(2) Asian Journal of Legal Education 182.
98 Bruce A. Kimball, 'The Proliferation of Case Method Teaching in American Law Schools: Mr Langdell's Emblematic "Abomination" 1890–1915' (2006) 46(2) History of Education Quarterly 192, 193.
99 Maxeiner views this as an adaption in James R. Maxeiner, 'Educating Lawyers Now and Then: Two Carnegie Critiques of the Common Law and the Case Method' (2007) 35(1) International Journal of Legal Information 1, 44–45.
100 Bruce A. Kimball, *The Inception of Modern Professional Education: C.C. Langdell, 1826–1906* (University of North Carolina Press 2009) 142.
101 Russel L. Weaver, 'Langdell's Legacy: Living with the Case Method' (1991) 36(2) Villanova Law Review 517, 524–525; Matthew T. Bodie, 'Open Source and the Reinvention of Legal Education' in Edward Rubin (ed), *Legal Education in the Digital Age* (Cambridge University Press 2012) 35.
102 Weaver (n 101) 524–526.
103 Dhar and Dhar (n 97) 182.
104 Kimball (n 98) 194.
105 ibid.
106 Ralph Michael Stein, 'The Path of Legal Education from Edward I to Langdell: A History of Insular Reaction' (1981) 57 Chicago-Kent Law Review 429, 452; Weaver (n 101) 539.
107 Kimball (n 98) 193, 195–196.
108 Lee Shulman, 'The Signature Pedagogies of Law, Medicine and Engineering, and the Clergy: Potential Lessons for the Education of Teachers (Math Science Partnership Workshop, Teacher Education for Effective Teaching and Learning, National Research Council's Centre for Education, 6–8 February 2005) 7–8.
109 For the history of clinical legal education in Australia, refer to Jeff Giddings, 'Clinical Legal Education in Australia: A Historical Perspective' (2003) 3 International Journal of Clinical Legal Education 7.
110 See, Ainslie Lamb, John Littrich and Karina Murray, *Lawyers in Australia* (3rd edn, The Federation Press 2015) 34–35.
111 See, Kate Galloway and others, 'The Legal Academy's Engagements with LawTech: Technology Narratives and Archetypes as Drivers of Change' (2019) 1(1) Law, Technology and Humans 27.
112 Sternin and Choo (n 89) 15; Goldstein, Hazy and Lichtenstein (n 56) 121, 125–146.
113 Marsh and others (n 88) 1177.
114 Uhl-Bien, Marion and McKelvey (n 54) 311; Uhl-Bien and Arena (n 70) 99.
115 Goldstein, Hazy and Lichtenstein (n 56) 104.
116 ibid 104, 121.

117 ibid 121.
118 Uhl-Bien, Marion and McKelvey (n 54) 311.
119 ibid; Uhl-Bien and Arena (n 70) 98–99.
120 ibid.
121 Uhl-Bien and Arena (n 70) 99.
122 Julian Birkinshaw and Cristina Gibson. 'Building Ambidexterity into an Organization' (2004) 45(4) MIT Sloan Management Review 47, 51; ibid; Jonas Hermann Shulze and Felix Pinkow, 'Leadership for Organisational Adaptability: How Enabling Leaders Create Adaptive Space' (2020) 10(3) Administrative Sciences 37, 45, 53; Stella Howden, Marie Beresford-Dey and Linda Martindale, 'Critical Reflections on Academic Leadership During Covid-19: Using Complexity Leadership Theory to Understand the Transition to Remote and Blended Learning' (2021) 9(2) Journal of Perspectives in Applied Academic Practice 118, 124–125.
123 Birkinshaw and Gibson (n 122) 53; Shulze and Pinkow (n 122) 45, 53.
124 Amy Edmondson, 'Psychological Safety and Learning Behaviour in Work Teams' (1999) 44(2) Administrative Science Quarterly 350, 354.
125 Deanna de Zilwa, *Academic Units in a Complex Changing World: Adaption and Resistance* (Springer 2010) 130, 132.
126 Goldstein, Hazy and Lichtenstein (n 56) 81–90.
127 ibid 28, 104–105.
128 ibid 111.
129 ibid 104, 111–112.
130 George Siemens, Shane Dawson and Kirsten Eshleman, 'Complexity: A Leader's Framework for Understanding and Managing Change in Higher Education' (2018) November/December Educause Review 27, 38.
131 Page, *Diversity and Complexity* (n 48) 146–147.
132 ibid.
133 ibid 147.
134 ibid 145.
135 Hazy, Goldstein and Lichtenstein (n 60) 10.
136 Michael Fullan, *Leading in a Culture of Change* (2nd edn, Jossey-Bass 2020) 62, 75, 100.
137 ibid 75, 127.
138 ibid 121.
139 Page, *The Difference* (n 47) 131–174, 239–296; Page, *Diversity and Complexity* (n 48) 146–147; Page, 'Where Diversity Comes from and Why It Matters?' (n 39) 275–277.
140 Page, *Diversity and Complexity* (n 48) 11, 13–17.
141 Mary Uhl-Bien, 'Complexity and COVID-19: Leadership and Followership in a Complex World' (2021) 58(5) Journal of Management Studies 1400, 1402–1403.
142 ibid 1402.
143 ibid 1401.
144 ibid.
145 Howden, Beresford-Dey and Martindale (n 122) 123.
146 ibid 124.
147 Law Admission Consultative Committee (LACC), *Model Admission Rules 2015* (Revised December 2016, LACC 2015) <https://www.legalservicescouncil.org.au/Documents/model-admission-rules-2015.pdf> accessed 7 November 2021. For an example of the enactment of these requirements, see the Legal Profession Act 2004 (NSW), s 24, and the Legal Profession Admission Rules 2005 (NSW), rr 43(4) and 95.
148 LACC (n 147) 6–12.
149 ibid.

150 ibid.

151 Margaret Thornton, *Privatising the Public University* (Routledge 2012) 37.

152 Michael Adams, 'Developments in Australian Curriculum and Teaching Across the Various Law Degrees' (Forum 1 'What Do We Teach and How?', Sino-Australian Law Deans Meeting, Hangzhou, 28 September 2014) < https://cald.asn.au/wp-content/uploads/2017/11/Adams-Michael.-Paper-presented-at-the-Sino-Aust-Law-Deans-Meeting-28-29-Sept-2014.pdf> accessed 7 November 2021, 11–12.

153 Dan C. Lortie, *Schoolteacher: A Sociological Study* (first published 1975, University of Chicago Press 2002) 61.

154 ibid 61–63.

155 David M. Moss and Debra Moss Curtis, 'Essential Elements for the Reform of Legal Education' in David M. Moss and Debra Moss Curtis (eds), *Reforming Legal Education: Law School at the Crossroads* (Information Age Publishing 2012) 223.

156 Philip G. Altbach, Maria Yudkevich and Laura E. Rumbley, 'Academic Inbreeding: Local Challenge, Global Problem' in Maria Yudkevich, Philip G. Altbach and Laura E. Rumbley (eds), *Academic Inbreeding and Mobility in Higher Education: Global Perspectives* (Palgrave MacMillan 2015) 1.

157 Angela Melville, Amy Barrow and Patrick Morgan, 'Inbreeding and the Reproduction of Elitism: An Empirical Examination of Inbreeding within Australian Legal Academia' (2020) 30(1) Legal Education Review 1.

158 ibid 1, 3–5.

159 See, for eg, Goldstein, Hazy and Lichtenstein (n 56) 55–65.

160 Michael W. Doyle, Johanna Fine and Matthew Moneyhon (eds), *Report of the First Global Colloquium of University Presidents on Academic Freedom and International Migration* (Global Colloquium of University Presidents 2005) 5.

161 Conrad Russell, *Academic Freedom* (Taylor & Francis Group 1993) 44.

162 For recent examples, see Robert S. French, Independent Review of Freedom of Speech in Australian Higher Education Providers (March 2019) (the French Report), Sally Walker AM, Report of Independent Review of the Adoption of the Model Code on Freedom of Speech and Academic Freedom (December 2020), and *Ridd v James Cook University* [2021] HCA 32.

163 For a summary of the Australian regulatory and policy framework, see Carolyn Evans and Adrienne Stone, *Open Minds: Academic Freedom and Freedom of Speech in Australia* (La Trobe University Press 2021) 33–40.

164 For a summary of the French Report (n 162) and the responses to that report, see Evans and Stone (n 163) 41–43. For a summary and discussion of the Federal and Full Federal Court judgments in *Ridd* (n 162), see Adrienne Stone, 'The Meaning of Academic Freedom: The Significance of 'Ridd v James Cook University' (2021) 43(2) The Sydney Law Review 241.

165 For example, Uhl-Bien, Marion and McKelvey (n 54) 311 discuss the importance of establishing an environment in which agents respect difference and Uhl-Bien and Arena (n 70) 99 discuss the importance of establishing mutual confidence. In order to ensure these conditions, and others, there must be limitations.

166 Eric Barendt, *Academic Freedom and the Law: A Comparative Study* (Hart Publishing 2010) 22–49; Evans and Stone (n 163) 54–56.

167 Evans and Stone (n 163) 54.

168 ibid 54–55.

169 *Ridd* (n 162) [31].

170 Evans and Stone (n 163) 47.

171 Mostafa B. Abdel-Motaal, 'Academic Freedom and Civil Society: Some Personal Reflections' (2002) 15 Higher Education Policy 365, 369.

172 See, for eg, Terence Karran, 'Academic Freedom: In Justification of a Universal Ideal' (2009) 34(3) Studies in Higher Education (Dorchester-on-Thames) 263, 275–276.

173 A point that is also made in Andrew Norton, 'Academic Freedom by the Book: Complex in Theory and Practice', The Australian (Online, 11 May 2021) <https://www.theaustralian.com.au/>. Norton reviews and provides commentary on Evans and Stone (n 163) emphasising the authors's support of academic freedom in serving the common good. See Evans and Stone (n 163) 47–48.

174 See, for eg, Liviu Andreescu, 'Academic Freedom: A Guide for the Academic Leader (2013) 3 Leadership and Governance in Higher Education 1, 20–23. See also, for eg, Nick James, 'How Dare You Tell Me How to Teach!: Resistance to Educationalism within Australian Law Schools' (2013) 36(3) University of New South Wales Law Journal 779, 804.

175 Michael Fullan and Geoff Scott, *Turnaround Leadership for Higher Education* (Jossey-Bass 2009).

176 Kathleen Lynch and Mariya Ivancheva, 'Academic Freedom and the Commercialisation of Universities: A Critical Ethical Analysis' (2015) 15 Ethics in Science and Environmental Politics 71, 77.

177 Margaret Thornton, 'Legal Education in the Corporate University' (2014) 10 Annual Review of Law and Social Sciences 19, 19, 29–30; Margaret Thornton, 'The Law School, the Market and the New Knowledge Economy' (2007) 17(1) Legal Education Review 1, 25; Evans and Stone (n 163) 75–77.

6 Re-Thinking Assessment in Law

Alex Steel

The legal curriculum is staggering under the weight of increasing and arguably impossible expectations. There is a sense it must teach more detail and more skills in less time and with an increasing burden of assessment. Changes to how teaching is timetabled and moves to more formative assessment have increased levels of assessment at the same time that the impact of technology on the student cohort has made them less prepared for traditional assessment forms. The impact of COVID-19 sees the curriculum and the assessment of student learning at a tipping point. Old shibboleths have been challenged and at least partly overcome. As law schools seek to return to a 'normal' approach to teaching, could there be changes in the way law students are assessed that might provide more space and flexibility in the curriculum?

This chapter outlines those challenges and then critically analyses the contours of assessment in law. It identifies the various dimensions, environments, formats and approaches to grading typically used. For each aspect, the chapter considers alternative approaches that might better aid student learning and reduce academic workloads. The chapter concludes with a suggestion for a radically different approach to assessment in legal education.

I. The Current Landscape

A. More and More to Learn

There is more law than there has been in previous generations, and understanding it is more complex.[1] Common law jurisdictions lean heavily on the concept of precedent, and so much authority for current interpretations depends on a nuanced understanding of previous caselaw, both of common law and statute. Courts developing that precedent craft their judgments with a focus on the needs of the parties and the issues put before them. They do not see themselves as providing content for new editions of textbooks on the law. Consequently, any new case that resolves or develops a point of law is unlikely to fully describe the whole area of law in which it sits. This requires lawyers, and law students, to study previous decisions in order to see the new decision in context.

In the last century, law schools developed the case-method approach to teaching.[2] Students are asked to read full or extracted appeal cases – to see the law as

DOI: 10.4324/9781003175216-7

primary sources – and to construct a complete understanding of the area of law by a compilation of the various legal decisions. Often this involves a critical parsing of the judgments to sift obiter dicta from ratio decidenda. This approach to learning builds reading and analytical skills as well as legal knowledge. But it takes up significant time in a curriculum. A single lecture can cover the main points of an area of law in under an hour, but reading and discussing the key cases – and then extracting the principles – takes much longer.

As courts continue to develop law, and more areas of law become significant for legal practice, there is increasing pressure to reduce the length of extracts that can be read by students, the amount of time in class that can be spent analysing them and indeed the number of areas of law that can be covered.[3] The facts of the cases are also often more complex than in previous generations. Corporate structures and the digital economy can militate against a simple, concise explanation of the facts underlying the issue.

Additionally, legislation is constantly being created by Parliaments. Again, the legislation is not getting simpler and is increasingly interconnected. This means that if students are to appreciate the web of legislative provisions, significant time must be spent reading and analysing Acts as a whole rather than as isolated provisions.[4]

The increase tends more towards the exponential than the linear. This is largely due to technology. In previous generations, written law was relatively scarce. Acts were printed in volumes, and caselaw was selected and edited for printed law reports. Law from other jurisdictions could take months to arrive on boats. Today, judgments at all levels of the court hierarchy and across the world are potentially available instantly; hearings and judgments may be streamed live. Similar instantaneity applies to Parliaments and legislation.

Beyond law itself, there are increasing commissions of enquiry, law reform bodies, activist and academic interventions and a whole world of peer-reviewed theoretical, doctrinal and empirical legal and socio-legal publication. All of these are now instantly available on computer screens worldwide, rather than being locked up in libraries or only available on application. Large-scale digitisation projects have brought to the internet primary materials stretching back decades and sometimes centuries.

A law school curriculum thus battles increasing volume and complexity in law and a digital stream of information that is not easily edited and prioritised – not only by academics in constructing classes but also by students in researching assessments.

This deluge of information is replicated in practice. Lawyers no longer need to be able to learn the arcane skills of a legislation citator reference book, the catalogue system of their firm and the Law Society's library in order to find the hidden precedent for their case. Instead, they need critical analysis and logic skills to construct boolean text-string searches in databases. They need to read quickly across digital texts to find key passages but with an ability to keep in their minds the logical structure of the publication they are reading. They need to be able to know when a source distributed through social media – and often professional social media – is reliable. Increasingly they will rely on AI to manage their workloads.[5] These skills are on top of the traditional legal research skills. Despite claims that younger generations are 'digital natives', many of these digital skills need to be learned in law school.[6]

Traditional legal communication skills must still be learned. The ability to craft extended legal advice, the ability to verbally articulate a logical argument and the ability to respectfully listen and respond in non-emotional ways remain key skills for a lawyer. In some ways, particularly in relation to written outputs, the requirements of legal practice are divorced from the way business is conducted and secondary school is taught. There is thus an increased need to emphasise and practice skills in which previous generations may have already been partly proficient. Those skills also need to be translated to other digital formats, such as formal writing in emails. In short, the scope of technical skills required in the curriculum has expanded.

Finally, law schools and the profession are also now recognising the need to provide soft skills and life skills alongside the analytical aspects of university study. Many students undertake university straight out of school and are in a vulnerable transition phase from childhood to adulthood, from dependent to independent study and life. There is an increasing realisation that law schools have a responsibility to equip students with skills to enable them to be resilient and thrive in a quickly changing world.[7] Skills of digital communication, time management, reflection and maintaining wellbeing are increasingly being taught explicitly.

Together, these factors have created a highly crowded curriculum. It seems to inevitably lead to compromises on content and skills and on breadth and context in the curriculum.[8]

In terms of assessment, these crowded curricula can have a range of effects. If content is dealt with at speed or in a summary fashion, it becomes difficult to set complex or analytical questions, and the tendency can be instead to focus on proof of knowledge retention. It can be difficult to ensure academic integrity in such assessment without invigilation – and this then leads to a tendency to set stressful, time-limited and supervised examinations.

For students, covering a wide range of material at speed can also make it stressful to study and increase the pressure to rely on others' notes – whether borrowed or purchased. This then undervalues the role of the class readings and discussion and tends to produce increasingly uniform assessment answers and issues of academic integrity. Finding space to properly assess research skills and other soft skills is also made more difficult by the felt need to assess the mass of content covered.

B. Less Time to Do It In

The last few decades have seen fundamental changes to the way legal education is set up. Most universities taught year-long courses in the 1970s, broken into terms.[9] By the 1990s, universities had moved to semesters.[10] A growing number are now teaching in discrete terms or trimesters.[11] Some are experimenting with 'intensive'[12] or 'block model'[13] approaches, whether face to face or online. At the postgraduate level, intensive teaching has become commonplace, operated within semester frameworks.

How a student's learning year is divided up has significant implications for assessment. The usual approach to tertiary education for many years has been to teach discrete subjects or units that are the same length as the teaching term. Assessment is also commonly weighted towards the end of the term, with 'finals' occurring after teaching concludes and constituting a majority of the percentage of the final grade. A few decades ago, that might have been a 100% final examination.[14] Today, more in-term summative assessment occurs, but there remains an inevitable emphasis on a final assessment.[15] The movement towards more in-term, low-stakes and formative assessment are intended to provide better scaffolding for student learning – sometimes described as 'assessment for learning' rather than 'assessment of learning'.[16] This is an important and laudable aim. But when it is combined with shorter teaching terms, it often leads to over-assessment. There is a tendency to set the same number of assessments per subject irrespective of its length. A final exam for a one-year length subject or a 6-week length subject is still likely to be 2–3 hours, yet the coverage is unlikely to be the same. No matter the length of the subject, there will be one or two in-term assessments. There are not likely to be significant differences in the amount of preparation or research required.

On paper, a year-long subject taught two hours per week and a half-year subject taught four hours per week or four subjects taught over a semester and four subjects taught in intensive blocks and sequentially over the same period all seem to have the same content and teaching time. But research shows that the cognitive load is different, and students' abilities to absorb, synthesise and reflect on their learning are more limited in intensive teaching modes.[17] As a learning experience, it can be immersive and transformative. But as experienced teachers know, students just don't have the time to do all the pre-reading required, and the more compressed the subject, the less content can be covered. This then impacts the scope of what can be assessed.

C. Changing Students

Today's students are very different to those of previous generations. The internet and smart devices have brought entertainment and distraction into almost all facets of learning and studying. Constant streams of information and info-tainment through social media have produced an 'always on' society.[18] The constant flicking from one screen to another, from one platform to another, has also built a facility and preference for multitasking, though the evidence suggests that this is at the loss of deeper learning.[19] This militates against extended periods of quiet reflection or content revision, against what Csikzentmihaly called 'flow'.[20] Our work worlds are now largely reliant on instant search and retrieval of information rather than memorisation. There is some evidence that this has changed the way we remember things.[21]

These developments mean that students can find it more difficult to absorb large sections of complex text.[22] Yet often, assessment remains centred around large-scale, memory-based tasks in time-limited formats[23] that neither reflect the way students learn nor how they will work in the profession. These skills arguably remain important foundational abilities, but as already mentioned, students are less prepared than in previous generations.

Students often come to university with a concretised approach to test-taking. For many, regular testing and sorting by apparent ability from those tests is an experience they have had since kindergarten.[24] Matriculating to university is likely to have involved repetitive learning of notes prepared by others and inculcation into a culture of looking to coaches or tutors for the 'correct' answer.[25] Many of the 'innovative' approaches to assessment in universities will have already been experienced in secondary school, and not all experiences will have been positive.

Particularly in law, students are likely to have been high achievers in secondary school and at least partly define themselves around their test results.[26] This may be combined with a fear that labour markets are competitive, and they will need to sustain high grades to be employed in the profession. This ingrained approach to test-taking and fear of failure is likely to mean students are risk-averse and anxious about any approach to assessment that is not clear-cut or based on rigid rubrics.

D. Competing Demands on Staff

Academic staff have also faced significant changes in recent years to how they are involved in assessment. Teaching loads and class sizes have increased as law schools grow in size. Increasing numbers of law staff are now employed as 'teaching focussed' or as casuals with higher teaching loads than full-time staff with research commitments.[27] Those attempting to undertake research face a battle to prioritise their teaching over the need to comply with research output performance metrics. Shorter teaching terms leave less time to mark and develop new assessment. High workloads lead to exhaustion and a lack of enthusiasm for innovative practices.[28]

In order to try to deal with these workload issues, staff are driven towards assessment that is quick to mark. Questions with predetermined answers and based on the assessment of knowledge rather than reasoning – such as multiple choice or short answer questions – have increased attraction. There is a tendency to retain and re-use questions leading to both issues for assessment integrity and also limiting students' ability to learn from their performance because of the need to prevent students from retaining the question.

E. The Enduring Impacts of the Pandemic

COVID-19 has fundamentally disrupted education, and it remains unclear what environments we will settle back into. However, some things appear to have changed irrevocably. Online learning and assessment have moved from a fringe aspect of higher education to the core.[29] While face-to-face learning will remain a treasured aspect of legal study, it is likely there will now be a significant online component. The pedagogies of online learning and teaching are different to face-to-face. They require technical skills significantly beyond the ability to use a pen and a whiteboard marker, and they require approaches to interaction and engagement that can be quite different to face-to-face techniques. Online and remote assessment also upends many assumptions about high-stakes assessment. Where face-to-face assessment is by its nature amenable to time limits, invigilation and closed book, remote assessment works best over longer time periods (to guard against internet connection failures), open book and without invigilation. Assessment questions are easily retained by students either with approval via downloads or surreptitiously via screenshots and photos by phones. This undermines attempts to develop reusable banks of multiple-choice questions. The ability to undertake internet searches on the exam-taking device, or another device, severely limits the utility of short answer questions for which defined knowledge-based answers exist.

II. Dimensions of Assessment

Together, these are seismic changes to the way we teach and the way students learn. This chapter suggests similar seismic changes should occur to the way we assess.

A. Atomistic – Programme Level, Programmatic

Law schools have traditionally built degree programs against a list of 19th-century doctrinal categories.[30] Once a student understood the basics of the legal system and had a modicum of research and writing skills, they passed from doctrinal course to doctrinal course with a final exam to assure knowledge prior to each transition. Some of the courses were built on assumed knowledge, but largely no knowledge of earlier courses was expected. There has been no final assessment in Australia at the end of the degree for many decades.[31] As a result, overall competence was, and is, demonstrated by overall grade averages and, for informed employers, how well a student went in 'tough' subjects. For students, this means no need to retain any detailed knowledge of a subject from one year to the next, and also the ability to increasingly take the subjects in whatever order is most convenient. This is currently reinforced for law schools in Australia by the fact that schools are accredited against eleven Prescribed Areas of Knowledge (known as the Priestley 11).[32] Nothing is expected of the law schools beyond ensuring graduates are competent in these discrete doctrinal areas, though in recent years, some accrediting bodies have begun to require a grounding in statutory interpretation.[33] It is important to note, however, that government regulators require a more holistic approach to assessment[34] and legal scholars have argued for capstone assessments for some time.[35] Yet, the atomistic sentiment prevails.

As the time spent on courses gets shorter and assessment tasks increase, there is a danger that learning is being atomised into a series of incremental achievements that are never synthesised into a larger whole. The alternative is to see the student journey through the degree as an arc rather than a series of disconnected achievement points. Achievements and skills should build on each other – and should be expected and used in later subjects. This means decoupling assessment from individual subjects. Rather than defining the degree by the subjects studied, the subjects could be background building blocks of an overall program-level approach to assessment and achievement. For example, low-stakes assessment of knowledge attainment can be a part of those subjects, but higher-stakes assessment that combines multiple subjects into one assessment can be set annually. Problem questions combining contracts and torts, ethics and criminal law are possible examples. If low-stakes testing of knowledge has already occurred, that knowledge can be assumed in the larger assessments which can focus on critical reasoning or communication skills.

The first stage in this development is to see assessment from a program perspective. Thus, at some point in the program, students must be assessed against the key areas (such as the Priestleys), but the timing of that assessment is not tied to the attending of classes for that subject area. Breaking that link allows for assessments that combine topics and for moving high-stakes assessments to a time of the year that better suits student and staff workflows.

A second stage is to introduce programmatic approaches to assessment.[36] This involves identifying skills and attributes that are formed by students throughout a degree but not fully developed until the end. Assessment is based around formative and low-stakes tasks that demonstrate the development of the skill or attribute. In law, the most obvious are legal analysis and research skills and communication and self-management skills. Programmatic assessment of these skills can complement program-level assessment of doctrinal knowledge. Whereas program-level assessment would emphasise high-stakes assessment at different points in the degree to assure learning, programmatic assessment would only assure learning at the end of the degree. Programmatic assessment is also often associated with assessment portfolios.[37] Portfolios curate a series of student outputs and allow a holistic assessment of achievement at the end of a degree, even when the task was completed earlier in the degree.

In fact, Australian law schools already have the basis for programmatic assessment in place. Australian universities are required by legislation to have learning outcomes for all degree programs. Most law schools have adopted the Law Threshold Learning Outcomes (TLOs),[38] or a variant thereof. The TLOs set out levels of competence, skill and achievement that all graduates should have on graduation. Law schools will have mapped these outcomes to some extent to their existing curriculum. The awkwardness of fit in these exercises is due to the need to shoehorn them into a subject-dominated assessment strategy.

But if the assessment can be wrested free from the subjects, a very different set of assessment expectations could be crafted. Currently, the Priestley 11 lists legal content only – there is no reference at all to any underlying reasoning skills, research ability or critical thinking. By contrast, the TLOs only refer to legal content in one of six outcomes. Those others speak of the skills and attributes of a lawyer. Yet legal doctrinal knowledge remains implicit in all. One cannot advise a client without knowing the legal issues; one cannot undertake legal research without understanding what is being read. Assessment could be arranged around the TLOs and inserted into stages of the degree, leaving the doctrinal aspects to be building blocks to these larger, integrated assessments.

B. Summative-Formative

Over the last decades, there has been a growing emphasis on formative forms of assessment. That is, an assessment task is seen not just as a badge of achievement – where the ultimate score obtained is all that matters – but, instead, as a structured way to provide feedback for students on how their learning is progressing, explaining the nature of the errors they have made and how to resolve them, and also providing encouragement and praise for tasks done well. It is sometimes described as the difference between 'assessment of learning' and 'assessment for learning'.[39] In law, most summative assessment tasks now include formative aspects.[40] A research essay will involve both a final mark and also formative feedback – at times in the style of a rubric. There is sometimes complaint from academics that students only care about the mark and fail to read or learn from the feedback.

In large part, the failure of students to learn from the feedback on assessment is because the atomistic nature of assessment means that students do not think the feedback will ever be of direct assistance in the rest of their degree – instead seeing it as a justification for the mark given. The feedback is interpreted in light of the mark – a good mark means any negative feedback can be discounted and vice versa.

One way to subvert this is to set far fewer summative assessments – that is, far fewer assessments where a mark counts towards the final grade. Instead, assessments can be entirely formative – where students only receive feedback on their performance with an indication of the grade they might have got or no grade indication at all. This would make the feedback the only way students could assess their progress. Students could hand in substandard efforts without formal penalty, but then the stress levels going into summative assessments with higher weighting would increase as students would be less certain of their capacity to pass. Staff in formative assessments would not need to worry about constructing overall grades or class rankings – instead just providing advice for improvement.

Formative assessment also lends itself to peer assessment.[41] This is an often-underappreciated form of assessment and feedback. For it to be effective, though, students need to be trained in how to give feedback. This training then can develop into a graduate's ability to give respectful feedback and critically assess others' work. Peer review of assessment provides multiple benefits. A primary benefit is that students see more papers than their own or their friends. This helps students to understand how their work sits in the broader cohort – to see excellent and poor work – and to encourage more engagement through the responsibility of critiquing their peers.[42]

So why do we set so many summative assessments? It appears to be a mismatched combination of student welfare and staff convenience. Some decades ago, 100% final examinations were common. There was justifiable concern that this meant students were being unfairly assessed – assessed at only one point in time and often only in one assessment format. As a reaction, summative assessment has been spread across the term with limits on the weighting that can be given to any one assessment. This is a significant improvement for students, though it increases the workload on academics.

On the other hand, the myopic focus on assessment inside individual subjects has been largely for the convenience of academics. If the Law School wishes to assess student learning in a subject, the simplest way to do so is to create a test during or at the end of that subject and only assess students on materials taught in that subject. This means that in the academic setting, the designer of the assessment only needs to have detailed knowledge of the material in that subject and has no responsibility for assessing the overall learning to that point in the degree. Students can be directed to quite specific materials needed to prepare for the assessment (e.g., set readings), and this alignment also assists in producing largely standardised answers that make marking quicker.

However, if program-level assessment is developed as discussed above, the summative assessment of the subject need not be during the subject, and students could take it when they have completed all the subjects that made up the exam coverage. These assessments that combine subject areas need not only be final exams. They could be cross-subject research papers or authentic experiential assessments. Student welfare would not be diminished by the removal of the number of summative assessments if an equivalent number of formative assessments remained, and students could use these to build confidence and competence towards the major summative assessments.

C. Random – Aligned

Moving the balance of assessment away from summative to formative is predicated on the need to align assessment not only to subject learning outcomes but across the degree. Assessment in individual subjects is often set without any reference to other subjects. This leads to a lack of obvious relevance of feedback for later tasks discussed above. It means that it is not clear to students how feedback on performance in an assessment in one subject could assure them that they will succeed in a subsequent assessment in a different subject.

Instead, assessment across the degree should be set with intentional alignment towards major summative moments. The assessments should build on each other – each subsequent task assuming the use of knowledge and skills assessed in earlier assessments. This then makes feedback critical for students to understand what their learning gaps are. Assessment can also move towards program perspectives on skills. For example, expertise in statutory interpretation is unlikely to be achieved in one term but can be seen as a group of distinct sub-skills that build on each other throughout a degree. The ability to apply advanced jurisprudential models of interpretation builds on basic analytical skills.[43] Students need not be required to complete summative tests on each of these skill levels but instead could be offered formative tasks to self-test their ability and be clearly told the level of skill required for each larger stake summative assessment. A later capstone assessment could form a summative assessment of all of those skills.

D. Secret – Open

One significant issue post-COVID-19 is the question of integrity in assessment – particularly if taken remotely.[44] Students are motivated to cheat if the outcome of an assessment is a mark contributing to their final degree or a hurdle they need to overcome to proceed. The greater the marks or the hurdle, the greater the incentive to cheat. Because of the significance of these high-stakes summative assessments for attesting student competence and attainment, it is paramount that there is integrity in the assessment. This involves both an attestation of the identity of the person undertaking the assessment and that they have only used permissible means to complete the assessment. Partly, this is achieved by assessment design, but a significant basis for integrity is often secrecy. This requires that the questions are not known to students before the time of the assessment and, once used, cannot easily be reused because of the advantage that would accrue to those who may have practised using those questions.

Conversely, there is very little incentive to cheat if the test is entirely formative. Indeed, looking at someone else's answer to the test may have positive educational benefits – particularly if the student attempts the answer themselves first. In a formative assessment that does not result in any summative grade, the saying 'you are only cheating yourself if you cheat' rings true. Further, in a formative assessment, there is no need for secrecy. As grades are not involved, there is no unfair advantage to be gained from knowing the questions ahead of time.

This means that assessments can be easily re-used year after year while still relevant. This longer half-life of assessments means academics can justify investing more time into developing them – and in a digital environment, they can also develop automated or pre-prepared feedback. Longitudinal analysis of the assessment items becomes possible, allowing the opportunity to identify students who are finding aspects of learning more difficult than a usual cohort.

Having open assessments with automated feedback also means that students can re-do assessments until they have reached a level of proficiency that gives them the confidence to tackle the summative tasks. Academic staff are also relieved from marking burdens for these multiple attempts. However, it is critical to ensure that the student's overall assessment burden does not increase. So, the introduction of formative assessment means fewer summative tasks.

III. Assessment Environments

The ability to reimagine the assessment structure in law school is also strongly influenced by the types of assessments that are set for students. Many of the standard assessment types in law have both advantages and disadvantages for students' learning and for staff workloads. Identifying the underlying reasons to use each assessment type can help to streamline assessment but still enhance learning outcomes. It is helpful to see assessment tasks as differentiated by both the environment in which they are undertaken as well as the nature of the task that is required.

A. Formal Limited Time Examinations

Exams taken by students in exam halls during a final exam period is a time-honoured assessment practice. Yet it is possibly the assessment setting most removed from any real-world situation. Students are restricted in the material they can use in the exam, even in an open book exam, the students cannot access any material they have failed to take in with them, they are unable to collaborate or seek assistance, and they have a time limit placed on their answer. While in some workplace emergency situations a time limit might apply, the usual work environment is to craft the best advice possible for a client using all means available and as much time as is needed.

Limiting exams to two or three hours is a modern practice largely due to logistical timetabling issues and staff concerns about marking workloads.[45] There seems to be a marginal educational benefit in ranking students in higher education on how quickly they can write. Limited time exams encourage quick surface responses over deeper critical thinking, and they encourage the production of standard notes and third-party 'tutoring' services.

Given that limited time becomes the most pressing aspect of these exams, it seems that the main contributions of formal time-limited examinations to the learning outcomes for students beyond the university are building competence in note and time management, writing better first drafts, building resilience in the face of stressful situations, and in assessing the value of notes prepared by others.

B. Open Book/Open Web or Closed Book

The range of materials a student can access when completing an assessment can fundamentally change the learning outcomes of the task. The range of options is wide. They include no-materials exams; limited materials, sometimes involving materials provided by the examiner such as a list of cases or legislative extracts; open book, where students can use any printed material they bring to the exam; and open web where the students have access to any printed or online materials they can find.

While there is nothing to constrain the form of questions asked in closed book exams, the fact that a student is unable to access supporting material means there is a strong temptation to ask questions that test short-term knowledge. These questions can be an important way of encouraging the learning of basic concepts that are practically needed to be rote learned in order to efficiently solve higher order problems. But beyond the first year, it is questionable whether such knowledge should be tested or just assumed. In law, in particular, there are few concepts that benefit from rote learning. By contrast, law is characterised by skills of analysis that assume no two situations are exactly alike.

Limiting materials also involves the costs and security issues of invigilation, discussed below. It is obviously easier to write a question based on readily available material if that material is denied to the students taking the test, but it is artificially divorced from what a graduate lawyer would be asked to do in practice. The challenge is to construct questions that require students to synthesise in novel ways the information that is readily available.

C. *Invigilation*

Invigilation is a form of assessment security generally believed to ensure the authenticity of the candidate and integrity of the assessment response. Authenticity can be assured if the invigilator is the class teacher and has verified the identity of the student on multiple occasions. However, invigilation is easily compromised by the use of forged identity documents in large formal examinations. This can be overcome by scanning programs that compare the proffered identity card to a central copy, assuming the original is not compromised, and a second system or person is able to correctly match the cardholder to the photo or biometric match. Such systems are likely to be expensive and involve difficult privacy considerations.

If the assessment is a closed book exam, the integrity of assessment is also compromised if the invigilator does not see the additional material snuck into the venue. Classic low-tech options include hiding notes on the person and accessing them in a toilet, but these methods are now supplemented by a wide range of technological devices that students can easily purchase online. If the assessment is being conducted remotely, there are services that offer remote proctoring through webcams and keystroke analysis. But there are even more ways to subvert those systems, including the use of notes out of the view of the camera, mirrors, virtual desktops, etc. The low-tech option of going to the toilet remains – enhanced by the ability to store notes in the toilet. There are even greater privacy issues with room 'inspection' by the invigilator. While invigilation in face-to-face assessments is largely effective in preventing group collusion, that becomes more problematic in remote assessments where students have more ability to engage in surreptitious forms of communication.

Invigilation is expensive and, with the introduction of technology, is fast becoming an 'arms-race' between invigilating and cheating vendors. It is clear this will become increasingly expensive for law schools, even as the efficacy of invigilation remains unclear.

In law, examinations have traditionally been invigilated, but not research essays. This is interesting because it demonstrates that law has long accepted that not all high-stakes assessment need invigilation to assure the integrity of an overall degree program. Invigilation is also mostly used for time-limited assessments – it is difficult to imagine how a student could be invigilated across a week-long research task.

There are alternatives to the traditional approach to invigilation. For longer forms of assessment, students can submit drafts of their work, they can be asked to discuss their progress with teachers and they can be required to peer-assess drafts (building a sense of trust and community). As discussed above, there may no longer be a real justification for time-limited assessment in law. But where it is justified, randomisation of questions, higher level complex questions for which answers do not pre-exist, similarity checking software and submission of files showing drafts across the time period are all options to assure integrity. All these options are also available for longer form assessment.

D. Individual, Assisted or Group Work

A common environmental stipulation is that the task is to be undertaken individually and without assistance. These two stipulations, often implicit, are central drivers for invigilation and other integrity measures. It is, however, possible to construct tasks without the need for invigilation. Strongly formative assessment that focuses on student learning rather than grades, assessment that relies on student presentation or dialogue-based discussion of student work[46] can be agnostic as to the method by which the student chooses to learn.

Assessing students in groups is a common alternative. Exactly how the contributions of individual students and group outcomes are assessed remains contentious, but there is general agreement that collaborative learning outcomes are really only achieved or measurable through group tasks.[47]

Indeed, in the real world of legal practice, it might even amount to professional malpractice for a lawyer to fail to seek assistance or work in a group to solve complex problems. Individually focussed assessments may be important for the integrity of claims of student competence, but they are not necessarily effective introductions to workplace activities.

E. Point in Time or Ongoing Assessment

The placement of assessment tasks in a degree is also a significant environmental consideration. Traditionally, exams were at the end of a year or term to assess, at one point in time, the student's accumulated learning. Assessment at the end of a stage of learning allows for responses that more fully synthesise the learning across that stage. Weekly assessments can create a positive learning environment via the 'testing effect' but often struggle to assess synthesis, and focus on lower order knowledge-based areas.[48] Both approaches are assessment tasks that are conducted at a single point in time. This can have a number of negative impacts. It can mean that a student who is 'off their game' on that day is penalised though they performed well at other times. It can mean that students focus on 'cramming' for these tasks rather than focusing on other subjects or areas of their learning. Students can find the assessment regime stressful if either the focus is only a small number of high-stakes assessments or alternatively on a large number of summative tests through a subject.

Alternatively, assessment can be seen as an ongoing form of appraisal throughout a course, where student work builds towards a final mark and where there is flexibility in both the scoring and the timing of work submitted or activities undertaken. Class participation is one example often found in law;[49] others are research projects or experiential subjects. Finding the appropriate balance between formative and summative aspects of continuous assessment is important and complex. Poorly designed continuing assessment can have all of the negative impacts of weekly testing,[50] and conversely, weekly testing can at times ameliorate uncertainty caused by vaguer continuing assessment scoring. What is ideal will vary by subject, but often a blend of continuous and point in time is optimal. Avoiding an excessive assessment burden for staff and students is also critical.

F. Authentic Classroom or Workplace Assessment

There has been increased interest in moving where possible to forms of authentic assessment – that is, assessment that approximates real-world conditions.[51] Student engagement has been linked to a sense that the assessment tasks are similar to what they will be asked to do as graduates. Law is intrinsically linked to real-world issues, so assessment in law has always been strongly problem-based and, therefore, authentic. A truly authentic assessment would involve large amounts of documentation, interviews and legal bureaucracy, which cannot be directly replicated in a university assessment environment. As a result, law has long simplified fact scenarios and often created unrealistically disastrous scenarios to cover as much material as possible in one task. It's arguable that the unrealistically disastrous nature of these problems, in fact, makes them more engaging for students. But there is probably a limit to the extent to which such assessments should be used. Mixing in more complex case studies with primary documentation, setting open-ended, messy tasks with no clear answer, having students answer in the form of briefs, letters, advice or judgments are all innovations law schools have used to increase authenticity.[52]

The increased availability of experiential learning, either as discrete subjects or as excursions inside courses, also creates significant opportunities to bring real workplace experiences into assessment tasks. Reflective work based on actual legal work in clinics is a gold standard, but there are many imaginative ways to bring something from outside the classroom into the way a student's learning is assessed. Court reports are a simple method to do this, but almost any community activity can be analysed in legal terms and add an authentic element.

IV. Formats

There is a range of formats of assessment traditionally used in law and a wide variety of innovative formats. It is beyond the scope of this chapter to attempt to consider the strengths and weaknesses of each format. Instead, a few approaches to critiquing assessment types are suggested. The main focus of such a critique is to understand exactly what aspects of learning are actually being assessed. Most assessment types involve a number of learning outcomes. Designing an assessment strategy for a program involves looking for the most efficient and effective way to assess those learning outcomes. Some complex learning outcomes may require repeated assessment, but others may be inadvertently over-assessed. Some tasks may be focused on outcomes that are not central to the program and are therefore not properly aligned.

Fundamentally, the format of the way in which the assessment response is produced emphasises, or de-emphasises, particular skills or learning outcomes. Every assessment task will assume that by the end of the task, the student will have accessed a set of information, often been required to manipulate it in some way and have produced some form of response. The task may also mandate a particular method for each of these components.

The way in which a student accesses information can vary from a quick test of memory recall, through an assessment of how well a student's notes have been arranged, to a discovery-based research question. The degree to which the information accessed is the same for all students has implications for how easy it will be for students to gain the information from others, and so has implications for the need for invigilation or randomisation. If it is a rich source of information from which students can individually choose to use aspects, these needs are lessened. The difficulty of the means of accessing the information also has research skills learning outcome implications. For example, some quick quizzes on assigned reading will require that the assigned material be read, but other quizzes on broadly known principles or facts might be able to be more easily accessed via Wikipedia. Assessment should assume students will use the most convenient way to access the information.

The way in which a student is asked to manipulate that information has strong links to assessing skills of synthesis, analysis and critical thinking. Identifying with some precision exactly what analytical processes a student is required to undertake can give insights into the learning outcomes of the assessment. Tasks that merely ask for the identification of key facts may not test the understanding of how those facts fit in a broader context but may be appropriate as first tasks. Tasks that ask for the application of law to hypothetical scenarios may require students to critically imagine outcomes that cannot be found already analysed elsewhere. More complex assessment tasks may even ask for iterative or cumulative forms of analysis – such as when a research essay asks for law in an area to be summarised, its flaws highlighted and reform suggested. Each of these is a separate skill and illuminates the complexity of the task assigned.

The way in which the student is asked to respond is also critical and possibly the most important aspect of assessment tasks. By way of example, the American Bar Association admission tests are a holistic test of a student's entire law degree. They are based around real-world fact scenarios. Yet they are closed book exams, and the questions are multiple-choice. The closed book environment means the knowledge accessed is merely memory recall. The manipulation ranges across a number of professional skills but is limited to manipulating the candidate's remembered facts. Significantly, because the response is multiple choice, there is no evidence of how the candidate reasoned to a conclusion. Nothing in the paper can distinguish whether the student correctly reasoned to the answer, incorrectly reasoned to the answer, or randomly guessed. Instead, examiners rely on probability to indicate that it is very unlikely that guessed or wrongly reasoned answers form a large part of a candidate's overall correct answers.[53]

At the other end of the assessment scale is the academic essay. While it is a format of response that is rarely required in business, it is arguably the assessment response format that contains the greatest number of skills and learning outcomes of any common assessment type. It is this complexity that makes marking essays so time-consuming. Longer research essays can be seen to contain the need for a student to demonstrate in their answer: evidence of wide reading and research with an implicit or explicit research methodology; the ability to summarise, synthesise and critique a range of long, complex sources written for different audiences; analysis of raw data; the ability to accept and reflect on other voices on an issue and to appropriately give them primacy; the need to balance opposing views before setting out one's own; the development of an authentic, yet respectful and professional voice of one's own; the ability to construct logical arguments and maintain them across complex terrains; and the ability to write persuasively and with a particular audience in mind.[54]

Separating out all the learning outcomes required in such responses can assist with more explicitly explaining marking to students, often via rubrics.[55] It can also help to better allocate marking workloads across programs by demonstrating the complexity of the marking task in comparison to other tasks.

V. Grading

Summative assessment ranks and sorts students. It raises and lowers students both in relation to others in their cohort and across other students across geography and time. At the degree level, it can have significant impacts on students' life choices and job prospects and on their own sense of achievement and self-worth. Failing to achieve minimum grades during the degree can lead to the cancellation of scholarships or visas for international students. The need to repeat failed subjects leads to tuition and living costs.

Consequently, it is important to ask what and why we are grading. It is useful to separate what we are grading into two distinct areas: competence and excellence. Sporting competitions focus on excellence: both comparative and objective. In each competition, there is a forced ranking from first to last, and records and statistics are then used to measure that achievement in light of previous cohorts. A gold medal in the Olympics and a world record are separate measures of excellence. There is only one opportunity to achieve a ranking in each competition. However, in each competition, there is an opportunity to increase a career-best score and perhaps attain a record.

Motor vehicle driving licence tests focus on competence. A score of 100% or close to it is required. No one is licenced for achieving a pass of 50% competence. There are no limits to the number of times a test can be taken. Equally, there are no special considerations that can lower the bar to pass.

In higher education, these two distinct approaches are conflated. Students are routinely graded out of 100 but allowed to continue through the degree and to graduate with grades of 50%. Students who fail to pass, however, are considered incompetent and are required to retake the subject from the beginning. Usually, there is no opportunity for multiple attempts at tests. Those who complain of 'soft marking' regularly allege that incompetent students receive degrees but rarely consider what percentage of an assessment a student can get wrong before they are deemed incompetent. This is further confused by the practice of seeing a grade of over 90% as very exceptional. If a course has made it possible for a student to achieve all the learning outcomes set, it might, in fact, be that there is a systemic failure in the teaching if students do not regularly get close to 100%.

For law schools, at least in Australia, the professional accrediting authorities have a set of competencies all students must attain. But like driving tests, the authorities do not look for a grade. Instead, they expect a level of competence. Competence is not assessed on a range of grades. It is assessed as Pass/Fail. This means that if we are assessing students for the admitting authorities, we should only be assessing on a Pass/Fail basis and, importantly, lifting the pass point to one that requires broad competence. We should also allow students who fail to achieve that level to retake the test. Re-doing the whole subject might be optional.

Employers, at least those in the legal profession, expect all graduates to be competent against the accrediting body standards. Beyond that, they look for differentiating factors to identify appropriate employees. All that a university provides for this purpose is a set of subjects with a grade out of 100 against it. Employers cannot determine from this the learning outcomes assessed, how the student did on the various tasks or if the tasks set were a fair reflection of the student's abilities. Often the tasks set will be testing skills only indirectly related to the tasks the employee will perform. If we are assessing students for employers, we should instead be offering a range of skills against which our students have been assessed. It would only be a specialist employer who was specifically interested in achievement in a distinct subject area. Instead, employers would be looking for program-level attainment in the areas highlighted by the Threshold Learning Outcomes – research, analysis, collaboration, self-management, professional responsibility and ethics. The legal content of the individual courses is assumed by the accreditation. These considerations are even more compelling if the majority of law graduates do not enter the legal profession or do not stay there for long. The legal aspects of the degree become less important than the approach to reasoning and research that the degree provides.

Then there is the academic argument for ranking. Our best students need an academic ranking to pursue further studies, get prestigious scholarships and win prizes. For this, excellence in rigorous academic assessments and consistent excellence across courses is needed – particularly in those areas in which they intend to study further. These rankings are close to the hearts of academics, rankings that were self-defining for many of us. They are the rankings we are most comfortable with, the ones we have used for many years and have tradition behind them. They are also the rankings that closely align to the conveyor belt of grading through secondary school, which the students have come to expect. Nostalgia, affinity and acculturation aside, though, the academic reasons seem the least compelling.

Australia has nearly 40 law schools, all grading on the same basis. But if the accrediting authorities only require a Pass/Fail competence basis, then there is enormous scope for law schools to create distinctly different approaches to assessment. Some schools may choose to focus on developing local practitioners with a strong emphasis on practical skills assessment. Others may seek to become an academically elite school with an emphasis on research papers and law reform. Assessment can be a driver for distinct offerings.

VI. Possible Futures

With all of these factors in mind, law schools have much to consider about their approach to assessment. Here is one possible approach.

Assessment in the law degree is separated from subjects. Students undertake formative assessments in the subjects and can retake them until they achieve competence. These tasks are not time-limited, are remote and not invigilated. They must, however, be completed. The formative assessments build skills towards larger summative assessments. The tasks are automatically marked, with significant investment in developing adaptive testing with feedback to guide and appropriately challenge students. Multimedia stimuli and design concepts from online gaming are used to increase the authenticity of the tasks.

A range of mid-level assessments is set on a Pass/Fail basis. These may be group work based and focused on skills development. These may focus on the application of knowledge learnt in subjects. There is an opportunity to retake these assessments if the student fails. Primarily, these Pass/Fail assessments demonstrate competence against the accrediting standards. These assessments are manually marked by academic staff, and feedback is given against learning outcome rubrics. But as the overall grade is Pass/Fail, staff can concentrate on assessing the constituent elements rather than a ranking. One such assessment is in each subject, but its timing can vary, as can the format. Some subjects may have a final problem question, others a mid-term essay or report. Failure in the assessment would not prevent progression to a subsequent subject, but students would receive advice as to whether this was wise, and a discretion to prevent progression could be applied to students who appeared to be struggling.

Larger stage or capstone assessments are set in teaching breaks. Students can take them when they feel competent, but some are hurdle requirements to progress to later stages of the degree. These larger summative assessments combine more than one subject area and require extended answers. Staff are separately assigned to set and mark these assessments. The combination of subject areas in the larger assessments means that students do fewer such assessments. Each assessment would typically be different. There may be an opportunity to take these assessments a second time if students wish to improve their marks. These assessments are marked out of a full range of 0–100 marks. Results in these assessments provide an academic ranking of students. There is a required pass mark for these assessments, and failure to achieve that grade would prevent progression to later stages or graduation.

Integrity is assured by extending the range of assessment types to include dialogic forms of assessment – such as through vivas, class discussions and presentations. The larger assessments would have the greatest emphasis on integrity measures. Some might be traditionally invigilated.

Student achievement is reported not only through subject grades but also against competencies and skills which are assessed programmatically throughout the degree. Students are aware that feedback on one task will assist with performance in the next task linked to that competency and that this will be in a later subject. Where possible, assessment responses are collected in e-portfolios and advertised to employers as a more textured way to appreciate student achievement and differentiation. Students see their major assessments as public artefacts that they strive to be proud of and that demonstrate their achievement.

This is one way of combining the suggestions explored in this chapter, but there would be others. Law schools could adopt one or more of the ideas in an incremental approach to change. A number can indeed be adopted by convenors in individual courses. Most of these suggestions lead to a reduction in academic staff workload, though not all do. But all are intended to increase the value of assessment to a student's learning. At the end of the day, we are here to help students learn, not to rank them for others. Holding fast to that idea may be the most subversive idea of all.

Notes

1 See generally the discussion in Alex Steel and others, 'Critical Legal Reading: The Elements, Strategies and Dispositions Needed to Master This Essential Skill' (2016) 26 Legal Education Review 187; Alex Steel, 'Reflections on Approaches to Drafting Regulatory Standards: Finding Ways to Quicken, Not Deaden, the Spirit of Legal Education' in Kevin Lindgren, François Kunc, and Michael Coper (eds), *The Future of Australian Legal Education* (Thomson Reuters 2018).

2 A leading review of legal pedagogy can be found in William M. Sullivan and others, *Educating Lawyers: Preparation for the Profession of Law ["the Carnegie Report"]* (Jossey-Bass 2007).

3 For an analysis of criminal law coverage see Helen Gibbon and Alex Steel, 'Are We Reading Enough Crime? Examining the Content and Depth of Criminal Law Courses' (2019) 44(2) Alternative Law Journal 151.

4 Issues for the curriculum are discussed in Jeffery Barnes and others, 'CALD Good Practice Guide for Teaching Statutory Interpretation' (Council of Australian Law Deans 2015) <https://cald.asn.au/wp-content/uploads/2017/11/Council-of-Australian-Law-Deans-Good-Practice-Guide-to-Teaching-Statutory-Interpretation.pdf> accessed 6 October 2022.

5 Zhiqiong June Wang, 'Between Constancy and Change: Legal Practice and Legal Education in the Age of Technology' (2019) 36 Law in Context. A Socio-legal Journal 64.

6 Kate Galloway, 'A Rationale and Framework for Digital Literacies in Legal Education (2017) 27 Legal Education Review 117.

7 Randall Kiser, *Soft Skills for the Effective Lawyer* (Cambridge University Press 2017); Julie MacFarlane, The New Lawyer – How Clients Are Transforming the Practice of Law (*UBC Press* 2017 2nd Edition).

8 Steel (n 1).

9 Committee of Inquiry into Legal Education in New South Wales, 'Legal Education in N.S.W.: Report of Committee of Inquiry' December 1979, 271–278.

10 In the mid 1980's five law schools had moved to semesters Dennis Pearce, 'Australian Law Schools: A Discipline Assessment for the Commonwealth Tertiary Education Commission' (Australian Government Publishing Service 1987), 88.

11 Universities Australia, 'Teaching Calendar, 2021' (*Universities Australia*) <https://www.universitiesaustralia.edu.au/our-universities/teaching-calendars/> accessed 6 October 2022.

12 See the summary in Sarah Moulds, 'Visible Learning at Law School: An Australian Approach to Improving Teacher Impact in Intensive and Online Courses' (2021) 55(2) The Law Teacher 1.

13 Tim Todd, 'Block Teaching Comes of Age at Victoria University' (*Victoria University | Melbourne Australia,* 21 October 2020) <https://www.vu.edu.au/about-vu/news-events/news/block-teaching-comes-of-age-at-victoria-university> accessed 6 October 2022.

14 Pearce (n 10) 173.

15 That is because assurance of the learning in the final weeks of the term is considered necessary, because the later the assessment the more the learning over the term can be assessed in a synthesised way, and logistically because if teachers are marking, there is more time to do this when teaching has ceased.

16 Dylan Wiliam, 'What Is Assessment for Learning?' (2011) 37 Studies in Educational Evaluation 3.

17 Suzan Burton and Paul Nesbit, 'An Analysis of Student and Faculty Attitudes to Intensive Teaching' (2002) <https://research-management.mq.edu.au/ws/portalfiles/portal/17151315/mq-1583-Publisher+version+%28open+access%29.pdf> accessed 6 October 2022; W. Martin Davies, 'Intensive Teaching Formats: A Review' (2006) 16 Issues in Educational Research 1; Marilyn Mitchell and Sven Brodmerkel, 'Highly Intensive Teaching in Tertiary Education: A Review of Recent Scholarship' *Stagnancy Issues and Change Initiatives for Global Education in the Digital Age* (IGI Global 2021).

18 Derek E. Baird and Mercedes Fisher, 'Neomillennial User Experience Design Strategies: Utilizing Social Networking Media to Support "Always on" Learning Styles' (2005) 34 Journal of Educational Technology Systems 5.

19 See, for example, Eileen Wood and Lucia Zivcakova, 'Multitasking in Educational Settings' in *The Wiley Handbook of Psychology, Technology and Society* (Wiley 2015) 404.

20 Mihaly Csikszentmihalyi, Sami Abuhamdeh and Jeanne Nakamura, 'Flow' *Flow and the Foundations of Positive Psychology* (Springer 2014).

21 Joseph Firth and others, 'The "Online Brain": How the Internet May Be Changing Our Cognition' (2019) 18 World Psychiatry 119.

22 Cf Alexandra N. Spichtig and others, 'The Decline of Comprehension-based Silent Reading Efficiency in the United States: A Comparison of Current Data with Performance in 1960' (2016) 51(2) Reading Research Quarterly 239–259.

23 While some law schools have used open book exams for years, this is not uniform and many continued to run closed book exams prior to 2020.

24 Cf Val Klenowski and Claire Wyatt-Smith, 'The Impact of High Stakes Testing: The Australian Story' (2012) 19 Assessment in Education: Principles, Policy & Practice 65.

25 Arathi Sriprakash, Helen Proctor and Betty Hu, 'Visible Pedagogic Work: Parenting, Private Tutoring and Educational Advantage in Australia' (2016) 37 Discourse: Studies in the Cultural Politics of Education 426.

26 Cf Massimiliano Tani and Prue Vines, 'Law Students' Attitudes to Education: Pointers to Depression in the Legal Academy and the Profession' (2009) 19 Legal Education Review 3; Rachael Field, James Duffy and Anna Huggins, 'Supporting Transition to Law School and Student Well-Being: The Role of Professional Legal Identity' (2013) 4 The International Journal of the First Year in Higher Education 15.

27 Belinda Probert and Judyth Sachs, 'The Rise of Teaching Focused Academics in Universities' (2015) 4 International Journal of Chinese Education 48; Belinda Probert, 'Teaching-Focused Academic Appointments in Australian Universities: Recognition, Specialisation, or Stratification?' (Office for Learning and Teaching 2013) Report <https://ltr.edu.au/resources/Teaching-focused_academic_appointments.pdf> accessed 6 October 2022.

28 Susan R. Hemer, 'Finding Time for Quality Teaching: An Ethnographic Study of Academic Workloads in the Social Sciences and Their Impact on Teaching Practices' (2014) 33 Higher Education Research & Development 483.

29 Olasile Babatunde Adedoyin and Emrah Soykan, 'Covid-19 Pandemic and Online Learning: The Challenges and Opportunities' (2020) Interactive Learning Environments 1; ibid.

30 AWB Simpson, 'The Rise and Fall of the Legal Treatise: Legal Principles and the Forms of Legal Literature' (1981) 48 The University of Chicago Law Review 632.

31 For topics in admissions examinations up to the 1950's see Committee of Inquiry into Legal Education in New South Wales (n 9) 269.

32 Law Admissions Consultative Committee, 'Prescribed Areas of Knowledge' <https://www.legalservicescouncil.org.au/Documents/prescribed-academic-areas-of-knowledge.pdf> accessed 6 October 2022.

33 Barnes and others (n 4).

34 Tertiary Education Quality and Standards Agency, 'Guidance Note: Course Design (Including Learning Outcomes and Assessment)' (25 September 2017) <https://www.teqsa.gov.au/latest-news/publications/guidance-note-course-design-including-learning-outcomes-and-assessment> accessed 6 October 2022.

35 Sally Kift and others, 'Conceptualising a Capstone Experience for Law Students' (Australasian Law Teachers Association 65th Annual Conference 2010, 4–7 July 2010, University of Auckland, Auckland).

36 Tim J. Wilkinson and Michael J. Tweed, 'Deconstructing Programmatic Assessment' (2018) 9 Advances in Medical Education and Practice 191.

37 Val Klenowski, Sue Askew and Eileen Carnell, 'Portfolios for Learning, Assessment and Professional Development in Higher Education' (2006) 31 Assessment & Evaluation in Higher Education 267.

38 Sally Kift, Mark Israel, and Rachael Field, 'Bachelor of Laws Learning and Teaching Academic Standards Statement' (Australian Learning and Teaching Council 2010).

39 Wiliam (n 15).

40 D. Royce Sadler, 'Formative Assessment and the Design of Instructional Systems' (1989) 18 Instructional Science 119.

41 Brent Carnell, 'Aiming for Autonomy: Formative Peer Assessment in a Final-Year Undergraduate Course' (2016) 41 Assessment & Evaluation in Higher Education 1269.

42 D. Royce Sadler, 'Beyond Feedback: Developing Student Capability in Complex Appraisal' (2010) 35 Assessment & Evaluation in Higher Education 535.

43 See, for example, the approach set out in Jeffery Barnes and others, (n 4).

44 See generally Phillip Dawson, *Defending Assessment Security in a Digital World : Preventing E-Cheating and Supporting Academic Integrity in Higher Education* (Routledge 2020).

45 Cf the approach to exams at Harvard in the 1970s in Scott Turow, *One L : The Turbulent True Story of a First Year at Harvard Law School* (Macmillan 2014).

46 See, for example David R. Carless, 'The 'mini-viva' as a Tool to Enhance Assessment for Learning' (2002) 27(4) Assessment & Evaluation in Higher Education 353.

47 Sandra Clarke and Michael Blissenden, 'Assessing Student Group Work: Is There a Right Way to Do It?' (2013) 47 The Law Teacher 368; Alex Steel, Anna Huggins and Julian Laurens, 'Valuable Learning, Unwelcome Assessment: What LLB and JD Students Really Think About Group Work' (2014) 36(2) Sydney Law Review 291.

48 Cf Jeffrey D. Karpicke and William R. Aue, 'The Testing Effect Is Alive and Well with Complex Materials' (2015) 27 Educational Psychology Review 317.

49 Alex Steel, Julian Laurens and Anna Huggins, 'Class Participation as a Learning and Assessment Strategy in Law: Facilitating Students' Engagement, Skills Development and Deep Learning' (2013) 36 University of New South Wales Law Journal 30.

50 Anna Huggins and Alex Steel, 'The Relationship Between Class Participation and Law Students' Learning, Engagement and Stress: Do Demographics Matter?' in James Duffy, Rachael Field and Colin James (eds), *Promoting Law Student and Lawyer Well-Being in Australia and Beyond* (Ashgate 2016).

51 Verónica Villarroel and others, 'Authentic Assessment: Creating a Blueprint for Course Design' (2018) 43 Assessment & Evaluation in Higher Education 840.

52 See, for example Noeleen McNamara, 'Authentic Assessment in Contract Law: Legal Drafting' (2017) 51(4) The Law Teacher 486–498; Cormac McGrath, Annelie Gunnerstad, Christine Storr and Åsa Örnberg, 'Making the Case for Virtual Law Cases: Introducing an Innovative Way to Teach Law' (2021) 55(2) The Law Teacher 198–212.

53 Deborah Merritt, 'Validity, Competence, and the Bar Exam' (*Faculty Perspectives – Association of American Law Schools | The Association of American Law Schools*) <https://www.aals.org/about/publications/newsletters/aals-news-spring-2017/faculty-perspectives/> accessed 1 September 2017; Andrea Anne Curcio, Carol L. Chomsky and Eileen R. Kaufman, 'How to Build a Better Bar Exam' (2018) New York State Bar Association Journal 37–41.

54 Daphne Barak-Erez, 'Writing Law: Reflections on Judicial Decisions and Academic Scholarship' (2015) 41 Queen's Law Journal 255.

55 Phillip Dawson, 'Assessment Rubrics: Towards Clearer and More Replicable Design, Research and Practice' (2015) 42 Assessment & Evaluation in Higher Education 347.

Part II

Subverting the Higher Education Sector

7 Can Law Schools Provide Students With a Subversive Legal Education in an Online Learning Environment?

K. E. Powell and Nicole J. Siller

I. Introduction

Legal education is rife with challenges of how we teach law and legal problem-solving to encourage both the protection and the development of society. In their book *Teaching as a Subversive Activity*, Neil Postman and Charles Weingartner aver that the rapidly changing nature of our world requires educators to engage with their students subversively by (in part) teaching them to question the status quo through learning how to ask the right questions. They conclude that the roles of teacher and student and 'the *nature* of the classroom environment' must evolve if a student's learning is to serve them throughout their lifetime in an ever-changing world.[1] Postman and Weingartner's 1969 conclusion—a proposed model of 'new education'[2]—is that preparing students to be lifelong learners, equipped to thrive after their studies, is to use the inquiry method to support a thriving learning environment.[3] As they explain:

> Knowledge is produced in response to questions. And new knowledge results from the asking of questions; quite often new questions about old questions. Here is the point: *Once you have learned how to ask questions—relevant and appropriate and substantial questions—you have learned how to learn, and no one can keep you from learning whatever you want or need to know.*[4]

The problem is that this teaching practice of rigorous engagement between student and teacher, or the facilitated engagement among students, has largely failed to translate into current offerings in online legal education. The value of employing subversive teaching activities, essentially active learning practices such as the inquiry method or critique within legal education, has long been recognised by academics, practitioners and governing bodies. After all, such teaching and learning practices foster some of the most important qualities of a good lawyer: the ability to think critically, problem solve and communicate the solution to key parties. Yet, the implementation of active learning in online education lacks resources to provide required focus and rigour.

So, why do we see a large-scale failure to implement active learning online? The most recent impediment is the transformation of Australian higher education in the

DOI: 10.4324/9781003175216-9

context of scope, governance structure and its relationship with both society and the economy. Specifically, the incremental corporatisation of Australia's public university decision-making, driven by federal funding models in decades past,[5] has resulted in the 'massification' of higher education, with law being no exception.[6]

As explained by Thornton, in legal education, this mass system shift was the catalyst for a series of educational sacrifices.[7] Among others, two of these sacrifices by law schools to accommodate federal financial modelling are key drivers of failed active student engagement. First, massification has led to large student numbers and lower academic support (higher student-to-staff ratios).[8] Second, the student has become the consumer, and the law school, in desiring to gain funding, must respond to student demands.[9] Among other responses, this includes offering forms of flexible delivery of educational content.[10] For many students, legal education delivery has moved from the classroom (consisting of large-scale lectures) to a digital platform (in both synchronous and asynchronous formats).

We posit that the current use of online learning platforms further inhibits law academics from fostering a subversive legal education through active engagement between students and educators. When the 'medium is the message', we must deeply consider what environment our online teaching platform creates for learning.[11] Arguably, the environment is not creating learning but rather is at least partially driven by the messaging of the university. That is, the learning management platform is the environment that allows for 'flexibility in learning'. Such flexibility in learning may enable a learner to access a variety of educational content at any time, but the current method of online learning is primarily passive—to provide static video lectures, readings and other activities within a learning management system (LMS) available to enable students to study at their own pace. Active learning via classroom and inquiry methods has been reduced. Live engagement may happen via video at certain times of the week if enough students attend the live session (as recordings again allow students to opt-out).

Moreover, students are time poor, fitting in online study between other life requirements, whether that be work, family or both, leaving online students as transactional learners. Students memorise black letter law via online asynchronous lectures to prepare for an exam, whereas in person, even in large lectures, teachers had the ability to interweave the inquiry method of teaching, which provided active engagement in learning. However, key digital factors prevent even this limited form of subversive learning, resulting in disengaged students attempting to finish assessments for graduation purposes. Therefore, this type of flexibility for students, to date, has led students to assume that flexibility in learning also allows for disengagement from active learning. Such assumptions have been somewhat reasonable when students receive an asynchronous dissemination of knowledge, and accreditation of law programs in Australia has meant little more than the assessment of specific legal content via exam. Such accreditation-based requirements leave insufficient room for active learning, for a teacher to be subversive and for students to learn via the inquiry method.

We begin with the premise that subversive teaching and learning (by way of some form of inquiry method as an active learning methodology) is essential for the production of competent law graduates, given the skillset it develops in a law student.[12] Section II addresses the rise of the student-consumer resulting in universities offering more flexibility in study options, including online learning. Unfortunately, this has led students to develop unrealistic expectations when undertaking legal studies. In Section III, we briefly discuss why.

In section IV, we discuss how online legal education is presently preventing the use of subversive teaching and learning methods. Finally, in Section V, we seek solutions at both the educator and institutional levels. Specifically, we explore to what extent, if any, the subversive nature of legal education can endure on a digital platform. We then posit whether shifting an accreditation focus to address learning outcomes in a course, as opposed to black letter law, might provide immediate support for a more subversive education.[13] While this contribution focuses on legal education in Australia, there are global implications for any legal program desiring to engage in subversive teaching and learning with students in an online environment.

II. Flexibility and Unrealistic Expectations in Online Education

Large-scale federal funding changes in Australia enacted between 1988 and 1992 affected higher education institutions.[14] Consequently, rapid growth occurred in both law schools and the number of undergraduate law students by more than 60%.[15] The enlargement of student enrolments was charged on a full cost recovery basis,[16] while the government allocated law schools the lowest level of per-student funding.[17] This funding model has continued in a substantially similar form since the early 1990s.[18]

As more students accessed higher education, the diverse cohort increasingly comprised working students, students raising families or both.[19] For example, if just over 70% of students are studying full time, a significant percentage (28%) are therefore studying part-time.[20] To capture this greater student demographic, a flexible education model spurred the move to the study of law online. In 2016, of the 1.4 million students studying in Australia, 15% studied wholly in the cloud, while 12% studied both in the cloud and in person,[21] and the numbers continue to increase.

In 2020, the COVID-19 pandemic required law students to transition to online learning for a portion of the year. This experience was not unique to Australia or the higher education sector. In fact, the United Nations Educational, Scientific, and Cultural Organization (UNESCO) estimated that 1.37 billion students of all ages experienced educational disruption, with many educational providers turning to technology to assist in teaching and learning.[22] The next few years will determine whether the move to online learning or blended learning becomes permanent for some or all universities and how teaching and learning will look in a post-COVID-19 world.[23] Among other recent trends in Australian higher education since this health crisis, an increased student acceptance of online study and the restructuring of universities and their workforce appear to signal that online learning will endure.[24]

More now than ever, the marketing of a 'flexible' anytime online education that can fit between work and family, performed asynchronously in a lockdown environment or on the beach, easily sways a student. This leads to a new type of student consumer, who is time poor, ready for employment, but perhaps lacking the time and resources for the active engagement needed for a high quality legal 'education'. Whether it be for flexibility reasons or the operation of an institution during a pandemic, one thing is certain: studying law online is here to stay.

The consumer-driven model has led to the creation of unrealistic expectations of students and emboldened their demands on educators. This 'false advertising' that one can learn the law from anywhere in a silo leads to a variety of problems. Specifically, students are unprepared for the volume of work in a law degree, and they do not have the time or space for inquiry learning, problem-solving or critical thinking (that, at a minimum, was touched on in campus learning). These unrealistic expectations can set them up for failure at the start of their legal studies.

As consumers move to an (often part-time) online asynchronous experience, our students frequently complain that any inquiry learning, problem-solving, or critical thinking is not what they were led to believe this educational experience would bring them. In large part, students expect to listen to lectures (all recorded and accompanied with PowerPoint slides) when it suits them and be provided with a plethora of additional resources, including practice exams with model answers. They expect their exam will be based on those lectures and in a similar style to the practice exam questions they were given. They expect there is only one right answer, and they focus on the 'solution' to a legal problem as opposed to the analytical journey undertaken to reach a conclusion. Because of the transactional learning experience, many students have less experience with the inquiry method of learning in tutorials and do not find the time to engage in optional moot court experiences or clinical legal education opportunities to partake in client interaction or other practical simulated work during law school. In essence, students believe they can complete their degree and secure a law job while simultaneously working and managing family life.

Student expectations fail law students in two critical ways. First, when Universities imply that students can study on a beach or in a completely flexible manner, it is a mismatch with legal accreditation requirements, for which each law school class expects a minimum of 10 hours per week per subject of independent reading, critical thinking, problem-solving and engagement with studies. Further, Universities do not adequately support the costs of academic time for online active engagement of law students. The drop in University funding for law students will only exacerbate this problem. Additionally, student surveys of educators penalise instructors for engaging in supporting students' learning of problem-solving and critical thinking.[25] Together, the current online efforts leave students with a transactional and passive learning experience. Second, the resulting failure to prepare online students adequately for the critical thinking, problem-solving and communication elements of legal employment, if they even completed law school, renders many students unsuited to and underprepared for the practice of law.

III. Why Is Flexibility Failing Law Students?

Online learning in the Australian model is designed to be flexible for students. However, a significant disconnect exists between the flexibility of online education and the identified necessary student learnings within the study of law. The practice of law is heavily regulated, in part because of the extreme danger to clients, the confidentiality of materials, globalisation and respect for the rule of law.[26] There are extensively required accreditation learnings via state legal accreditation boards, meaning the complete freedom to teach has never existed.[27] Complying with the requirements of accreditation while delivering legal education online in the current environmental challenges is the Postman and Weingartner approach of subversive education. In recent years, this conflict has become heightened with the university's requirements for online courses, changes in type and quality of contact and consultation hours and the characteristics of learning platforms, further preventing engagement in subversive teaching and learning.

A. What Is Needed of a Practising Lawyer?

A significant disconnect is evident between the flexibility of online education and the student learning needed to prepare for the practice of law. This has arguably only heightened the divide between student expectations of 'knowledge acquisition' (as transactional learners) and the legal practice expectation that universities foster the development of professional attributes needed to be a competent legal practitioner.

Like professionals in many occupations, those who excel within the legal profession possess many qualities and skills. In law, it is well-settled that in addition to knowledge of the law itself, some of the most important qualities of a good lawyer are the ability to think critically, problem solve and communicate the solution to key parties.[28] These qualities help to ensure one is competent—from an ethical and practice-based perspective—to practice law. What constitutes a competent lawyer is different from what the university is currently providing to students when delivering asynchronous black letter law lectures online. In essence, both the competency to practise law and the requisite competency for admission to practice focus on a lawyer who understands their chosen field, uses critical thinking and can problem solve and effectively communicate.

In Australia, like most common law countries, a practising lawyer is subject to strict regulation of their activities, including a duty of competency. Codified in Rule 4.1.3 of the Solicitor Conduct Rules 2015, it is the fundamental duty of Australian lawyers to 'deliver legal services competently, diligently and as promptly as reasonably possible'. While no further description of the concept of competency exists within the domestic Rules, the International Bar Association Principles on the Conduct for the Legal Profession describes competency in detail as encompassing knowledge, skills and capability to practise law.[29] The explanatory note to Principle 9 states competency:

> is founded upon both ethical and legal principles. It involves more than an understanding of legal principles: it involves an adequate knowledge of the

> practice and procedures by which such principles can be effectively applied, and includes competent and effective client, file and practice-management strategies.[30]

Such standards are the bare minimum for Australian legal practitioners, and the effect of competency failure is not one that solely affects the practitioner.[31] As for most jurisdictions that license practising lawyers, competency failure can cause catastrophic effects on the client, from a loss of legal rights, finances or freedoms depending on the matter.

Australian law schools attempt to address this competency by teaching the required core subjects. In Australia, these are entitled the 'Priestley 11' subjects, and they comprise specifics of criminal law and procedure, torts, contracts, property, equity, company law, administrative law, constitutional law, civil procedure, evidence, ethics and professional responsibility.[32] In line with federal funding and accreditation expectations, Australian law schools have also adopted specific standards of threshold learning outcomes that are designed to produce competent law graduates. Created in December 2010 as part of the Learning and Teaching Academic Standards (LTAS) project, key members of the legal profession and law academics developed a set of six threshold learning outcomes (TLOs) for the Australian Bachelor of Laws degree.[33] These TLOs frame the academic requirements specified for the purpose of admission to practise as a legal practitioner and are used by university law schools. The standards were adopted by the Council of Australian Law Deans (CALD) and implemented in law schools.[34]

The six TLOs for the Bachelor of Laws are TLO 1: Knowledge, TLO 2: Ethics and professional responsibility, TLO 3: Thinking skills, TLO 4: Research skills, TLO 5: Communication and collaboration, and TLO 6: Self-management. TLOs 1–5 are directed at the specific legal skills and knowledge necessary for the practice of law, while TLO 6 provides the necessary direction for legal practitioners to manage their career path. When taken together, the TLOs

> represent what a graduate is expected to know, understand and be able to do as a result of learning or, in the words of the Australian Qualifications Framework, the "set of knowledge, skills, and the application of the knowledge and skills a person has acquired and is able to demonstrate as a result of learning".[35]

The TLOs are set forth in the LTAS Statement, which includes an expansion on each learning outcome. The statement notes that the TLOs 'were defined in terms of minimum discipline knowledge, discipline-specific skills and professional capabilities including attitudes and professional values that are expected of a graduate from a specified level of program in a specified discipline area'.[36] The statement further comments that:

> [a]s the Australian Law Reform Commission noted in 2000: In a changing environment, the best preparation that a law school can give its graduates is

> one which promotes intellectual breadth, agility and curiosity; strong analytical and communication skills; and a deep moral/ethical sense of the role and purpose of lawyers in society.[37]

The LTAS project is designed so that the six TLOs are all required as minimum standards for law students.

Therefore, every Australian law school (via CALD) committed to implementing a program demanding more of its students than acquiring knowledge of the existence of the law. The law school collective consciously determined it wanted its students to acquire skills needed to be subversive (i.e., to question, examine and analyse). However, a disconnect is apparent between the learning aspirations we have for our students and equipping our educators to fulfil such aspirations. The following sections address our contention that while the TLOs are designed to give law graduates key skills that 'promote intellectual breadth, agility and curiosity; strong analytical and communication skills',[38] the current online environment restricts such educational aspirations, thus further challenging methods used by subversive educators in a classroom setting.

IV. Online 'Classrooms' as Barriers to Employing Subversive Teaching Methods

This section briefly reviews and reflects on the rich body of research addressing the evolution of legal education in Australia to ascertain how legal education has reached the point of offering extensive online options. It is our contention that barriers to subversive legal education emerged at the start of university legal education and have only been further entrenched since the mass system shift in the late 1980s. A brief review of the history of legal education in Australia reveals that implementing subversive teaching methods received little support until the end of the twentieth century. While the potential benefits of this educational tool are now acknowledged, financial constraints, accreditation concerns and the consumerism of higher education often suppress its use in the classroom.

From the start, those entering the practice of law in Australia were trained by way of an apprenticeship. The notion that law should be a course of study at university was highly criticised.[39] Australian law schools did not emerge until the latter half of the nineteenth century. However, that did not stifle the ongoing debate on the role of law schools as true academic institutions or vocational schools.[40] Regardless, since 1936, every state capital has housed a university law faculty.[41]

As explained by Chesterman and Weisbrot, after having 'won the right to be the principal providers of legal education and socialisation, [Australian law schools] also inherited the imperatives of practice from the profession'.[42] Legal educators divided their time between teaching and legal practice. The content and delivery of the first law courses were 'strictly formalist and doctrinal'. As reported by James, '[l]egal education was little more than "the imparting of information in the form of legal principles, rules and propositions . . . to be committed to memory for examination purposes"'.[43]

After the Second World War, law schools began to hire full-time academic staff who took 'a scientific approach to teaching law [that] involved dividing the law into discrete conceptual fields, each with its own set of principles, while excluding questions of social policy, politics and the use of non-legal data'.[44] This new fleet of professional staff and their delivery of the law was still largely controlled by the profession, and 'any suggestion that the scientific approach might be deficient was regarded as "deeply subversive"'.[45] The call by some academics for their students to question legal institutions and the law itself in the 1960s and 1970s was the first real movement towards infusing subversive teaching and learning practices into the curriculum. Naturally, this approach was met with resistance.[46]

In 1985, the Commonwealth Tertiary Education Committee commissioned a report to evaluate Australian legal education. Submitted in 1987, the Pearce Report noted the important educational functions that both critique, as well as inquiry teaching and learning methods, serve in legal education. Specifically, the report called on law schools to 'examine the adequacy of their attention to theoretical and critical perspectives, including the study of law in operation the study of relations between law and other social forces'.[47] Further, it identified the merit in teaching students to question the status quo:

> A university law school is concerned to evaluate and criticise the law, legal institutions and legal processes and to ask of them 'what are you good for' and to assess whether they should be changed. In educating law students, accordingly, it is desirable to cultivate a student's intellect in a spirit of free enquiry and to encourage independent thought and enquiry about the law.[48]

In 1994, McInnes and Marginson reported that the Pearce Report has positively contributed to law schools' consideration of teaching weaknesses and lack of skill development.[49]

However, the findings of the Pearce Report did not result in a teaching and learning system overhaul in favour of subversive teaching and learning practices in the classroom. Instead, the government enacted massive changes to the federal funding model of higher education a year after the publication of the Pearce Report.[50] As a result, between 1988 and 1992, there was both rapid growth of law schools and rapid growth in the number of undergraduate law students.[51]

The explosion of law student numbers coupled with a reduction in government funding instigated a change in the law classroom to a large-scale lecture delivery method. As explained by Keyes and Johnstone, the 'traditional model' (teacher-focused – lecture style – content transfer) that emerged in the 1980s was problematic since it failed in 'enabling, stimulating, prompting and guiding students to develop their own conceptions and abilities'.[52] While this model has been repeatedly criticised, legal education research reports this approach has largely been retained within Australian law schools.[53] In the years that followed, the reduction of teaching weeks in a given term and academic workload upturns in the teaching, service and research output spaces only served to cement further the use of the law lecture to disseminate legal knowledge, often favouring content transfer over the learning process component of a classroom.[54]

To compensate for the shortcomings of the large lecture format, several universities added tutorials to allow for a portion of the contact hours to be in a smaller group (15–50 students) setting. The mode of delivery in these sessions often depended on the school and academics, ranging from another mini-lecture style to interactive delivery. Various forms of interactive learning included student-led discussion, problem-based learning, inquiry-method teaching and learning and role-playing.[55]

To compensate for the funding deficit, law schools amplified their marketing game to ensure students chose their institution over many other competitors vying for full-fee-paying students.[56] Accordingly, the law school has now become a consumer-driven model,[57] enticing post-secondary students with high ATAR scores and access to HECS funding to choose their university.[58] To do so, universities promote themselves to students (as consumers) based on a variety of selling points, including student satisfaction, flexibility in study options and employment rates of their graduates to drive increased enrolment numbers and revenue.[59] This discussion focuses on the challenges of flexibility in study options.

While universities attempt to create flexibility in law degrees, there is still an overarching accreditation requirement. As noted previously, the practice of law is highly regulated. The increased number of universities educating an increased number of law students has also witnessed an increase in professional accreditation bodies wishing to develop uniformity of curricula offered in law schools.[60] The Legal Profession Uniform Admission Rules 2015 sets out the current learning requirements for admission to practice.[61] The Rules identify two types of competencies for entry-level lawyers: academic and practical legal training (PLT).[62] Satisfaction of the academic competency will typically occur by submission of an academic transcript that indicates the candidate successfully completed the Priestley 11.[63] These prescribed academic areas of knowledge are identified in Schedule 1 of the Legal Profession Uniform Admission Rules 2015. Given the central role the Priestley 11 play in determining an applicant's competency to practise, the Law Admissions Consultative Committee (LACC) has dramatically shaped subject offerings at every law school in Australia.[64]

The following subsections discuss in greater detail two current barriers to subversive teaching and learning of law online: the university's control of the teaching space (i.e., the online classroom) and concern over the misuse of data amassed by the LMSs used to facilitate online learning.

A. University Control Over the Educator and Online Classroom

In online legal education, another influential component not recognised is the university and its control over the technological and bureaucratic system.[65] In a traditional classroom setting, a brilliant teacher could manage university attempts to infiltrate the learning space and 'control' the classroom to engage with students for an inquiry methodology of teaching and learning. Within that space, students could experience (in both a challenging yet fairly safe way) learning via an inquiry method. However, the online presence means greater institutional control of the inner workings of each offering and less influence from the educator on the student journey. As required by the university, much of the information is posted long in advance of student access and is primarily static (videos, readings and perhaps some additional materials). When accessing the materials, students may do so in their own time and in an order of their choosing, but they do not have access to 'live' instructors at most hours of the day. In recent years, universities have devoted significant resources to the creation of this type of digital infrastructure and online network used to allow law students to study from online lectures and seminars, review class resources and submit assessment tasks. During the COVID-19 health crisis, this mode of delivery was compulsory. Universities are putting increasing funding into technology (instead of bricks and mortar).[66]

This use of pre-recorded material, presented asynchronously, fails to allow for student engagement or authentic use of the inquiry method. It prevents instructors from using current events or other related information and materials to draw students in and render concepts more relatable because online materials are designed to be used for more than one iteration of teaching. With set materials, students lose much of their interaction with instructors, and instructors cannot engage in organic interactive learning opportunities. The added requirement for educators to master the online learning technology, comply with (ever-changing) blanket guidelines concerning the platform and use the system as the primary medium of communication with students steals more time away from engaging uniquely with students and employing subversive teaching and learning methods.

Not only does the university manufacture more control over the educator by imposing the online learning environment, but also its use of student evaluation of teaching is a significant external factor in influencing methods of teaching and learning delivery, including preventing authentic use of inquiry-based teaching methods. Performance management of educators is now subject, in part, to student evaluation of teaching. Regardless of the fact that student evaluations of tertiary level educators are biased and disadvantage womxn, people of colour, non-native English speakers and non-heterosexual instructors, Australian universities continue to use them for performance analysis of academics.[67] Further, federal funding is now tied, in part, to student evaluation of their instructors.[68] While this might be of use if such evaluations actually relate to student learning, extensive research demonstrates that student evaluations cannot be correlated to student learning.[69] In fact, at least one study indicates that student surveys that are positive are inversely tied to student learning.[70]

B. Data Collection and Potential Dissemination

As previously discussed, universities have devoted significant resources to the creation of digital infrastructures and online networks used to allow law students to engage in legal study in a vacuum, that is, to study from pre-recorded online lectures and seminars, review unit resources and submit assessment tasks.

However, these platforms and networks do more than facilitate the online learning environment. They are also used to collect an enormous amount of data from users, including where a student is located, the number and quality of logins to a unit site and personal identifying information about the users.

The system further records interactions between students and teaching staff, adding to the digital footprint of all classroom participants. For an educator, every word, nuance and engagement may be reviewed, leading to little flexibility, engagement with a student in the moment or discussion of challenging or topical material without fear of reprisal, as well as the onerous task of reproducing (recording and editing) the digital media.

The online experience provides a significant ability for the instructors and the university to closely track the education experience—in real-time, later and, in fact, at any juncture. Billed as a 'benefit', this causes two key problems. First, flexibility for students has led to prescriptive 'teaching' tied to arbitrary benchmarks (e.g. progress through the materials on a unit site) that are the descriptions of learning (and not the actual active learning per Postman and Weingartner), such as class learning outcomes and graduate learning outcomes. This framework supports Thornton's comment:

> [t]he central role of the university in safeguarding and transmitting a society's culture is now passé. Today, a functional role of an altogether different kind has been assigned to universities, that is, to serve the state through the market. This role has been effectively secured through perpetual under-funding from the public purse in conjunction with regimes of audit and compliance, which require particular targets and levels of productivity to be met in order to qualify for parsimonious hand-outs.[71]

Secondly, this prescriptive teaching also creates a framework that does not enable 'off-script moments' or the messy exercises of actual active learning through discussion. Teachers cannot determine when a student may need support, additional information or a challenge, or even encourage an off-topic conversation learning opportunity. From a student perspective, students are afraid to be caught on camera or discussion boards forever, seeming not to understand. The remote nature of online learning also means they cannot look to other students to determine whether they are ahead or behind or to form study groups, and they rarely have access to a live human to support their learning at the time they engage with the required material.

V. Solutions, or Must We 'Abandon Hope All Ye Who Enter Here'? (Dante's *Inferno*)

We now turn to some potential solutions to the current challenges of online legal education. We begin by noting that this chapter addresses the work that can be done directly by legal academics within their institutions. Before we address that, it is critical to note this chapter is not intended to place additional burdens on academics already facing extreme stressors. First, the chronic underfunding of legal education will likely become more dire with the impact of COVID-19 on Australia's higher education system. While it is beyond the scope of this chapter to address this crisis, we cannot in good conscience leave such a crisis without mention.[72] The precarity of employment for casual and permanent staff places stress on research and teaching, which cannot be overemphasised. In addition to the structural challenges facing higher education, we also note the individual challenges already facing many legal academics, especially womxn and academics of colour in research, service and teaching.[73] The stressors now on the academic profession are profound, and as of yet, the extent is unknown.

Yet, law academics, by the very nature of their profession, must not be dissuaded from subversive teaching. First, for law academics who have practising certificates, training as competent lawyers requires that we not yet abandon all hope even in light of the restrictions in legal education. Second, for those research-focused academics, rigorous debate and inquiry must not be lost to a mere recitation of black letter law. Finally, if law academics at all buy into Postman and Weingartner's call for subversive teaching, we must also engage in the inquiry method to teach subversively in law schools.

As noted by Postman and Weingartner, '[t]he basic function of all education, even in the most traditional sense, is to increase the survival prospects of the group', and '[s]urvival in a rapidly changing environment depends almost entirely upon being able to identify which of the old concepts are relevant to the demands imposed by the new threats to survival, and which are not'.[74] As educators, we must then find engaging ways to educate online, and to do so subversively, not only for the field of law but also for the future of a strong society.

We turn now to what specific changes to legal education might serve to enhance student learning. As subversive legal educators, we know that 'subversion is a risky business', and as lawyers, we are in the risk management business.[75] As our training has demonstrated, we cannot and should not approach this challenge from a singular perspective of a solution (returning to the past) or with the idea that all is lost (no future for the inquiry method). Rather, we must put our 'crap-detecting' skills and problem-solving abilities to work to be subversive educators since the next generation of lawyers must be developed in the current environment. In the following sections, we address the current learning environment and future considerations in the context of institutional change and subversive teaching.

A. Institutional Change

First, it is worth considering what might allow for subversive teaching within the existing structure. There is little chance the funding model, accreditation and online learning will change in the short term. As noted by Thornton previously in this contribution, parsimonious handouts are based on targets and productivity.[76] It is thus critical to focus efforts on legal academics requiring law schools to focus current and future resources on properly implementing existing standards. While this argument is not sexy, nor does it feel at first subversive, we can and should use this argument to demand resources within the current system to implement teaching requirements already in place within the established system. Doing so will direct current resources to more engaging teaching practices.

In the Australian context, academic focus TLOs 2–6 developed by the CALD as opposed to education relating to the academic areas of knowledge (i.e., Australia's Priestley 11 subjects) can better safeguard subversive teaching and learning in the law curriculum, including educational opportunities on digital platforms. There is no doubt that subversive educators must take to heart the LTAS Statement directive that all learning thresholds are of equal importance: knowledge, critical thinking, problem-solving, teamwork and self-reflection.

While TLO1 requires certain knowledge of the law, specifically that required by the relevant Australian admitting authorities, it is through the use of TLO2 and TLO3 that the inquiry method can safeguard the development of critical analysis, thinking creatively and exercising professional judgment.[77] Developing these skills goes beyond black letter law to create a truly competent legal counsel. The CALD has already indicated that law schools must teach, and students must learn, all of the threshold learning objectives since they are equally important for practice.

For example, consider TLO3 regarding thinking skills:

> Graduates of the Bachelor of Laws will be able to: (a) identify and articulate legal issues, (b) apply legal reasoning and research to generate appropriate responses to legal issues, (c) engage in critical analysis and make a reasoned choice amongst alternatives, and (d) think creatively in approaching legal issues and generating appropriate responses.[78]

Such critical analysis requires more than just knowledge of the law itself. Critical analysis requires that a student perform high-level analysis and engage in agreement or disagreement by identifying a myriad of advantages, disadvantages, strengths, weaknesses, accuracies and flaws in an individual and in toto. For example, TL03 notes:

> Engage in critical analysis and make a reasoned choice amongst alternatives: 'Critical analysis' is the practice of examining a text, claim or argument and identifying the hidden structures: for example, legal and non-legal issues; premises and hypothesis; factual, theoretical and ideological assumptions; undisclosed biases and prejudices; and so on. The word 'critical' emphasises that analysis is a high-level, conceptually analytical activity; it does not mean simply being confrontational or negative—the outcome of critical analysis can be agreement with the text, claim or argument. Making a 'reasoned choice among alternatives' involves critical evaluation of a text, claim, argument or response to a legal issue. It requires identification of the strengths and weaknesses, advantages and disadvantages, accuracies and flaws in a text, claim, argument or response (usually by comparing the text, claim, argument or response with one or more criteria such as truth value, doctrinal

> correctness, practicality, or consistency with an ideological standard such as the rule of law or social justice). The use of the word 'reasoned' emphasises that the choice must be justified, supported by evidence, and consistent with the critical analysis. Graduates must be able to explain the basis for adopting a particular point of view.[79]

Such analysis must be justified with evidence, and graduates should be able to articulate such analysis and evidence.[80] To review just one more aspect of critical analysis, thinking creatively for a law graduate requires lateral thinking and transferrable problem-solving applied to new issues. Graduates should be able to create new solutions using a variety of approaches, including formal and informal methodologies.[81] There is no doubt that law schools (and, by extension, universities) believe that such critical analysis is as important to a legal practitioner (and successful law student) as is knowledge. Therefore, there must be teaching and learning of critical analysis, with some level of assurance of student learning. Knowledge acquisition alone falls short of the legal education of students.

It is also important to flag that TLOs acknowledge the value in developing both oral and written communication. Students who study wholly online, with no requirement for synchronous engagement, will suffer in learning specific oral communication skills. As noted in the LTAS Statement, communication skills require 'an ability to understand verbal and non-verbal cues and also to engage with culturally diverse audiences; for example, through the use of active listening skills (such as questioning, summarising and paraphrasing)'.[82]

Thus, those of us teaching one of the 'knowledge'-based classes must consider how to integrate teaching *and* learning of the learning outcomes within our discipline. However, it cannot be solely the singular teacher's responsibility to integrate all learning outcomes into a single class. Rather, we should, with our colleagues, require the law school's institutional responsibility for student learning to demonstrate all learning thresholds in ways that can be tracked and measured.

In Australia, the most prevalent method of obtaining entrance into the legal profession is through a law degree followed by completion of a sanctioned PLT course, which earns those graduates a Graduate Diploma of Legal Practice.[83] While each university does use some method to target the learning outcomes for law students, there is no method for an applicant for a practising certificate to demonstrate acquisition of the skills acquired via TLOs 2–6 upon successful completion of their university study. The application for a practising certificate—the state-required accreditation for a practising lawyer in Australia—focuses on both a 'need to know' and 'need to do' but loses any metric on determining whether the applicant can demonstrate the 'how to think' criterion.[84]

While there is some expectation that such skills will be taught in the PLT course, the LTAS Statement was developed for student learning within legal education. The CALD themselves believe such standards are critical as the basis of legal education within a law school. It is illogical and unreasonable to expect students to learn critical thinking and problem-solving in a practical legal education course in the final six months before entering the legal profession, especially given the PLT courses focus more on teaching tangible matters to students such as which forms to use in a given situation. Thus, law schools, and by extension, their universities, can and must allocate resources to teach and benchmark student learning for all TLOs.

There is, of course, a strong argument for removing the Australian bureaucracy present in teaching and learning.[85] Over time, such bureaucracy has only grown to the detriment of the student and teaching experience. There has been little movement to lessen the model that requires auditing tied to funding. Thus, a pragmatic approach is, at the least, to choose the correct learning outcomes for audit purposes and confirm that law schools (and their associated universities) are meeting the educational thresholds expected of the degree. This shift of focus and resources will, at least in part, also encourage the movement away from the inappropriate use of student evaluations for judging the efficacy of teaching methodologies in the classroom.

While this chapter is not intended to address comparative legal education, we note that accreditation requirements in other jurisdictions may be indicative of stronger active learning opportunities for law students. United States accredited law schools mandate in-person attendance throughout their degree.[86] United States accreditation further requires that students engage in significant experiential education and limited online legal study.[87] Of note, law schools also only maintain accreditation if 75% of their students pass a bar exam. In Canada, a national committee on accreditation oversees both law school and lawyer accreditation.[88] Canadian accredited law schools must offer primarily in-person education with direct interaction between the students and teachers.[89] It is a further requirement that the law schools have both adequate resources and staff to educate students.[90] In contrast, Australia and the United Kingdom appear to offer extensive legal education in a wholly online context.[91]

It is incumbent upon Australian universities and their law schools to consider that merely funding a move to online learning is failing in developing the needed skills for competency in legal practice. With such consideration, academics who constitute the law schools within universities must truly consider how appropriate resourcing can occur when the federal government continues to restrict funding for law schools. Students studying law had their fees increased by 28% in 2021.[92] To counter such movement, law academics must adapt within the existing regulatory and accreditation framework to develop subversive teaching. Such action can occur within the university itself when law academics argue for resource allocation within the university, as well as inside a 'classroom' to teach students what is currently required for competency and employability within law.

B. Subversive Teaching and Learning in the 'Classroom'

Second, what is the role of law professors in paving new ways to teach within the virtual classroom? Besides supporting the learner to understand, digest and learn substantive legal knowledge, we are bound by the TLOs, as practising attorneys, research academics and subversive teachers, to teach students critical thinking, problem-solving and communication skills. So, how do we translate those skills from the inquiry method in a larger lecture hall to an inquiry method in online education?

Of course, Postman and Weingartner argue that education must be 'training centers for subversion'—teaching 'crap detection' as a requirement for a functioning democratic society.[93] There can be nothing more appropriate for the study and practice of law because our legal institutions are both the protector of the existing rule of law as well as the leaders for shepherding new ideas and ideals of society through challenging the status quo. Postman and Weingartner advocate that such education must be delivered through student-centred learning using the inquiry method to cultivate learners who are curious, challenging and learn through their own interests. There is nothing in such a context that prevents learning in an online context.

From a pragmatic perspective, we thus consider how to turn transactional learners into engaged learners in the current environment. We consider first the transparency considerations. Are we doing a sufficient job at explaining what skills students need to be good lawyers and then assessing our students on such skills? As law academics, we can explain, model and assess according to a student-centric model using existing and new online tools and all six TLOs. Such discussion can be embedded into online forums in a more explicit manner, transferred across multi-year learnings and linked to practice expectations. Much of the foundational work has been done in the drafting and implementation of TLOs. Now, the implementation of such work must occur across online platforms.

With that in mind, we explore how a subversive teacher might embed the inquiry method into online education. Learners learn by doing.[94] Even in online classes, we can learn to engage students so that they can learn to do. How might we do that? In general, many universities still engage with some type of tutorial experience, whether in person or online. This is the first place for employment of the inquiry method. With the increased use of signalling learning and engagement expectations to the students in their online material access (as discussed above), it is imperative that tutors follow through with rigorous student engagement through the inquiry method.

While there is extensive literature on methods for student engagement, we note a few since they relate to active learning in the inquiry method in a tutorial session. First, when asking a question, avoid telling the answer. Be prepared to sit with silence (that is, either student thinking or hostility, both of which can draw learning). As demonstrated by Carl Rogers, implement a discussion practice in which students cannot speak until they have restated the previous person's statement to the speaker's satisfaction.[95] Such a requirement in conversation or the inquiry method directs people to listen closely and engage with the points previously made. Determine whether we can offer teaching time that is not recorded and avoids becoming a shadow to active classroom discourse. That is to say, we do not suggest forgetting to record teaching but to be creative in our uses of technology for subversive manoeuvres.

Second, we can model such an inquiry method into our black letter law online. Use the same methods online that are used in the physical classroom deliberatively.

We might also design a more deliberative examination of communication skills in a written format—use online quick-write options, polls, active and compulsory discussion boards and other engaging activities. We can also push the universities and funding sources for virtual reality (VR) options and advanced technological support to encourage the creation of a 'functional online classroom' to engage students in modelling their future employment.

Finally, we might encourage a variety of learning methods that are employed outside of a 'traditional law classroom', encouraging law students to partake in supported experiential education, including clerkships, internships, research projects simulations, and other learning experiences. We can tie those outside experiences to the online learning experience by providing targeted online education to support (or be in tandem with) experiential education (e.g. law clinic cloud site).

As noted above, we support the notion that students must actively participate in their education to become subversive learners. To do so, we must engage students. In the interim, as we drive engagement, that engagement should be directive. By that, we mean urge a portion of the class to be compulsory for participation. Such an attended session should not be recorded and should be investigatory.[96] However, we also note that merely implementing compulsory attendance without acknowledging the needs of the current student cohort is not enough. There is no doubt that the need to increase university resource support and offer options at times that suit students is imperative to ensure the university itself has delivered on its promise of flexibility in learning. Without significant cost, for example, such compulsory and participatory experiences could happen at least once a week during the evenings and once a week during the day. Or, participatory experiences could be offered once during a teaching term but available for all-day drop-in. The participatory experience would include a session in which students come prepared to discuss a list of open-ended questions (provided in advance) in seminars to instigate policy debate or other legal investigations.[97]

Alternatively, it would be possible to engage a set of law academics to be available in a perpetual chat box 24 hours a day during the teaching period. The law schools would encourage students to hop on while studying and make use of a 'real person' on the other side of their virtual chat who can be trained in the inquiry method or could make such drop-ins a weekly requirement. Legal academics might bridge subject matters with a set of questions that are topical or driven by the weekly substantive materials.

To take such a model to the next level, students could be required to login to a chat box and live recording session at certain times. At that point, a tutor would engage in the inquiry method, testing students on the weekly reading. This would mirror what used to occur in the classroom, and students could be recorded and marked on their oral skills. Students might be required to attend such a session weekly or a certain number of times over the academic term.[98]

Normalising such methodologies for students not only provides student learners with true opportunities for learning but also combats the concern that students do not want to engage in the hard work and will penalise academics who do so with poor evaluations. When we normalise student engagement as an expectation and assess such an engagement, students will progress from being passive learners to more active learners, leading to the type of subversive learner needed for the development of society.

VI. Conclusion

Deep learning, the type needed for the competent practice of law, requires both educator and student engagement. Student engagement is a significant challenge and takes real work on the part of the educator. Yet, this chapter demonstrates that the facilitation of this learning is at odds with the status quo of higher education. As described by Thornton,

> the dominance of the market, with its inevitable inequalities and exploitative practices, favours a technocratic approach and induces a resistance to critique. This can be seen clearly by the pressure brought to bear by student-customers to slough off social and critical knowledge and produce a bare-bones package of orthodox and uncontentious knowledge that can be easily imbibed and regurgitated in examinations.[99]

The integration of technology into university coursework has led student cohorts to expect unfettered flexibility and accessibility of online resources, including asynchronous teaching spaces. The perceived ability to have wide discretion over one's pace of study and the choice to fashion one's own learning environment have become themes that many law schools across the country are selling and contemporary law students are buying.

These financial changes to higher education institutions have influenced law schools to act more like a business and treat students more like consumers. Current barriers are the manifestation of serving the student-consumer and set unrealistic expectations of what it means to study and practise law. To capture the law student market, promises of flexibility in learning are—currently—to the detriment of subversive teaching and learning. Both the university and students have allowed the promise of flexibility to become the premise of disengagement in their learning.

We agree with Postman and Weingartner's suggestion that implementing the inquiry method (Socratic method) in the classroom is of vital importance. In the context of law, we argue it is one of the best ways to develop a student's ability to think critically (crap detection), problem solve and communicate those solutions. We cannot, as subversive educators, become complacent in light of the extensive challenges to student engagement. Instead, a subversive educator must understand the need to support the kind of learning that leads to the improvement of our democratic society and supports our democratic ideals through urging changes across the university, teaching and student engagement.

It is rare that legal academics and law schools are at the forefront of technological development. Yet, online learning is here to stay and could be exactly the space where subversive teaching and learning could best develop. Employing new technologies for active learning and the enquiry method could lead to VR classrooms and courtrooms designed for student engagement. Activities that engage the enquiry method of learning, but could expand on experiences in the classroom, such as moot courts and mock trials, along with client interviews and negotiations, can occur 24 hours a day. With the expansion of VR, online platforms and technology, a university can seamlessly encourage and even require engagement with students both within and outside a classroom. Thus, technology is not a barrier to this type of learning; rather, it is the expectation barrier from the university that prevents proper resourcing of technology for engagement. Nonetheless, the universities' own marketing strategies may save us. If one university normalises and properly resources student engagement, leading to better employment outcomes and student learning, the bar will rise, and all universities will also rise up once again to capture student revenues.

Notes

1 Neil Postman and Charles Weingartner, *Teaching as a Subversive Activity* (Delacorte Press 1969) 205.
2 ibid ch 12.
3 ibid ch 2. See pages 23 (learning how to ask relevant questions), 31–33 (do not need to have a final absolute answer), and 196–197.
4 ibid 23.
5 Department of Employment, Education and Training, 'Higher Education: A Policy Statement' (Australian Government Publishing Service 1988); see also Nickolas John James, 'Australian Legal Education and the Instability of Critique' (2004) 28(2) MULR 375, 378.
6 Margaret Thornton, *Privatising the Public University: The Case of Law* (Routledge 2011).
7 ibid. On a positive note, this change also enabled greater accessibility of this field to the population, with a more heterogeneous student population. However, see Timothy Higgins, 'The Higher Education Contribution Scheme: Keeping Tertiary Education Affordable and Accessible' in Joannah Luetjens, Michael Mintrom, and Paul 't Hart (eds), *Successful Public Policy: Lessons from Australia and New Zealand* (ANU Press 2019) 61: '[w]hile absolute increases in participation numbers were higher among more advantaged students, there was little change in the proportions of applicants from different socioeconomic groups'.
8 Margaret Thornton, 'Legal Education in the Corporate University' (2014) 10 ARLSS Sciences 19.
9 ibid 19; Thornton (n 6).
10 Thornton (n 6).
11 Postman and Weingartner (n 1) s III.
12 ibid.
13 The concept of learning outcomes in an Australian context will be discussed in greater detail in section 3.
14 See Gwilym Croucher, Simon Marginson, Aandrew Norton and Julie Wells (eds), *The Dawkins Revolution 25 Years On* (Melbourne University Press 2013). As discussed in chapter 4 (on page 97), the federal government's contribution to a university's income (excluding HECS) reduced from 83% in 1987 to 56% in 1993.
15 Eugene Clark, 'Australian Legal Education a Decade After the Pearce Report: A Review of McInnis, C. and Maginson, S. Australian Law Schools After the 1987 Pearce Report' (1997) 8(2) LER 213, 216. The Labour government's reform of higher

education triggered an increase in the number of law schools, corresponding with the significant increase in the proportion of the population seeking tertiary education (i.e. 'massification' of education). Key reports on the growth of law schools as part of the massification of education include: Dennis Pearce, Enid Campbell, and Don Harding, 'Australian Law Schools: A Discipline Assessment for the Commonwealth Tertiary Education Commission' (Australian Government Publishing Service 1987); and Craig McInnes and Simon Marginson, 'Australian Law Schools After the 1978 Pearce Report' (1994) 3(2) LED vii. See also David Barker, 'An Avalanche of Law Schools 1989–2013' (2013) 6 JALTA 1.

16 This income-contingent scheme is one in which the government (through the *Higher Education Funding Act 1988 (Cth)*) provides students with funds to cover educational costs to undertake study. The repayment occurs as a tax levy after students have ended their studies. Students are only required to repay the agreed-on costs when their income reaches the national average. Introduced as the Higher Education Contribution Scheme (HECS), this program is now called FEE-HELP. For more information on the evolution of this funding system, see David Weisbrot, 'Recent Statistical Trends in Australian Legal Education' (1990–1991) 2(1) LER 219. See also Bruce Chapman and Jane Nicholls, 'HECS' in Gwilym Croucher, Simon Marginson, Andrew Norton, and Julie Wells (eds), *The Dawkins Revolution 25 Years On* (Melbourne University Press 2013) 108–125.

17 For a discussion of this history, see Richard Johnstone and Sumitra Vignaendra, 'Learning Outcomes and Curriculum Development in Law' (Report Commissioned by the Australian Universities Teaching Committee, Commonwealth of Australia 2003).

18 David Kemp and Andrew Norton, 'Review of the Demand Driven Funding System—Final Report' (The Australian Government Department of Education 2014).

19 Extensive student data is available on the 'Universities Australia' webpage <www.universitiesaustralia.edu.au/stats-publications/student-stats/> accessed 22 March 2021. See also David Weisbrot, 'Recent Statistical Trends in Australian Legal Education' (1990–1991) 2(1) LER 219.

20 'Student Statistics' (Universities Australia 2021) <www.universitiesaustralia.edu.au/stats-publications/student-stats/> accessed 22 March 2021.

21 ibid.

22 '1.37 billion students now home as COVID-19 school closures expand, ministers scale up multimedia approaches to ensure learning continuity' (UNESCO 2020) <https://en.unesco.org/news/137-billion-students-now-home-covid-19-school-closures-expand-ministers-scale-multimedia> accessed 15 July 2021.

23 Chrysi Rapanta, Luca Botturi, Peter Goodyear, Lourdes Guàrdi, and Marguerite Koole, 'Online University Teaching During and After the Covid-19 Crisis: Refocusing Teacher Presence and Learning Activity' (2020) 2 PSE 923.

24 Gwilym Croucher and William Locke, 'A Post-Coronavirus Pandemic World: Some Possible Trends and Their Implications for Australian Higher Education' (Melbourne Centre for the Study of Higher Education 2020).

25 While outside the scope of this chapter, we note the critical research work demonstrating the punitive nature of student evaluations of teachers on their career advancement, especially affecting womxn and academics of colour. This impact intensifies the already disadvantageous effects of academia on those academics who are not white cisgender males. Linda Trinh Vo, 'Navigating the Academic Terrain: The Racial and Gender Politics of Elusive Belonging' in Gabriella Gutierrez y Muhs, Yolanda Flores Neimann, Carmen G. Gonzales, and Angela P. Harris (eds), *Presumed Incompetent: The Intersections of Race and Class for Women in Academia* (University Press of Colorado 2012) 93–113.

26 Historically, the legal profession in Australia was largely self-regulated. This has changed in recent decades with federal and state oversight entities and laws (e.g. Law

Council of Australia and Australian Solicitors' Conduct Rules). On the discussion of regulation, see Laurel S. Terry, Steve Mark, and Tahlia Gordon, 'Trends and Challenges in Lawyer Regulation: The Impact of Globalization and Technology' (2012) 80(6) FLR 2661.

27 Margaret Thornton, 'The Idea of the University and the Contemporary Legal Academy' (2004) 26(4) SLR 481, 494.

28 See Australian Solicitor Conduct Rules; Legal Professional Uniform Law 2014 s 296–297; International Bar Association, 'International Principles on Conduct for the Legal Profession' (International Bar Association 2019); Sally Kift, Mark Israel and Rachael Field, 'Bachelor of Laws Learning and Teaching Academic Standards Statement' (Australian Learning and Teaching Council, 2010). See also Johnstone and Vignaendra (n 17) 10, listing ten fundamental skills, which include problem solving, legal analysis and reasoning, and communication.

29 International Bar Association (n 28), Principle 9.

30 ibid.

31 Consequences of failure to meet such standards can trigger a finding of unsatisfactory professional conduct or professional misconduct. See Legal Professional Uniform Law 2014, ss 296–297.

32 L. J. Priestley, 'Uniform Admission Requirements: Discussion Paper and Recommendations' (Centre for Legal Education, Sydney, 1994). Named after the 1992 chair of the Law Admissions Consultative Committee (LACC), Lancelot John Priestley, this committee identified the minimum study requirements of a law degree to be qualified in Australia. This list of 'prescribed areas of academic knowledge' is set out in Schedule 1 of the LACC Uniform Admission Rules 2015.

33 LTAS Statement (n 28).

34 JD TLO Sub-Committee, 'Juris Doctor: Threshold Learning Outcomes' (Endorsed by the Council of Australian Law Deans 2012).

35 LTAS Statement (n 28).

36 ibid.

37 ibid 8, citing Australian Law Reform Commission, 'Managing Justice: A Review of the Federal Civil Justice System' (ALRC Report 89, 2000), 153.

38 David Weisbrot, 'From the Dean's Desk' (1994) 3(1) SLSR 1.

39 Linda Martin, 'From Apprenticeship to Law School: A Social History of Legal Education in Nineteenth Century New South Wales' (1986) 9 UNSWLJ 111.

40 Nickolas J. James, 'A Brief History of Critique in Australian Legal Education' (2000) 24(3) MULR 965, 967.

41 ibid.

42 Michael Chesterman and David Weisbrot, 'Legal Scholarship in Australia' (1987) 50 TMLR 709, 714.

43 James (n 40), citing Committee on the Future of Tertiary Education in Australia 'Report on the Future of Tertiary Education in Australia to the Australian Universities Commission' (Australian Universities Commission 1964) [11.27]– [11.38].

44 James (n 40) 967, 968.

45 ibid, citing Rob McQueen, 'Is There a Critical Legal Studies Movement in Australia? Innovation in Australian Legal Education after the Pearce Report' (1990) 2(1) Culture and Policy 3, 5.

46 James (n 39) 969–972.

47 Pearce, Campbell and Harding (n 15).

48 James (n 40) 973, fn 54 citing Dennis Pearce, Enid Campbell and Don Harding, 'Australian Law Schools: A discipline assessment for the Commonwealth Tertiary Education Commission' (AGPS, 1987) ('Pearce Report'), volume 1, 21.

49 McInnes and Marginson (n 15) vii–viii; Mary Keyes and Richard Johnstone, 'Changing Legal Education: Rhetoric, Reality, and Prospects for the Future' (2004) 26(4) SLR

537, 550. See also Johnstone and Vignaendra (n 17). In 2003, Johnstone and Vignaendra documented the efforts made by law schools in the 1990s to infuse critical perspectives into the curriculum (47–48). In the last 20 years both Thornton and James have discussed the marginalisation of teaching critique. See, for example, James (n 5); Margaret Thornton, 'The Law School, the Market and the New Knowledge Economy' (2008) 17(1&2) LER 1.

50 See Department of Employment, Education and Training (n 5).

51 Clark (n 15). The Labour government's reform of higher education triggered an increase in the number of law schools, corresponding with a significant increase in the proportion of the population seeking tertiary education (i.e. 'massification' of education). Key reports on the growth of law schools as part of the massification of education include: Pearce, Campbell and Harding (n 15); and McInnis and Marginson (n 15). See also Barker (n 15).

52 Keyes and Johnstone (n 49).

53 Kate Galloway and Peter Jones, 'Guarding Our Identities: The Dilemma of Transformation in the Legal Academy' (2014) 14(1) QUTLR 15, 19.

54 Postman and Weingartner (n 1) 19. On this issue, the authors state, 'The medium is the message'. It implies that the invention of a dichotomy between content and method is both naïve and dangerous. Further, *it implies that the critical content of any learning experience is the method or process through which the learning occurs.*

55 Johnstone and Vignaendra (n 17).

56 Margaret Thornton and Lucinda Shannon, '"Selling the Dream": Law School Branding and the Illusion of Choice' (2013) 23(2) LER 249. Introducing a JD program has also assisted remedying the funding shortfall. See, Donna Cooper, Sheryl Jackson, Rosalind Mason and Mary Toohey, 'The Emergence of the JD in the Australian Legal Education Marketplace and Its Impact on Academic Standards' (2011) 21(2) LER 23.

57 Keyes and Johnstone (n 49).

58 ATAR stands for Australian Tertiary Admission Rank. In Australia, a student's ATAR score is part of the ranking system used among universities across the country to select graduating high school students into a course of study (e.g. Law, Arts, Engineering, etc.). The HECS scheme is discussed above in n 16.

59 Andrew Harvey, Lisa Andewartha, Daniel Edwards, Julia Clarke and Kimberly Reyes, 'Student Equity and Employability in Higher Education' (Centre for Higher Education Equity and Diversity Research, La Trobe University 2017) 20; Thornton and Shannon (n 56).

60 For a history of accreditation practices modelled against curriculum changes, see Clark (n 15).

61 Legal Profession Uniform Admission Rules 2015.

62 ibid.

63 ibid sch 1. In 1992, the Law Admission Consultative Committee (LACC) identified the 11 subjects (the 'Priestley 11') a candidate is required to complete successfully during their studies before entering legal practice. It should be mentioned that the LACC also identified a list of skills (called the Priestley 12) that candidates should sharpen or acquire during their practical legal training.

64 Thornton (n 27).

65 Postman and Weingartner (n 1) chapter III.

66 Stephen Matchett, 'The Future for Campus is Digital First: Universities Will Consider Selling Real Estate to Fund Digital Programmes and Research' *Campus Morning Mail* (Sydney, 22 February 2021) <https://campusmorningmail.com.au/news/the-future-for-campuses-is-digital-first/?utm_source=sendgrid.com&utm_medium=email&utm_campaign=website> accessed 29 March 2021.

67 Britt P. Tevis and K. E. Powell, 'Student Evaluations of Teaching: An Unlawful Barrier to Women's Professional Advancement in Australian Universities' (2020) 37(1) HLELJ 1.

68 ibid 3.
69 ibid 13 citing Bob Uttl, Carmela A. White, and Daniela Wong Gonzalez, 'Meta-Analysis of Faculty's Teaching Effectiveness: Student Evaluation of Teaching Ratings and Student Learning Are Not Related' (2017) 54 SEE 22, 22, 24 (highlighting a SET conducted by Clayton in 2009, where the ratings showed that student learning is not directly related to higher scores on the survey.
70 ibid 13, citing Scott E. Carrell and James E. West, 'Does Professor Quality Matter? Evidence from Random Assignment of Students to Professors' (2010) 118(3) JPE 409, 412, 430.
71 Thornton (n 27) 498.
72 Current government funding initiatives again increase costs to higher education students, drive cuts to university staff and increase the precarity of casual teaching staff.
73 While research data are still emerging, initial studies note the additional burden placed on womxn in academia during COVID-19. Marwa Shalaby, Nermin Allam and Gail Buttorff, 'Gender, COVID and Faculty Service' (Inside Higher Ed 2020). <https://www.insidehighered.com/advice/2020/12/18/increasingly-disproportionate-service-burden-female-faculty-bear-will-have> accessed 31 March 2021. Further, the intense purging of casual and permanent staff will disproportionally impact colleagues of colour and those with non-traditional backgrounds.
74 Postman and Weingartner (n 1) chapter XIII.
75 ibid chapter XII.
76 Thornton (n 6).
77 LTAS Statement (n 28) 13.
78 ibid 10.
79 ibid 18.
80 ibid.
81 ibid 19, elaborating on the requirements for creative thinking in legal practice.
82 ibid 21.
83 In Australia, law graduates must complete a practical legal training course, which earns those graduates a Graduate Diploma of Legal Practice, required before acquiring a practising certificate. See, for example, Victoria's admission rules as memorialised in the Legal Profession Uniform Admission Rules 2015.
84 'Welcome' (Federation of Law Societies of Canada, National Committee on Accreditation 2021). <https://nca.legal/> accessed 31 March 2021.
85 Anna Huggins, 'Incremental and Inevitable: Contextualizing the Threshold Learning Outcomes for Law' (2015) 38(1) UNSWLJ 264, 278.
86 American Bar Association, 'ABA Standards and Rules of Procedure for Approval of Law Schools 2020–2021' (American Bar Association 2020) Standard 311.
87 ibid Standard 303, and Standard 304.
88 Federation of Law Societies of Canada, 'National Requirement' (Federation of Law Societies of Canada 2018), 5 (C.1).
89 ibid.
90 ibid (C.2).
91 It is beyond the scope of this chapter to consider how other regulatory structures may support or pervert subversive legal education in an online context. We suggest that further inquiry might assist in determining how online legal education could better serve Australian law students and the public.
92 Paula Karp, 'Humanities Students Will Pay up to 113% More for Uni Courses After Centre Alliance Backs Changes' *The Guardian* (Sydney, 6 October 2020) <https://www.theguardian.com/australia-news/2020/oct/06/humanities-students-will-pay-up-to-113-more-for-uni-courses-after-centre-alliance-backs-changes> accessed 31 March 2021.
93 Postman and Weingartner (n 1) chapter I.

94 John B. Biggs and Catherine Tang, *Teaching for Quality Learning at University* (4th edn, Open University Press 2011).

95 Carl Rogers, 'Personal Thoughts on Teaching and Learning' (1957) 3(4) MPQ 241. For more on Rodgers and legal education see, Paul Maharg, 'Rogers, Constructivism and Jurisprudence: Educational Critique and the Legal Curriculum' (2008) 7(3) IJLP 1.

96 We urge compulsory engagement to break the cycle of transactional learners, thus encouraging students to take charge of their learning. Once the culture of education has shifted, there may be more advanced methods of engaging students that do not require such overt participatory requirements.

97 Postman and Weingartner (n 1) chapter V.

98 For a short description of the Socratic method in a traditional classroom, see Edward J. Gac, 'Socratic Grading Method' (1984) 2(1) JLSE 76.

99 Thornton (n 27).

8 Hacking the Priestleys[1]

Kate Galloway, with Melissa Castan and Alex Steel

I. Introduction

According to commentary around the Priestley 11, the core mandated subjects of the accredited Australian law degree are either a dead hand or a 'surprisingly light hand'.[2] Despite a recent review of the formulation of the Priestley subjects, there has been no change. In the absence of a significant—and likely consensus—shift in the approach to law school accreditation, the Priestleys look to retain their long-standing formulation into the foreseeable future. Partly this is due to an ingrained textbook tradition of the law that, for many in the academy, the profession, and the judiciary, makes it difficult to imagine a 'coherent body of discipline knowledge' of the law in any other way. And partly, it is fear of creating an alternative and more onerous and intrusive form of law school regulation that would regulate pedagogy and broader educational aims.

Between the framing of the mandated curriculum and the unbundling, globalisation, and 'technologization' of legal services,[3] what *is* a lawyer in the 21st century? What type of lawyer is the mandated curriculum serving? Assuming that legal education continues to serve the administration of justice, the underlying question, and the focus of this research, is whether it is possible that alternative law curricula might also serve society and the administration of justice through diverse conceptualisations of the threshold knowledge and skills of the graduate lawyer.

The Priestley 11 compulsory knowledge areas are determined by the judiciary, embodied in legislation, and enforced by the practitioners' admissions boards in each state and territory.[4] They are also looking increasingly dated. In the US, an American Bar Association committee recommended a significant reduction in the number of areas of law in the Bar Examination—the core of the US admission process.[5] The UK admission requirements now see doctrinal knowledge as part of a more applied approach to legal practice.[6]

Given Australia's top-down and dated approach to the accredited law curriculum, this chapter critiques the current curriculum regulations and reports on a project of collective reimagination of the core law curriculum—'hacking' the Priestleys. In describing the variety of responses to an 'ideal' law curriculum, it highlights diverse conceptions of what it means to be a graduate lawyer in the

DOI: 10.4324/9781003175216-10

context of rapid and paradigmatic social, economic, environmental, political, and technological change.

Part II outlines the influence of Priestley 11 on the Australian law curriculum and its inherent relationship with the essence of what it means to be a lawyer. Part III describes the project we undertook to 'hack' the Priestleys. Part IV discusses the outcomes of the project before concluding.

II. Australian Law Curriculum as Preparation for Being a Lawyer

For an Australian law school to offer a pathway to admission to practice law, they must have their law degree accredited by their state legal practice board. The requirements of the accredited degree are set out in various statutes, approved by the Supreme Court in each jurisdiction. These requirements include a list of prescribed areas of knowledge (the Priestley 11) and include particularised topics within each subject area.[7]

All applicants must have completed a university-level qualification offered by a law school[8] that is accredited by these bodies. Fundamentally, law schools are accredited on the basis of sufficiently rigorous teaching of eleven doctrinal content areas, the 'Priestley 11'.

These areas arose out of the 1982 McGarvie Report on legal education.[9] Sandford Clark notes:

> The Report also set out 'topics which will ordinarily be treated as necessary parts of the required area of knowledge'. These were drawn from the current handbooks at Melbourne and Monash. Importantly, however, they were only meant to help law schools know what an admitting authority would 'ordinarily' look for and were offered in an attempt to help law schools meet its expectations more easily than it might otherwise do. But the lists were intended merely to be indicative, not prescriptive. Because Professor Jack Goldring, then Head of School at Macquarie, thought it was necessary to guard against the possibility that they would be wrongly interpreted as prescriptive, a second, more general formula was added to each description to ensure the intended flexibility.[10]

Since 1979, the Legal Admissions Consultative Council (LACC) has served as a peak body of state and territory admitting authorities.[11] LACC is an advisory body only, and state accrediting authorities may add additional requirements, but it is recognised that LACC has the carriage of any review of the development of the Priestleys. Most recently, LACC led a review of the framing of the existing 11 subject areas that sought to update the content of the knowledge areas without changing the names of those areas,[12] but which it has decided to defer implementing.[13]

An alternative regulatory approach exists. Australian university degrees are required to develop a set of learning outcomes that match levels in the Australian Qualifications Framework (AQF). Law is aided in achieving this requirement by the existence of the more broadly based discipline Threshold Learning Outcomes (TLOs).[14] These were developed under the aegis of the Australian Learning and Teaching Council, which was commissioned by the Australian Government to support the development of disciplinary-based elaborations of the AQF requirements.

The TLOs provide significant support to law schools in devising program-level learning outcomes as required by Tertiary Education Quality and Standards Agency. The TLOs attempt to make a break from the Priestleys by formulating outcomes in terms of the threshold of graduate knowledge, skills, and attributes that constitute a lawyer. They relegate the importance of doctrinal knowledge to one outcome that itself extends more broadly than the prescribed knowledge areas of the Priestleys:

> TLO 1: Knowledge
>
> Graduates of the Bachelor of Laws will demonstrate an understanding of a coherent body of knowledge that includes:
>
> a) *the fundamental areas of legal knowledge*, the Australian legal system, and underlying principles and concepts, including international and comparative contexts,
> b) the broader contexts within which legal issues arise, and
> c) the principles and values of justice and of ethical practice in lawyers' roles.[15]

The commentary to the TLOs states:

> TLO 1 has been drafted to encompass the current 'prescribed academic areas of knowledge' known as the 'Priestley 11' and to be flexible enough to allow for subsequent developments as negotiated between [the Council of Australian Law Deans] and the law admitting authorities.[16]

Despite embracing the threshold outcome of knowledge, the external (professional) requirements for accreditation mean that the TLOs will always exist in the shadow of the Priestleys. The commentary to the TLOs makes clear that the Priestleys retain their primacy, but the TLO anticipates a future beyond them. That future has not yet arrived.

Given the complexity of the higher education environment, there are multiple other variables informing curriculum: each state and territory regulator's interpretation of the Priestley requirements, each of those decision-maker's own conceptions of what makes a lawyer, vague factors such as the culture of the profession, and of course universities' own policy imperatives. Given the complexity of the system, the relationship between the Priestleys and legal education is inevitably multidirectional. Although the Priestleys might be considered to reflect the profession's image of itself as the key regulatory organising structure for educating lawyers, it may also be sufficiently internalised as the coherent body of knowledge necessary to constitute the baseline of legal education.[17] The Priestleys are 'within us' as *constituting* legal education.

As legal education is driven by the peak accrediting bodies who control lawyers' entry to the legal system, their approach to how to interpret or contextualise the Priestleys—or to fail to seek to renew or replace them—implicitly determines the substantive meaning of what it is to be a lawyer through what is required to be taught in the accredited degree. While prescribing core knowledge areas is one way of organising curriculum, our affinity with knowledge of identifiable core doctrinal subjects as a proxy for what it is to be a lawyer can inhibit the scope in order to teach a range of other knowledge, skills, and attributes that apparently the profession desires in the 'work-ready' graduate.[18] Yet the meaning of what it is to be a lawyer is increasingly open to interpretation in the professional literature across common law jurisdictions.[19]

Lawyers tend to use 'the profession' as a catch-all phrase to signify the institution of those admitted to practice, as well as what has emerged as a broader legal services industry. It is also, in general terms, a means of describing the source of regulation of legal education. More precisely, however, the primary source of accreditation body membership is the judiciary, largely drawn, of course, from the ranks of the bar—a subset of a subset of the broader profession. The design of legal education more broadly is informed by stakeholders, including solicitors who employ graduates in their businesses, the courts as gatekeepers to admission, the public as consumers of legal services, and students as learners and future professionals.

More generally, if the 'work-ready' graduate is a goal of legal education,[20] the meaning of 'work-ready' is somewhat diffuse. In the first place, commentary offered by the profession offers a diverse list of additional knowledge and skills beyond the core—that itself remains vital.[21] Tellingly, the suggestions are not accompanied by the means of designing a curriculum to meet them all. The questions for any law school designing a work-ready curriculum are what exactly is the desired 'work-ready' outcome and how can the crowded curriculum accommodate what looks to be a wish list for graduates entering their first job. Of note, the TLOs[22] are capable of accommodating the enhanced skillset. However, as the TLOs are not prescriptive, and in the face of the emphasis on content in the Priestleys, they go only part of the way to assist in designing a curriculum to meet a radically broader skillset.

Without a clear articulation of what exactly they are educating for, law schools face the challenge of attempting to serve all stakeholders while also meeting other (educational) imperatives that intersect to an extent but are not the same. The proliferation of mooting and interviewing competitions, work-integrated learning programs, clinical programs, mentoring and internships, volunteering, international experiences, and hackathons and incubators both for credit and extra-curricular are all examples of attempts to value-add to the student experience in terms of employability skills. There is a cross-over between these activities and universities' contemporary emphasis on employability[23] also reflected in their framing of programs of study in terms of graduate attributes[24] and enterprise skills.[25] Law schools will also reflect their own university's particular branding[26] and design curricula aligned with that university's strategic intent and learning and teaching policies and priorities. This can lend a particular flavour to legal education independent of the imperatives of wider stakeholder groups.[27]

A further challenge for legal education in terms of graduate work-readiness (as a benchmark of knowledge, skills, and attributes of graduate lawyers) is that employers of graduates cannot necessarily articulate what is required or what they expect. Knowledge (such as is represented by the Priestley subjects) is a straightforward way to articulate what is expected and may perhaps explain why the profession is so enmeshed in the core curriculum as the driver of legal education both in a regulatory sense and in practice.

In the regulation of legal education, whether through accreditation requirements or through policy imperatives for law schools to engage with employability metrics (such as those imposed by the government),[28] the profession itself has identified an indeterminate field of skills and attributes. Within these skills and attributes, and lending to the ambiguity of the cited skill-set, there is no acknowledgement of the effect on skills of diverse types of legal service provision, the fragmented effects of technology on legal practice, and the changing nature of legal services altogether.[29] There is a general embrace of technology, for example, without any useful or actionable examination of what it means.[30] Finally, the profession has not clarified how it might contribute to the framing of the requisite skills or the education of its employees, who are necessarily the future of the profession.

The discussion about the nature and content of legal education, therefore, begs the question of the outcome sought. There are myriad types of lawyers with diverse skills and knowledge—but this is not recognised within the scope of the Priestleys and the current accredited curriculum.

Given that there are many types of lawyers and, axiomatically, many purposes for legal education, the idea that a prescriptive list of subjects and associated content will serve the justice system, the profession, or the community, cannot be assumed. But without a process of continuous evaluation and review, the existing structure, prescribed from the peak of the law's hierarchy, will remain in its own image. In this project, we seek to challenge the power inherent in the prescribed curriculum by drawing on the experience, expertise, and informed beliefs of a range of legal educators to test the universality of the law curriculum as manifest in the Priestleys. In crowd-sourcing a new curriculum—or curricula—this project subverts the expectations in the model of a universal curriculum and the power vested in its pronouncement.

III. Hacking the Priestleys

One meaning of 'hacking' is the gaining of unauthorized access to data in a system or computer, widely recognised as a subversive activity. According to Tréguer, for example, 'the Internet has enlarged the public sphere, opening a space where once excluded citizen groups can act at its outskirts to challenge dominant discourses and resist power.'[31] So-called 'insurgent citizenship practices' arise online based on the construction of the internet as an extension of the public sphere. Its ready accessibility to all, including the marginalised, provides a new and democratised platform for resistance and expression that challenges mainstream ideas and discourse. 'Hacking' in this sense describes, for us, the subversion of the power of pronouncement of the only acceptable curriculum that is emblematic of the law itself.

Hacking also has an older, broader meaning of a technical expert who overcomes the limitations or standard uses of systems of objects using non-standard means.[32] In this sense, hacking describes, for us, the expertise legal academics have to re-use and re-imagine the elements of the Priestleys to form innovative curricula.

A. Method

The purpose of the study is to answer the research question, what is the ideal law curriculum to develop the graduate lawyer of tomorrow? To answer the question, the project involved a multimodal method situated as a (semi-)naturalistic inquiry to gather data in a fairly controlled setting.[33] The data to be gathered included participants' vision of a graduate lawyer; the style of curriculum that would achieve such a graduate; and core elements of that curriculum.[34]

Given that we are seeking to uncover 'the description of activities [the law curriculum] in relation to a particular cultural context [the law school] from the point of view of the members of that group themselves',[35] we adopted an ethnographic approach, broadly speaking, as a form of social research used to examine curriculum design through the eyes of the participants. Ethnography as a research method, 'grasp[s] the point of view of the native [sic], his [sic] view of the world and in relation to his [sic] life.'[36] For our purposes, illustrating the breadth of possible curricula depends upon engaging a diverse group of experts in framing the law curriculum in a way that is meaningful to their interpretations of what it means to be a lawyer and what is the purpose of legal education.

Although we are cognisant of the paradox, and therefore limitations, of a 'naturalistic' approach in a contrived environment, we maintain that the nature of the inquiry—into experts in the law curriculum in an academic context—limited the constraints, such that the data produced would be valid.

The participant group was self-selecting—law academics who were present at the UNSW Legal Education Conference, held on 27–8 November, 2019, and who chose to attend. This may seem somewhat limiting, notably, in that we did not specifically recruit law deans or associate deans of education or ensure a wide representation of law schools. Indeed, it is likely that many law academics could not afford to attend the conference, and the group may have had an over-representation of Sydney-based academics.

On the other hand, the conference was going to draw those who were at least interested in legal education and more likely to be engaged in questions of legal education than the broader law academic population. In electing to participate in this session, we were likely to have the most interested and most dedicated group of relevantly qualified experts. We believe that in light of the nature of this inquiry, the method of selection is valid to provide us with the data we need. This is in line with our second understanding of hacking, i.e. iconoclastic experts without loyalty to established approaches.

University research ethics approvals were sought and granted. With the permission of the organisers, we advertised the session in advance, together with information sheets and related materials pursuant to our ethics approval. The group that attended the session were then informed of the nature of the research and process and signed consent forms agreeing to participate and for us to use the resultant data. All participants were free to leave the session at any time, although to the extent that their (unnamed) contribution was to that point intermingled with other text, it was not possible to extract the contribution they made prior to their departure.

Participants recorded the data as text and diagrams through a facilitated series of scaffolded, individual, and small group activities designed to simulate a curriculum design process. We transcribed the results, consolidating them into the tables produced below.

B. The Facilitated Activities

Tasks and stimuli were designed to encourage participants to identify their vision of graduate lawyers and the curriculum that will generate that type of lawyer. The group of participants commenced as individuals. As tasks progressed, members joined into small groups with a common interest and, through additional tasks and stimuli, articulated that the groups agreed on core components of curriculum relevant to achieving their ideal graduate.

Task 1: Identify Graduate Competencies. The first task required identifying words describing what that participant believed were the top three graduate competencies. We provided a list of words (Table 8.1), but participants could use any word. The words are very general, and some are ambiguous. It was open to participants to interpret the words according to their own parameters. Participants were invited to write one word per post-it note.

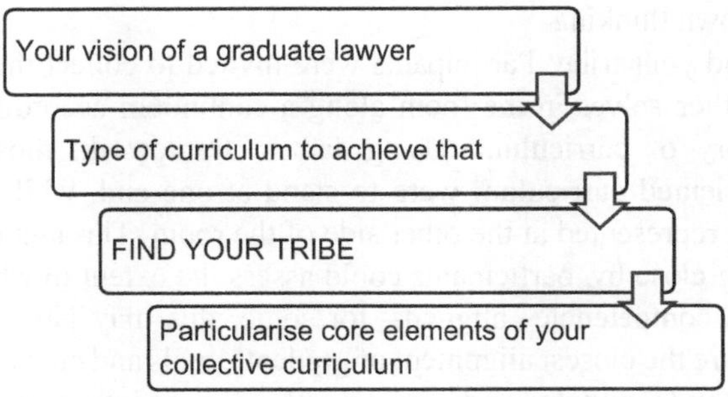

Figure 8.1 Scaffolded tasks

Table 8.1 Desirable graduate competencies—stimulus words

Commitment to rule of law	Creativity	Project management	Legal problem-solving	Knowledge of First Nations contexts
Ethical	Effective communication	Global-orientation	Commitment to justice	Legal writing
Tech-savvy	Learned in law	Leadership	Advocacy	Self-confidence
Resilience	Reflective	Adaptable	Coding proficiency	Entrepreneurship
Legal design	Client-readiness	Effective collaboration	Self-awareness	Critical thinking
Curiosity	Legal drafting	Business skills	Digital literacy	Work-readiness
Social awareness	Cultural intelligence	Intellectually capable	Independence of thought	High-level research skills

Task 2: Frame your curriculum goal. As an introduction to this task, we introduced participants to various frames of thought about curriculum in terms of its purpose (Table 8.2). Each framing has its own context, but in our view, there are overlaps and similarities. Expressing the four frames in a table allowed us to represent the common themes running through.

Table 8.2 lists the work of four authors, each of whom has engaged in the analysis of curriculum according to categories. Using Schiro's categories of types of curricula as the starting point, the rows group together similarly themed categories within the work of the authors in each column. These are not exactly correlated but, in our view, represent sufficiently similar thematic underpinning to be seen as broadly on the same lines.

We observe an overlap, or alternative grouping between corporatism and doctrinalism, discipline, and status professionalism—largely arising from the corporate nature of the prescribed law degree and the focus on graduate destinations in 'BigLaw'.[43]

The purpose of presenting participants with these curricular frameworks was to promote reflection on the type of curriculum a participant might see as generating their ideal graduate. These categories both provide the language to describe curriculum goals or purpose, as well as to stimulate thinking about key differences in approach to the law curriculum. They are not intended to be definitive, and the suggested correlations are open to contestation—this in itself might stimulate participants' own thinking.

Task 3: Find your tribe: Participants were invited to collect their post-it notes and position themselves in the room along a continuum according to their preferred category of curriculum. Using James' framework, those preferring a doctrinally oriented curriculum were to stand at one end, while the pedagogic approach was represented at the other side of the room. Through discussion with those standing close by, participants could assess the extent to which their desirable graduate competencies aligned—for some, this may have involved some sorting to assure the closest alignment of graduate goals and curriculum approach. Thus, this method facilitated participants' self-selecting into groups with a similar attitude to graduate competencies and curriculum.

Table 8.2 Frames of interpretation of curriculum purpose

Curriculum: Schiro (2008)[37]	*Discourses: James (2004)*[38]	*Curricular emphasis: Galloway (2011)*[39]	*Narratives of 'lawtech' in curriculum: Galloway et al. (2019)*[40]
Scholar academic	Doctrinalism	Discipline-based	Status professionalism
Social efficiency	Corporatism		'Death' (of the profession) (Susskind)[41]
	Vocationalism	Practical skills	Disruption (Christensen)[42]
	Liberalism		
Social reconstruction	Radicalism	Service to community	Adaptive professionalism
Learner-centred	Pedagogicalism	[Serving a particular cohort, e.g.] external students	

Task 4: Build your curriculum. The next task, undertaken in small groups, involved building the desirable curriculum. We used a simple table (Table 8.3) to promote targeted thinking of the knowledge, skills, and attributes of the graduate lawyer necessary to achieve the curriculum goals—to a maximum of four each.

Table 8.3 Knowledge, skills, and attributes to achieve curriculum goals

	1	*2*	*3*	*4*
Knowledge				
Skills				
Attributes				

Task 5: adopted a concentric framework (Figure 8.2) to help participants identify subject areas for their curriculum that they felt would develop the knowledge, skills, and attributes, according to whether each subject would be at the core or outside that as an 'intermediate' subject, or one that was peripheral.

C. Results

Participants formed seven groups based on their ideal graduate and curriculum. Each group clarified their curricular purpose, as well as the key knowledge, skills, and attributes necessary to achieve that purpose. The data is presented below.

Graduate competencies were fairly widely spread, as indicated in Table 8.4 below. In collating this data, we grouped similar competencies and counted the incidence with which they were recorded. Some groups recorded three, and some recorded six.

The highest incidence of a desirable competency was legal problem-solving and adaptability, both appearing in four groups. This was followed by effective

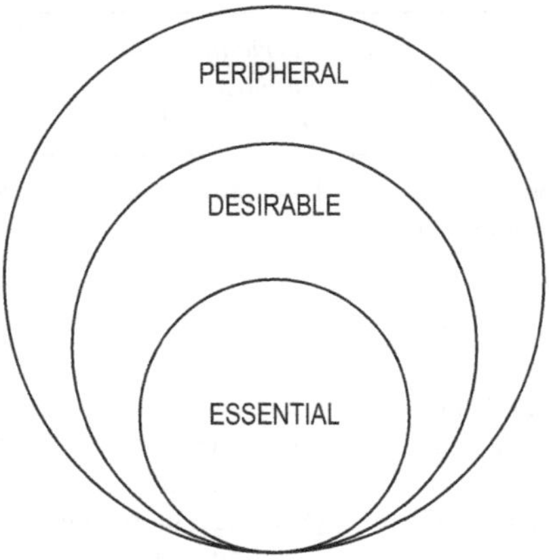

Figure 8.2 Prioritising subject areas relative to achieving curricular goals

Table 8.4 Incidence of desirable graduate competencies

Number of responses	*Graduate competency*
4	legal problem-solving
4	adaptable
3	effective communication
3	ethical
2	democratic citizen; service to community
2	empathy; cultural intelligence
2	critical thinking
2	creativity
2	intellectually capable
2	self-management; reflective
2	high-level research skills
1	effective collaboration
1	disruptive
1	advocacy
1	global orientation
1	work-ready
1	rule of law
1	broad legal knowledge

communication and ethical disposition at three instances, with a number of desirable competencies nominated by two groups.

In tabulating the curriculum approaches, we present the raw data in Table 8.5. It includes the particular curriculum approach adopted by that group and the knowledge, skills, and attributes that group saw as the goals of that approach. While we had encouraged limiting these to four goals for each aspect of curriculum, we have recorded all goals proffered.

Table 8.5 Knowledge, skills, and attributes for curriculum approaches

Knowledge	Skills	Attributes
Status professionalism		
Knowledge	**Skills**	**Attributes**
• Doctrinal • Ethical • Service delivery • ‘How-to”’professional knowledge • How to best acquire and use knowledge; ‘meta-knowledge’	• Research • Critical evaluation • Communication • Conflict resolution • Problem-solving	• Professional identity • Self-management • Resilience • Adaptability • Technologically agnostic
Liberalism		
Knowledge	Skills	Attributes
• Interdisciplinary knowledge: politics, economics, culture, theory, history, etc. • Holistic legal knowledge; connection between theory and practice	• Comparative and international legal skills • Integrated learning • Critical thinking skills • Research • Writing • Applied practical skills • Theoretical skills • Ability to make connections between individual and collective legal ideologies	• Globally-minded; ability to make connections to broader context • Critical thinking • Cultural competency • Emphasis on social justice and ethics
Service to community		
Knowledge	Skills	Attributes
• Ethical foundations • Law in action • Positive law • Theoretical framework	• Self-awareness • Cultural competency • Professional and ethical competence • Interpersonal skills	• Commitment to justice • Commitment to rule of law • Tenacity • Resilience • Kindness
Adaptive professionalism		
Knowledge	Skills	Attributes
• Ethics • World awareness: disruption, climate change and social evolution • ‘Known unknowns’ • Legal discourse, including rule of law	• Ethics • Technology-based skills • Self-management across work, social, justice, and interpersonal contexts • Critical thinking	• Ethical disposition • Adaptive • Agile • Self-awareness • Social justice

(*Continued*)

Table 8.5 (Continued)

Status professionalism		
Disruptive, creative professionals		
Knowledge	Skills	Attributes
• Public interest litigation subjects • Technology • Global legal frameworks • Work integrated learning	• Plain English writing • Critical analysis • Problem identification and solving • Digital literacy	• Adaptability • Good communication • Creativity • Collaboration
Radicalism		
Knowledge	Skills	Attributes
• Foundational concepts • Justice • Morality • Ethics • Law's failings and limitations • Law as an agent of change	• Critical thinking • Interpersonal skills: connective, communicative, and collaborative skills • Ethical skills • Persuasion • Advocacy	• Curiosity • Creativity • Intellectually capable • Reflective • Adaptable to change and during uncertainty
Environmental sustainability		
Knowledge	Skills	Attributes
• Knowledge of diverse political theories • Transdisciplinary literacy across politics, philosophy, science and economics • Knowledge of legal principles • Rights and obligations with respect to land (property and environmental law) • Torts and contracts (harm, remedies, restitution, agreement, and negotiation) • International law (private and public) • Transdisciplinary environmental and climate literacy • Corporations law • Administrative law	• Ability to read and write at a very high level • Communication • Critical thinking • Ability to actively listen • Collaboration • Ability to translate technical information to non-specialists • Boundary spanning • Integrative thinking • Facilitation, mediation and negotiation	• Respect for differences • Curiosity and openness to new experiences • Empathy • Conscientiousness/discipline • Cultural competency • Critical and independent-mindedness • Creativity

Table 8.6 Incidence of topic categories in curriculum as essential, desirable, peripheral

	Categories	*Specific topics include . . .*	*X-ref*	*Essential*	*Desirable*	*Peripheral*
KNOWLEDGE						
K1	Context (incl Global legal frameworks, Political knowledge, legal history and institutions, Future of law, critical perspectives on law (e.g., according to contexts of class, race, gender, and environment))		D3	7	2	
K2	Doctrine	doctrinal areas; thematic, i.e. legal principle across doctrinal areas; 'law'; [peripheral: Priestley 11]	D1	4	1	3
K3	Rule of law, Protections of citizens in the 'halls of power', Sovereignty and power		D1; D2	3	-	-
K4	Statutory interpretation			2		
K5	List of specific doctrinal fields	Contract law + human rights; Civil obligations law (Ethical) Criminal law		2	1	
K6	Legal theory, Jurisprudence			2	2	
K7	Foreign law			-	-	1
K8	Other disciplines	Interdisciplinarity generally; named fields; includes languages	S6	-	-	5
SKILLS						
S1	Critical thinking/ critique		K1	2	-	-
S2	Communication		S2	1	-	-
S3	Lawyering; legal skills		D1; D2; S3	1	3	1
S4	Project management; business skills		S4	-	1	1

(*Continued*)

Table 8.6 (Continued)

	Categories	*Specific topics include . . .*	*X-ref*	*Essential*	*Desirable*	*Peripheral*
S5	Other thinking skills (design-orientated thinking; Innovation, creativity)		S6	-	2	
S6	Technology-based skills		K1; S2; S6	-	1	2
DISPOSITIONS						
D1	Ethics	justice, morality, social justice, professionalism	K1	7		
D2	Public Interest Litigation; Pro bono law		P1	2		
D3	World awareness		P6	-	-	1
PEDAGOGY						
P1	Project style teaching spanning multiple areas	Capstone	D2	1	1	
P2	WIL	Public interest litigation	D2	2	2	-
P3	Starting each course with real-life case studies (as opposed to High Court judgments)		P2	1	-	-
P4	Interpersonal study			-	1	-
P5	Industry mentors/ networks		S2	-	1	-
P6	Study exchange		D3; K1; K7	-	-	1

In the final part of the curriculum development activities, groups identified the core, intermediate, and peripheral curricular topics that they felt necessary to deliver on that group's vision of curriculum for the graduates they envisage. This is presented in Table 8.6.

In examining the data, we saw that they fell into categories of knowledge, skills, dispositions, and pedagogy. This echoes the data shown in Table 8.5 above. We have grouped specific responses together under a general category but provide in the table some details of the variety of specific topics included in that category.

Each topic is given a number to permit cross-referencing with topics that cross boundaries. We had the choice to aggregate some responses under one category but, in some instances, felt the specificity of response warranted keeping a separate category. The aim of the table is to identify broad themes (categories) whilst retaining some of the individuality in the responses. In the columns essential/desirable/peripheral, we indicate the number of incidences of that category in the responses.

IV. Discussion

A. Competencies

While participants were asked to prioritise attributes, it is interesting that given the doctrinal imperatives of the accredited law degree, and the prevalence of *legal problem-solving* in law programs, legal problem solving appears in only four of the seven groups. Notably, however, *legal problem-solving* does not appear together with the competency of *intellectual capability*. It may be that the latter competency implies an ability to solve legal problems.

The balance of the competencies largely, and perhaps unsurprisingly, reflects the TLOs.[44] What this exercise illustrates, however, is that designing a curriculum requires the prioritisation of particular competencies. While other competencies might be incorporated throughout a curriculum, there is a complex filtering process designed to highlight the most desirable elements. Another feature of curriculum design is that competencies may be expressed at a greater level of generality (e.g., *intellectual capability*) that gives scope to embed diverse curricular elements under its umbrella (e.g., *thinking skills*, *problem-solving*, etc.). In the TLOs, there is a blend of higher-level and more specific competencies that provides a useful benchmark.

B. Curriculum Goals

As might be expected, curriculum goals varied somewhat between groups. However, there were some common features amongst the knowledge, skills, and attributes connected with each curriculum goal. For example, nearly all groups included *legal* and *ethical knowledge* as a component of curriculum to achieve desired goals. Similarly, *critical thinking* or *disposition* features in all approaches except *service to community*.

While most groups feature an academic or more theoretical approach to delivering on curriculum, of note *status professionalism* and *disruptive creative professionals* both focus on what might be described as 'work readiness'. *Status professionalism* seeks to deliver 'how to' knowledge with a service delivery emphasis. *Disruptive professionals* incorporate work-integrated learning as a core feature of knowledge in curriculum.

Despite different curriculum approaches, there is some agreement on a couple of core skills. *Communication* (including *writing* and *interpersonal skills*) and *critical thinking* both feature seven times and once more as an attribute. *Ethics* (or a variation thereof) appears three times and a further two as an attribute, while *self-management,* including a *reflective disposition,* appears a total of five times as a skill and attribute.

Given the emphasis in university graduate attributes on *cultural competency*, and more recently in the context of legal education itself,[45] it is perhaps surprising that it appears only once as a skill and twice as an attribute. The same might be said for *digital capabilities*[46] (or technology skills), appearing only twice. Otherwise, there is fairly significant diversity in the knowledge, skills, and attributes according to the particular curricular approach.

The diversity in knowledge, skills, and attributes featured in these curriculum approaches is unsurprising. Thinking about the law curriculum beyond doctrine and instead in terms of how we see our graduates engaging with the world will inevitably see a divergence in emphasis. What the participants' ideas illustrate, however, is that within any curricular approach, the select knowledge, skills, and attributes represent an internally coherent design—even if they do not align with an organisational method such as the Priestleys.

C. Curriculum Topics

By far, the most common topic nominated is *contexts of law*—though, as might be expected, this is expressed in a variety of ways. Considering the range of curriculum outcomes—from status professionalism through to radicalism—it is interesting to observe the importance attached to context. This is perhaps indicative of the way that law is taught—it is taught and learned beyond 'pure' doctrine and according to broader contexts.

The second most common topic we describe as a *general approach to doctrine* (four essential, three desirable, and one peripheral). This category warrants some explanation. Only one of the groups expressly identified the Priestleys as relevant to their curriculum, and then it was a peripheral matter only. Perhaps this suggests that the Priestleys, as such, would not be prescribed (but may be optional). The absence of Priestleys from the list of essential and desirable topics might be the strongest indication in this project of their perceived redundance as an organising concept for curriculum.

Despite this, two other groups indicated as essential what might be a *reframing of the Priestleys*. *Public and private law*, the *law of organisations*, *transactions*, *business*, and *dispute resolution*, all within one group's response, were the most comprehensive of these. Another group indicated *transactions*, *governance*, *remedies*, and *dispute resolution*. Group two felt that '*multiple legal areas*' would be essential, and group one identified '*coherent legal principles inside and outside the Priestley 11*'. Less specifically also, group 5 identified '*law*'. Only two groups gave circumscribed specific areas of doctrine—*contract* and *human rights* in one case and *civil obligations* and *criminal law* in another. Two groups named *statutory interpretation* as an essential standalone component of curriculum.

If doctrine as a general topic is aggregated with specifically nominated doctrinal fields to include K2–K5, then it is doctrine that forms the basis of curriculum topics. However, the different ways in which doctrine is represented highlight the challenges of retaining the dominance of the Priestleys in the face of preparing law students to be 21st-century lawyers. The variation in expression of doctrine, notably without citing the Priestleys, points to a wide variation amongst participants in the fields of law seen as essential to legal education. While the two most extensive lists provided might reflect the Priestleys, they moved away from naming doctrinal areas in favour of thematic approaches to the law. This offers an important insight into the possibilities for the law curriculum, even where it is expected to meet the existing doctrinal list. While many contemporary law courses do reconfigure their curriculum to some extent (e.g., the law of obligations, etc.), there is scope for a reconceptualization of how we teach and learn law beyond naming doctrinal fields.

Beyond doctrinal knowledge, there was a strong theme of *ethics* throughout the groups—on its own account and as *justice and morality*, *professionalism*, *social justice*, *pro bono*, and *public interest litigation*. Depending on one's perspective, ethics might be expanded to include *sovereignty and power*, *protection of the citizen*, and perhaps even *rule of law*—three other listed essential topics. These latter topics might also be considered to overlap with *contexts of the law*, which was another persistent theme. '*Contexts*' extends to *history and institutions*, *global legal frameworks* and *political knowledge* and may also include '*future law*'. Finally, there were two groups that listed *legal theory* and *jurisprudence*, respectively, as essential parts of curriculum.[47]

Two groups included skills—*critical thinking* and *communication*—in the essential column. There were also three pedagogies mentioned: *project-style teaching*, *public interest litigation*, and *work-integrated learning*. The somewhat sparser but still present inclusion of skills and pedagogies highlights the differential conception of what is essential for a lawyer to know and how they come to know it.

But the downplaying of doctrine in these potential curricula may be due to other subtler reasons. All of the aims of the curricula need some source materials to work on legal doctrine. The extent to which expertise can be developed in providing advice to clients, acting ethically, or thinking critically is likely to be limited by the degree of granularity with which a law student understands legal doctrine and the accepted rules for its manipulation. So, it is unlikely that any of the contributors to the session saw legal doctrine as unimportant. What is more likely is that there is a strong message that the learning of legal doctrine is not an end in itself but an enabler of the more complex and nuanced understandings and skills that these variants of lawyers need. While the Priestleys only refer to doctrine and make the broader skills implicit, our contributors, to varying degrees, subverted that approach and privileged the skills and attributes over the more instrumental doctrinal knowledge.

V. Conclusion

This chapter concludes that the subversion of power to create a law curriculum reveals the potential for alternative iterations of the core law curriculum adapted to the future that might otherwise be masked by a commitment to reproducing the past.

Our research suggests that doctrine remains a key element of legal education but that it should be seen only as knowledge. Importantly, knowledge and skills are necessary first steps towards greater educational goals. Those goals represent diverse images of the lawyer who will emerge at the end of their threshold university qualification. When those greater goals are brought to the forefront of curriculum, doctrinal knowledge may only be necessary to the extent it helps to achieve the overarching goal.

By letting go of knowledge areas as the organising category of the law curriculum, students can instead learn to independently access and interpret doctrine—resulting in less need for comprehensive doctrinal coverage in a degree. The Priestleys would, on that basis, move from a prescriptive role in degree accreditation back to illustration only.

Given the interesting array of approaches to curriculum illustrated in this project, it is clear that knowledge areas might sensibly give way to a more purposeful and targeted curriculum. Were accrediting bodies to listen to this subversion of the underlying entry requirements into the profession, they might no longer require law schools to 'give students fish'. Teaching students *how to fish* may instead hold the key to the future of legal education.

Notes

1 Some of the ideas in this chapter have been adapted from Kate Galloway, 'Is Legal Education Over-Regulated or Under-Regulated?' (Paper Delivered at Professional Legal Education Conference Plenary Panel Bond University, Friday 2 October 2020).

2 Cited in Richard Johnstone and Sumitra Vignaendra, 'Learning Outcomes and Curriculum Development in Law: A Report Commissioned by the Australian Universities Teaching Committee' (2003) 21.

3 Richard E. Susskind, *The End of Lawyers?: Rethinking the Nature of Legal Services* (Oxford University Press 2010); Mitch Kowalski, *The Great Legal Reformation* (iUniverse 2017).

4 See, eg, *Admission Guidelines No 1 of 2016* issued under Rule 9AA of the *Supreme Court (Admission) Rules 2004* (Qld).

5 National Conference of Bar Examiners <https://nextgenbarexam.ncbex.org/>.

6 Solicitors Regulation Authority <https://www.sra.org.uk/sra/policy/solicitors-qualifying-examination/sqe1-functioning-legal-knowledge-assessment-specification/>.

7 Set out in the Uniform Admission Rules 2015, Schedule 1.

8 The exception being the Diploma Law run by the Legal Profession Admission Board in New South Wales.

9 Academic Course Appraisal Committee, Council of Legal Education, *Legal Knowledge Required for Admission to Practise* (14 October 1982).

10 Sandford Clark, 'Regulating Admissions – Are We There Yet?' (2017) 91 Australian Law Journal 907, 909.

11 Law Admissions Consultative Committee Charter <https://www.legalservicescouncil.org.au/Pages/about-us/law-admissions-consultative-committee.aspx>

12 Law Admissions Consultative Committee, 'Redrafting the Academic Requirements for Admission' <https://www.legalservicescouncil.org.au/Documents/redrafting-the-academic-requirements-for-admission.pdf>.

13 Resolution of the Law Admissions Consultative Committee, September 2020, published on: Law Admissions Consultative Committee, 'About Us' <https://www.legalservicescouncil.org.au/Pages/about-us/law-admissions-consultative-committee.aspx>.

14 Sally Kift, Mark Israel and Rachael Field, 'Bachelor of Laws Learning and Teaching Academic Standards Statement' (Australian Learning and Teaching Council, 2010).

15 ibid 10 (emphasis added).

16 ibid 12–13.
17 See TLO 1, Kift, Israel and Field (n 14).
18 See, eg, the list identified in the Law Society of New South Wales, *Future of Law and Innovation in the Profession* (2017) ('FLiP Report') 78–79.
19 See, eg, Lisa Webley and others, 'The Profession(s)' Engagements with Lawtech: Narratives and Archetypes of Future Law' (2019) 1(1) Law, Technology and Humans 6.
20 Nickolas J. James, 'More than Merely Work-Ready: Vocationalism versus Professionalism in Legal Education' (2017) 40(1) UNSW Law Journal 186.
21 See, eg, FliP Report (n 18).
22 Kift, Israel and Field (n 14).
23 Ruth Bridgstock, 'The University and the Knowledge Network: A New Educational Model for Twenty-First Century Learning and Employability' in Michael Tomlinson and Leonard Holmes (eds), *Graduate Employability in Context* (Palgrave Macmillan 2017) 339.
24 Sharon Christensen and Sally Kift, 'Graduate Attributes and Legal Skills: Integration or Disintegration' [2000] 11 Legal Education Review 207; Ruth Bridgstock, 'The Graduate Attributes We've Overlooked: Enhancing Graduate Employability Through Career Management Skills' [2009] 28(1) Higher Education Research & Development 31; Andrew Litchfield, Jessica Frawley and Skye Nettleton, 'Contextualising and Integrating into the Curriculum the Learning and Teaching of Work-Ready Professional Graduate Attributes' (2010) 29(5) Higher Education Research & Development 519.
25 Brian Jones and Norma Iredale, 'Enterprise Education as Pedagogy' (2010) 52(1) Education+ Training 7; Elvir M. Akhmetshin and others, 'Acquisition of Entrepreneurial Skills and Competences: Curriculum Development and Evaluation for Higher Education' (2019) 22(1) Journal of Entrepreneurship Education 1.
26 See, eg: QUT's motto is 'University for the Real World' <https://www.qut.edu.au/>; UNSW Law motto is 'Where Law Meets Justice; Monash Law: Law for the Public Good' <https://www.monash.edu/law>; Griffith Law School: We Challenge the Rules <https://www.griffith.edu.au/arts-education-law/griffith-law-school>.
27 See, eg, Kate Galloway, 'Refreshed in the Tropics: Developing Curriculum Using a Thematic Lens' (2011) 4(1&2) Journal of the Australasian Law Teachers Association 119.
28 Australian Government, Department of Education, Skills and Employment, 'Performance-Based Funding for the Commonwealth Grant Scheme' <https://www.dese.gov.au/reviews-and-consultations/performancebased-funding-commonwealth-grant-scheme>.
29 Kate Galloway, 'Text to Bits: Beyond the Revolution in Law and Lawyering' (2 October 2016) <https://ssrn.com/abstract=2879220> or <http://doi.org/10.2139/ssrn.2879220>; Kate Galloway, Melissa Castan and John Flood, *The Global Lawyer* (Lexis Nexis 2020).
30 Kate Galloway and others, 'The Legal Academy's Engagements with Lawtech: Technology Narratives and Archetypes as Drivers of Change' (2019) 1(1) Law, Technology and Humans 27 <https://doi.org/10.5204/lthj.v1i0.1337>.
31 Félix Tréguer, 'Hackers vs States: Subversion, Repression and Resistance in the Online Public Sphere' (2015) 91(3) Droit et Société (Law and Society) 639, 642.
32 A well-known example is that of flatbed furniture 'hack' sites, eg <https://www.ikeahackers.net/>.
33 Described in Lawrence Manion, Louis Cohen and Keith Morrison, *Research Methods in Education* (Routledge 2007).
34 This project is conducted under Monash University Ethics Approval Project ID: 22071.
35 Graham Hitchcock and David Hughes, *Research and the Teacher* (Routledge 1989) 52–53.
36 Bronislaw Malinowski, *Argonauts of the Western Pacific: An Account of Native Enterprise and Adventure in the Archipelagoes of Melanesian New Guinea* (Dutton 1922) 25.

37 Michael Stephen Schiro, *Curriculum Theory: Conflicting Visions and Enduring Concerns* (Sage Publications 2008).
38 Nickolas James, *Power-Knowledge and Critique in Australian Legal Education: 1987–2003* (Queensland University of Technology 2004) <https://eprints.qut.edu.au/15910/1/Nickolas_James_Thesis.pdf>.
39 Galloway (n 27).
40 Kate Galloway and others (n 30).
41 See, eg, Richard E. Susskind, *The End of Lawyers?: Rethinking the Nature of Legal Services* (Oxford University Press 2010).
42 Clayton Christensen, *The Innovator's Dilemma* (Harvard Business School 1997).
43 For a discussion on 'big law' see, eg, George Beaton, *New Law New Rules: A Conversation About the Future of the Legal Services Industry* (Beaton Capital 2013).
44 Kift, Israel and Field (n 14).
45 See, eg, Marcelle Burns, 'Are We There Yet: Indigenous Cultural Competency in Legal Education' (2018) 28 Legal Education Review 1; Marcelle Burns, Anita Lee Hong and Asmi Wood, 'Indigenous Cultural Competency for Legal Academics Program data' (2019); Galloway, Castan and Flood (n 29) 71–94.
46 See, eg, Kate Galloway, 'A Rationale and Framework for Digital Literacies in Legal Education' (2017) 27 Legal Education Review 117; Galloway, Castan and Flood (n 29) 97–129.
47 We have previously identified these elements within taxonomies of research into legal education. See Kate Galloway, Melissa Castan and Alex Steel, 'Towards a Taxonomy of Legal Education Research' in Ben Golder and others (eds), *Imperatives for Legal Education Research* (Routledge 2020).

Part III

Subverting Through Courses

9 Value and Values in Higher Education

Some Reflections From the UK on the Subversive Dimensions of Historical Approaches in the Study of Law

Sarah Wilson

> It is the thesis of this book that change – constant, accelerating, ubiquitous – is the most striking characteristic of the world we live in and that our educational system has not yet recognized this fact. We maintain, further, that the abilities and attitudes required to deal adequately with change are those of the highest priority and that it is not beyond our ingenuity to design school environments which can help young people to master concepts necessary to survival in a rapidly changing world.[1]

I. Introduction

The very essence of this collection lies in promoting legal education as an educational endeavour which embeds lifelong learning for its participants and as a pathway with transformative capabilities that is able even to generate and foster world-changing thinking. The presentation of legal education as a pathway which is capable of creating meaning in the lives of those who engage with it belies a strong aspirational import and thus harbours perceptions that legal education currently fails to achieve these goals. In different ways, the conversations within this collection explore why legal education might be vested with such tremendous potential whilst also lamenting its current failure to deliver on these 'promises'. At the heart of all of them also lies a core idea that these arguments for change within legal education are subversive, and those who advance them are 'subversive teachers'.

Given its plain and ordinary meaning, subversiveness, of course, connotes the intention of disrupting established systems or institutions, and celebrations of subversiveness in legal education abound within this collection and also beyond it.[2] This contribution uses teaching *history* within undergraduate *legal* curricula to explore subversiveness and suggests that subversiveness of this kind – emphasising legal education's creative and transformative qualities – *should* be celebrated. Key premises for this lie in how 'Law and History' teaching might be considered subversive on account of its questionable place in learning regimes which are widely regarded as highly vocationally oriented learning environments and which

DOI: 10.4324/9781003175216-12

are positioned within a general setting for Higher Education whlch is widely regarded as strongly neoliberal and highly marketised. For this, the contribution draws on experiences of teaching 'Law and History' within legal education found in UK universities. It does so through reflecting on experiences of delivering the 'Law and History' module offered to finalist Law undergraduates at York Law School (YLS), University of York, in the UK.[3]

II. Background and Context

In reflecting on the Australian experience since the 1980s, in 2013, Raewyn Connell argued that education had been 'powerfully affected by the rise of a neoliberal political, economic, and cultural agenda'.[4] Connell's account of the 'Australian experience' of the 'market agenda' is presented as one of 'general reflection' on global trends,[5] and over the same broad timeframe, the neoliberal 'cascade'[6] into UK Higher Education has also been responsible for the replacement of the nurturing and developmental 'social process' of education with neoliberal structures for management and resource allocation, and values promoting hierarchies and competition.[7] The language of 'students as consumers', which now dominates UK Higher Education narratives, predated the recent creation of the Office for Students in 2018 by some significant time,[8] but this is not the totality of the relentless pursuit of neoliberalism within Higher Education in the UK setting. Indeed, Connell's proposition of the redefinition of universities 'as firms' is readily apparent in the highly visible 'business' agendas of UK university management, underpinned by managerialism and priorities largely embodied in the colloquialism of 'bean counting'. At the same time, the UK Higher Education sector has also borne witness to the replacement of traditional State focused, public utility models of funding with (student) fee income and competitive 'bidding' for public money for teaching and research,[9] speaking persuasively to Connell's account of the privatisation of public assets which has occurred in Australia.[10]

The vocational emphasis of legal education has always been a present force within its provision. This is understandable, given the embeddedness of the legal profession within many societies, and is not in and of itself insidious and inimical to ambitions for legal education to be meaningful and even transformative for its stakeholders. But this vocational emphasis *has* arguably acquired ever greater presence and heightened significance in more recent times and is a plausible companion for a general vista of Higher Education as marketised and commodified 'service provision' and a perceived retreat from conceptualisations of it as a public good or 'citizen right'.[11] The effects of these forces can be seen in their profound impact on how Law Schools present themselves in the market for student interest and for resource allocation following from this. As this general trend towards marketisation and privatisation of Higher Education has played out, there have been brutal consequences for some spheres of study. Some spheres – particularly in areas of Arts study – have struggled in the market for student interest, with this reflecting to some significant degree perceptions of their more marginal vocational value. Law Schools, on the other hand, have shown considerable resilience and even thriving capabilities. Law School resilience has been *underpinned by* student demand, but this has also led to the 'cash cow' problem, and, furthermore, Law School resilience has been *shaped by* student demand, with the reasons for this student demand also pushing a particular vision of legal education. This is a vision which strongly foregrounds vocational values.

UK Law Schools have typically responded to these forces by concentrating resources in particular ways. Resources are focused very strongly on perceived particular directions for the pursuit of legal careers in a number of different ways. Most Law Schools have extensive portfolios of Corporate and Commercial electives. More recent developments include creating curriculum space for the oft-claimed importance of 'commercial awareness' for aspiring practitioners, together with a notable push towards mainstreaming skills (emphasising strongly debating and mooting, and also drafting, negotiation, etc.) into universal learning activities. Much of this newer emphasis *is* being driven by anticipation of the introduction of the new SQE – Solicitors Qualification Examination – but is also associated with a more generalised and longer-standing trend of Law Schools looking to demonstrate 'value', or even a 'provider edge' in the market for student interest. Law Schools' strong market drive can currently readily be seen in the sector-wide preoccupation with ensuring 'SQE preparedness'[12] in anticipation of this shift to a centrally set and marked examination for gatekeeping entry to the solicitors' profession in England and Wales.[13] SQE has emerged as two sets of exams based on knowledge and skills and purports to ensure fairer entry and to promote diversity whilst setting a universal quality standard for new solicitors. Whilst its precise fall-out for Law Schools is as yet unknown, it is widely associated with risks for traditional university undergraduate 'Law degree' provision.[14] Indeed, (still) further intensification of vocational emphasis within undergraduate education is entirely plausible, but its implications for the very existence of the traditional 'LLB in Law' could be much further reaching.

A. *Law and History Teaching at YLS: Reflections on Its Current Place Within the Undergraduate Law Curriculum*

Yet, in this strongly vocationally-oriented and highly marketised setting, Law and History teaching came into being at YLS 12 years ago. And it is in this setting that this very self-consciously non-vocational emphasis continues to thrive. Remarkably so, perhaps. Indeed, most recently, the 'Law and History' module has even proven to be extremely resilient in the face of additional pressures as COVID-19 has arguably heightened the challenges presented for the UK Higher Education sector within an already highly competitive global market. This is so at a time when one might expect students to be particularly conscious of what could give them the 'edge' in an employment market which is now not only highly competitive but also brittle and uncertain as the longer-term dimensions of COVID-19 and 'Covid recovery' start to play out. Moreover, 'Covid encounters' add rich, and not entirely expected, dimensions to how students have traditionally responded to the module. This module lacks vocational emphasis entirely, and yet over the timeframe of a decade, it has been consistently popular with students and has generated very positive reflections from them. Arguably thus, Law and History 'performs' very effectively within the highly vocationally-oriented and highly marketised setting of the Law School. It would appear that its participants value interrogating law in ways which are very consciously non-vocational and consider this to be interesting and important.

In suggesting that for YLS students, the study of law beyond its present-day embodiment and application – facilitated by Law and History study – is considered an interesting and also important pursuit, this analysis draws on the module's key reference points and student engagement with its core themes. From this, it argues that there is a very important place for history within legal curricula taught at universities. The analysis engages directly with themes of subversiveness by suggesting that the 'pursuit of history'[15] and articulation of perceived benefits of orienting legal education in this way for the students' wider learning experiences might be considered subversive through challenging the way things are conventionally 'done' within Law Schools. And it will become apparent that in looking to challenge conventional approaches, as it is configured, Law and History teaching at YLS does seek to channel the aspirational agendas for legal education identified within these conversations and address questions of what 'being subversive' means when interrogating legal education. It also suggests that an even more subversive agenda still lies in proposing a more ambitious agenda for Law and History teaching. The latter is one which would see 'historical approaches' embedded within and across undergraduate Law curricula rather than confined to elective/optional study. The analysis advances that channelling ideas of subversiveness in this way helps to illuminate why student appetite for studying 'Law and History' might be so strong and that the reasons for this are complex and intriguing.

For the past decade, YLS finalist undergraduates have had the opportunity to enrol in a dedicated 'Law and History' module. Like all YLS modules, it is modelled on a 20-credit weighting, and like all YLS electives, it is a 'short-fat' module running over one term, and it has traditionally been available in the spring term – January-March – of the UK academic year cycle. In many respects, the module works well as a finalist option, given that it challenges students to engage with a different discipline and also given how it requires them to push their understandings of analytical approaches found within law. In other ways, the timing of the module's scheduling, both in being offered only to finalist students, and being available only at the very end of their studies, ensures that it can only ever have limited reach in encouraging law students to think about how engaging with history could impact on the ways in which they learn the law, and the understandings they come to through learning experiences. From bringing together key operating parameters of the Law and History module, and reflections on how it is received by students with current developments in legal history scholarship, an account of teaching history in Law Schools as subversive activity can emerge, as can different possible faces of subversiveness.

B. Locating Law and History Within the YLS Curriculum: Signposting Subversiveness

The dedicated Law and History module currently functions as a space for students to take stock of their legal education to date in terms of how YLS has encouraged them to think about law, its importance, and the ways in which these views have become formed for them from their learning experiences. YLS's unique Problem-Based Learning (PBL) pedagogy[16] strongly encourages 'real world' and legal practice-oriented understandings of law. Alongside this, the LLB program at YLS embraces the 'law in context' and socio-legal influences which have been profoundly felt across the UK legal education sector, particularly in the last two decades, and which have become powerful forces felt even within the most traditional law schools. YLS's relative youth and its distinctive ethos and outlook,[17] together with its strongly contextual and socio-legal underpinnings, have combined to provide students with learning experiences which are strongly real world *and* 'critical'. PBL learning, which occurs across what has traditionally been Foundation learning[18] and a number of elective subjects, acquires its intended real-world qualities through the emphasis on 'problems' in learning experiences, and where these problems are either drafted by legal practitioner tutors or by academic staff working closely with the former. Alongside the real-world emphasis, in every problem scenario, students are required to engage with *normative* considerations, reflecting on the law's fitness for purpose, what it could or should do better, and the complexities inherent in making such assertions.

By the final year of study, student consciousness of both real-world considerations and normative critique is very evident. The Law and History module asks them to take stock of these understandings of law and its importance and explore how engaging with 'law's past'; doing so in particular ways might lead to more confident and better-informed understandings of law as it is today. The module asks students to reflect on their learning experiences to date – in terms of how they have been encouraged to think about law and the ways in which they have been encouraged to analyse it – and on how thinking about law historically might be an interesting and important addition to a lawyer's analytical toolkit. For this, the module is grounded in law (as it *is*) today and its relationship with society and social change. YLS students are well-served with an introduction to 'law and society' themes, which occurs in year 1 study of the 'Introduction to Law and Society' (ILS) module. In turn, ILS themes of exploring law's interactions with morality, 'inclusiveness' and 'power' provide a strong foundation for how the students will be presented with law's real-world applications and challenges and normative critique throughout their studies. By their final year, students' confidence in their understanding of law and its importance and complexities is thus well-placed.

From this, Law and History asks students to build on these understandings by thinking about law and its interactions with society across long timeframes. Engaging with law's reflective and reflexive qualities – namely that law can reflect societal norms and social change and that law can also be an instrument of change for society – the module asks students to explore change and continuity *across* time, as well as at particular points in time. This is framed by looking to combine wisdom from conventional *legal history's* interest in the value of understanding law's own history for the present[19] with *modern history's* commentaries on the value of history for understanding society today.[20] In this setting, 'Law and History' is a term of art for how the module suggests that understandings of law can be enriched by exploring 'law and society' dynamics across time. This 'reach' beyond the discipline of law to how historians engage with the past and write history is the key reason for identifying the module as *Law and History* rather than *Legal History*. Support for this approach can be gleaned from within legal history scholarship itself and how it has traditionally self-identified as the study of 'law's history'. But as well as explaining to students that legal history scholarship is showing signs of pursuing very promising novel directions, it is equally important that they understand that traditional trends in legal history are broad ones rather than entirely homogenous ones.

C. Law and History's Origins/Genesis: Subversiveness in Legal Education in Action?

As signposted, reflections on the Law and History module are directed towards exploring how and why teaching history to law students might have subversive qualities. Here, the overall pedagogic ethos of YLS has provided important support for the aims of the Law and History module, but 'Law and History' *as an idea* started to take shape long before the module's introduction in 2010. It was even then an idea many years in the making and inspired by a personal academic journey marked by research activity and accommodating 'the past' in teaching across a wide sweep of legal subjects. In turn, the origins of this journey lay in undertaking legal education at a time when 'law in context' interest was starting to change legal education profoundly, and from this transpired an undergraduate education experience which was contextually rich whilst also being strongly traditional. Feeling excited by the possibilities for engaging with technical law in a variety of ways simultaneously stirred a curiosity about why there was so little emphasis on how and why present-day law and legal institutions might have come into being. The result of this curiosity was undertaking postgraduate study – at Master's and PhD level – in *History*.

In time, a post at YLS would allow for the creation of a discrete module which could bring together many years' thinking around 'Law and History' ideas, drawn from research interests and agendas and from teaching experience. By this point, the thinking underpinning it had become fashioned as ideas which have recently been expressed as 'theorizing' [law] with 'historical sensitivity'.[21] The module was envisioned as a dedicated space for seeking understandings of law which celebrated established analytical tools whilst seeking directions which *did* appear to be novel and could bring together a number of intellectual strands to embrace law's (seemingly) inherently historical character. What remained to be clarified was how this would take shape within the confines of a 20-credit elective for an undergraduate Law degree program. First and foremost, the task of assembling the module needed to privilege not just law itself but actually students' learning experiences. The thinking behind it was very much the connections which students are able to make with law through their studies. The most obvious pathway for this was for the new module to track established approaches in English law schools, which on account of the influences brought to bear by the legal professions,[22] have been[23] built on Qualifying Law Degree (QLD) foundational subjects.[24]

III. The Law and History Module in Outline: Key Operating Parameters and Aims

The resulting module paperwork would explain to students that, at all times, the module remains grounded in their studies (in law) and interested in their experiences of learning and understanding law. It would be necessary to explain this given the module's interest in combining 'history' found within legal scholarship with history as written by historians – on which more is said shortly – because whilst the module's content and direction would require students to engage with the work of historians, this was not a module in Modern British History. The module was instead designed to develop – and on occasions also to challenge – students' understanding of technical law and also law's importance for society. To achieve this, the module thus looked to track the QLD foundational subject requirements in several ways. Principally it does so by engaging directly with the so-called 'foundations' of legal knowledge[25] and with 'key themes' which can be drawn from them. The module is now structured around central thematic classes, which are conducted in a 'class discussion' format. Three of these relate directly to foundation subjects, namely the emergence of the Modern State and conceptualisations of Public Policy, Responses to Crime, and Innovations in Private Law. Complementary 'key themes' classes are based on ideas of the nineteenth century as the 'century of law reform' and examine the significance of 'individualism' in the western legal tradition. This 'key themes' emphasis also introduces the 'continuity and change' trope, widely used by historians (and explained shortly), exploring how this might be evident within and relevant for studies of law, focusing especially on the timeframe of the nineteenth century to the present.

A. The Importance Attached to Students' Experiences of Learning and Understanding Law – the Key to Subversiveness?

This combination of substantively focused and 'key themes' classes also looks to draw on elective modules which students have already studied or are currently studying, again to encourage students to connect with their wider learning experiences as much as possible. The module has also traditionally provided study opportunities for individual interests not formally found elsewhere within the curriculum. The latter has been very significant in YLS's own past, given its relative youth and the time it has taken to build staff capability across a range of substantive areas. But even as YLS has become better staffed, the impact of timetabling and staff research leave etc., can still leave gaps in what students wish to study, and so the module continues to support students in developing their own 'narratives of interest' in these circumstances. The emphasis which is placed on experiences of studying law and reflecting on these and the understandings of law acquired through them looks to underscore that the search for ever-greater enhancement and nuance in understandings of law is – and *should be* – a continuing pursuit. This experiences-based approach also reinforces that, for this, the module is asking students to engage with possibilities for making connections between law and society across time. From this, students are supported across a wide range of individual interests, which they are encouraged to explore and develop through the thematic classes. Individual interests also underpin the assessment, which asks students to comment on the value of history as an analytical tool for legal scholars. The question is set, but students are asked to illuminate their thoughts by drawing on 'an area of law', which is broadly defined,[26] and a further stipulation is that they must draw on primary historical source material.

B. The Significance of the Nineteenth Century for Exploring Connections Between the Past and 'Lives Lived' in the Twenty-First Century

The importance of the nineteenth century within the emergence of 'modern Britain' has been signposted and can now be explained as a further manifestation of the module's remit in encouraging students to make the connections between past and present which are *most relevant for* their studies. Students engage with materials which suggest that it was during the nineteenth century that law itself in use today, institutions, ideas, rhetoric, and language became clearly recognisable for today's scholars of law. The early parts of the module explain this and ensure the students understand why we only really engage with the emergence of modern Britain marked by industrialisation and how and why, from this, we put a great deal of emphasis on 'modern Britain'. This generates intense early focus on what historians identify as the 'Age of Reform',[27] and legal historians term the 'Century of Law Reform',[28] and the significance attached to the enduring legacy of these widely-conceived transformative times.[29] Communicating these messages is one function of the early parts of the module, which operate ahead of the substantive and 'key themes' classes commencing in earnest in week 5 (of a 10-week term).

The time allocated to the module during weeks 1–4 of the term looks to serve multiple introductory functions. These early weeks introduce the core idea of thinking about law and social change across time, and not only at particular points in time, and that this idea of using long timeframes is taken from the work of historians. Learning activities here also propose that this core idea might highlight the differences between 'legal historians' and 'historians' in terms of how some historians configure the importance of the past for present-day 'lives lived'. These earliest weeks also provide an introductory overview to the emergence of modern Britain, particularly following industrialisation, where industrialisation is itself historically contextualised and where emphasis is placed on applying this to building a vista of 'lives lived' in Britain in the twenty-first century. The importance of 'lives lived' in twenty-first–century Britain is premised on encouraging students to make connections between the law which they study and the society which generates, supports, or changes this law and interrogate the long timeframe influences which this current dynamic might embody. For this, presenting some key reference points in the emergence of modern Britain serves a number of functions, including importantly seeking to create a base level of understanding of key events and themes in the emergence of modern Britain across a cohort with typically varied previous experiences of studying history.

Many undergraduate LLB entrants will have studied history in the Advanced Level[30] (A Level) exams which typically gatekeep university entry, but others will not have done. The module's 10-year plus history has shown that studying history at A Level does not appear in and of itself to provide advantages for those who have done so over those without previous study of history to draw on. Indeed, the nature of A Level syllabi, and the scope of (provider and student) choice within this ensures that even those who study A Level History will often not have studied Modern British History. And even those who *have* done so will not have focused their studies on the 'law and society' dynamics championed by the module. Thus, the introductory overview of 'Britain since c.1750' is designed to ensure that everyone is familiar with key events and milestones for the emergence of modern Britain and can use these to help construct an understanding of key characteristics of 'lives lived' in twenty-first–century Britain. From this, the module proposes that a better understanding of lives lived in twenty-first–century Britain and the kind of society we are can sharpen appreciation for the importance of law for society and of the nature and importance of society itself.

An overview of the emergence of modern Britain assists in building this understanding through identifying key forces of change and the effect of change on key societal institutions – including law. These ideas are explored through themes of 'transformations' of Britain post-industrialisation which can help to trigger recognition of 'lives lived' today; namely: economic transformations; transformations in population, urbanisation, and social life; revolutions in transport; political transformations; transformation in innovation and ideas; transformations in work, education, and opportunity; and the emergence of the Modern State. From this, students can start to think about the importance of law for society and the dynamics of social and legal change. As students are encouraged to start to configure 'lives lived' in twenty-first–century Britain, assisted by exploring themes of 'transformation', as signposted, they are also encouraged to think about the importance of the historians' trope of 'continuity and change' for examining change *across* time. This proposes that at any given point in time, *continuity* and *change* are 'twin forces' which are 'always at work' in society.[31] This encourages the students to think about the possibility of finding continuities with the past, as well as change from it, in their emerging understandings of 'lives lived' in twenty-first–century Britain.

C. Is Law and History Different From Legal History and Why Might This Matter for a Subversiveness Agenda?

The module thus places great emphasis on 'lives lived' in the present for exploring 'law and society' dynamics across time. What needs now to be explained is *how* the students come to understand both the significance of 'lives [currently] lived' and the importance attached to curiosity about dynamics across time, rather than simply at specific points in time; and thus change – and continuity – across time. These emphases emerge from the module's in-depth early study of why legal analysis might usefully look to the discipline of history at all as part of how lawyers understand law. This is where students learn about the lengthy tradition of Legal History within legal scholarship and the 'promises' of illumination and understanding which its advocates believe it holds. Students are also invited to think about the proposition that legal history, as it has traditionally been practised, might not by itself provide the fullest and richest understandings of law which are possible to achieve, and this might justify exploring enrichment possibilities *for* legal analysis *from* the discipline of history. It is here that, in the earliest parts of the module, students are introduced to legal history's claims of being an essential tool for understanding law and the pursuit of 'confident' law reform.[32] Alongside this, students learn that for historians, the present we are living through can be configured as part of a 'trajectory . . . still unfolding' where past, present, and future lie on the same continuum of societal evolution and development.[33] It is from this amalgam of ideas from *legal history* and *history* as practised and written by historians that the module has become a study of how the pursuit of a 'Law and History' agenda in legal study and scholarship might provide a useful way for us to engage with law, through reference to our (collective and societal) past as we look to the future.

IV. Illuminating 'Legal History' Traditions and Parameters Within Legal Scholarship

It is very important for the students to understand that legal scholarship *does* have a lengthy and also rich tradition of examining and interrogating 'law's past'. This body of scholarship *does* exist, and it has much potential to contribute to 'making the case' for examining law beyond the present and across long timeframes at all. Further justification for setting out key parameters for 'legal history' at some length originates in the manifest absence of law's past – let alone ideas of an enduring legacy of this past – from studies of 'Law today'. The introduction to 'What is Legal History?' is initiated by asking students to reflect on how they have encountered law predating 'current law' in their learning experiences and how much emphasis has been placed on current law's *origins*. Conclusions that this is largely absent from their everyday studies provide a very effective 'lead into' the strong and lengthy academic tradition for insisting that engaging with law's history must not be viewed as a 'purely academic' and a marginal 'antiquarian' pursuit. The students interrogate the case made by legal historians and are encouraged to make connections between these claims made by 'legal history'; the absence of such perspectives from their own studies; and the proposition of a decline in Legal History's presence in legal study, and which appears to have accompanied the neoliberal 'march' on Higher Education commencing during the 1980s.

To make the value which legal historians attach to their craft relatable to the students, they are introduced to views from leading legal historian David Ibbetson that:

> Legal history is too important to remain within the domain of specialist legal historians. The structure of modern law is too heavily dependent on the legacy of the past for it to be marginalized as something of purely antiquarian interest. If we are to make sense of today's law we have to understand its history, and it is only when we can make sense of it that we can confidently begin to reform it.[34]

For the students' earliest introduction to what legal history is or might be, Ibbetson's reflections provide a touchstone for many themes which are central to exploring the possible relevance of the past for the present. This work identifies the importance of understanding and evaluating technical law and recognising law's continuing evolution and development through reform. This early scrutiny of legal history scholarship *does* thus touch on vocational aspects of what it means to be a lawyer, and for those destined for legal practice as well as those who are not alike, students are encouraged simultaneously to link ideas relating to *legal* change with ideas of *social* change. For this, Ibbetson's work provides early signposting for why we might search beyond legal history for *historically enriched* understandings of law. But equally, this work helps students to appreciate that advocating Legal History as the study of legal change[35] is not only a key trope of legal history scholarship but is also one of its key strengths; and that this is a key perspective which is currently largely missing from legal education. From this, and through Sir John Baker's work, students are encouraged to make connections between these ideas on the enduring importance of law's history for today and the very importance of law itself. For this, students engage with Baker's proposition that law is a highly valued societal institution and is properly regarded as something other than 'a body of randomly changing rules'.[36]

Baker's argument that 'Unless we regard law as no more than a body of randomly changing rules, its history must be an essential dimension in its study'[37] makes a powerful case for the importance of history within legal education, but students also learn that these protestations of importance are coming from a complex 'place', and in many ways a difficult place, for Legal History. As signposted, the module encourages students to situate how legal historians conceive their craft alongside a decline in Legal History's overall presence in legal study, which does appear to have 'tracked' the neoliberal 'cascade' in Higher Education. Perceived risks to Legal History's place within legal analysis abound within the work of both Baker and Ibbetson, with both expressing concern about its marginalisation, given that for them, its manifest significance for every student and scholar of law ensures that it is too important to remain within the 'domain of specialist legal historians'.[38] With reference to legal education specifically, Baker laments that with 'so many changes taking place in the law and the legal world', legal history is becoming perceived as being 'less relevant to a student's needs', which Baker naturally considers 'could hardly be more wrong'.[39]

Alongside the 'many changes taking place in the law and the legal world', if not actually a manifestation of this, is increasing subjugation of legal education to a generalised marketisation of Higher Education. As previously signposted, this (seemingly unstoppable) direction of travel within legal education has had profound consequences for the structuring of Law curricula and the staffing and resourcing of particular 'spheres of interest'. As these trends have gathered considerable pace in the past decades, this has concurred with concerns about legal history's decline. Resultant prioritisation of demonstrating vocational value and employability qualities makes for interesting discussions with Law and History students on their perceptions of their studies and why they have chosen to study *this* module. Students identify strongly with views from within legal history that within law curricula 'most if not all topics . . . are taught either without any historical sensitivity . . . or with but a passing nod to the 'origins' of some area of doctrine that is only ever at best recommended reading'.[40] For the author of this latter viewpoint, such a culture within legal education is the likely origin of the dominant 'side-lining' of law's history in legal scholarship.[41] For Law and History students, this is a jump-off point for exploring ideas of possible benefits accruing from scrutinising the history of legal *change* and whether it might even be a truism that law cannot be properly understood without doing so.

V. 'Finding' a Role for History From Understandings of 'Legal History'

From this, the module scrutinises these claims, directing them to Ibbetson's conceptualisation of legal history as the *history of* 'legal categories, concepts and doctrines; the mechanisms used by lawyers to organize their thoughts'.[42] Students also engage with Ibbetson's companion observation that whilst the meaning of legal history encourages division rather than consensus, the pursuit of legal history is in many ways a less complicated one than analysing 'law today' because law is 'fluid and dynamic', meaning that legal scholars are able to 'describe its history with more certainty than we can describe its state at any single point in time'.[43] Familiarising the students with such viewpoints also presents the opportunity to identify one related point of consensus rather than division – namely, the perception that legal history is considered to be distinguishable from law 'as law', and so thus that it is most persuasively configured as history rather than as law.[44]

From this, students start to engage with questions of 'what is history' or what might it be. Notwithstanding legal historians' identification of legal history as history rather than law, legal history has not always embraced the arguably considerable 'overlap between legal thought and the practice of history'[45] and instead might be considered to have adopted an altogether narrower approach to theorising with 'historical sensitivity'.[46] For some, legal history's approaches are part of a wider pattern of generalised continuing 'resistance to history' within legal scholarship.[47] But Law and History students learn that this *is* a generalisation, and analysing law with 'historical sensitivity' *can* be found,[48] albeit in ways which might best be understood as occurring in 'pockets' and being pursued through conversations conducted 'in whispers' rather than extensively and at the 'meta' level between disciplines.[49] The idea that much of legal history is written strongly as 'law's history' is explored through a portfolio of 'examples' of legal history writings and with reference to students' existing understandings of methodology and theoretical approach, working from the dominant UK doctrinal analytical tradition, and examining alternative approaches which might be termed contextual, critical, and socio-legal. Here, students explore why even very contextually-rich classic works of legal history such as Cornish and Clark's seminal *Law and Society in England 1750–1950*[50] have not necessarily embraced as fully as possible the capacity for law's history to function as 'an essential dimension in the social and intellectual history of this country'.[51] In making the latter reflections, Baker properly alludes to the pioneering work of FW Maitland (1850–1906), identifying Maitland as a legal scholar who worked as a *historian.* That for Baker, this was embodied in Maitland's extensive contextualisation of law and legal change with 'societal' considerations, and his use of primary historical sources[52] provides further steer for the students as to *what* 'history' might actually be.

VI. History and the Pursuit of Understandings of 'Social and Intellectual' 'Lives Lived' in Britain – Past, Present, and Future

For Law and History students, the argument is made that legal history is currently strongly 'law centric', and law is at the centre of 'its universe'.[53] The module asserts that, like many social science disciplines, Law has largely ignored the contributions which historians – and their 'complex and many-sided' understanding of the 'temporalities of social life' – could make to social science theory[54] and the scope for mutual enlightenment which can be achieved through bridging 'disciplinary divide[s]'.[55] Law and History studies explain that this typology of history exists in a setting where although there is, like within legal history itself, a spectrum of views concerning the objectives and limitations of historical study,[56] there *are* core endeavours connecting all historians and attaching to the aspiration of understanding the past on its own terms, and to the discovery of what happened in the past and what it was like to live in the past.[57] The students also learn that for some historians, this is not the 'end game' and instead that what is usefully termed a 'history as resource'[58] agenda looks beyond this and emphasises contributions which history can make to the understanding of the complexities of social life today.[59]

This latter model of history is itself premised on configuring the present not as the beginning and end of all that does and should concern us about our 'lives lived' but instead as a point in time forming part of a 'trajectory' which is still 'unfolding'.[60] This is itself underpinned by ideas of a collective social journey which has been made for a society to reach this point; a journey which is underpinned by an 'inventory' of alternative directions and choices which have been possible thus far[61] and, where attaching value to a collective past for enriching understandings of the present, can garner appreciation for future possibilities.[62] This is the 'promise' of what is known by historians as 'historical process'.[63] This idea does not consider the past as a 'blueprint' for the future,[64] and instead, in the presence of regard for cardinal principles of historical difference[65] and historical context,[66] historical process can alert us to possibilities for future directions and provide hope for the future through championing ideas of freedom from conceptions of pre-determined outcomes.[67]

Through championing the use of ideas from the discipline of history, the module has sought to distinguish itself from many manifestations of the broad church that is Legal History. Legal History has, in different ways, manifested 'top down' accounts and also illuminated law's history 'from below',[68] with much of this written in the doctrinal tradition, grounded in law's strong self-identification with ideas of inherent coherent 'internal' logic and self-evident rationality, and freedom from external 'non-legal' influences.[69] Whilst Legal History has also embraced contextual[70] and critical traditions[71] – and also shown socio-legal tendencies, for example, through engagement with philosophy[72] – its engagement with the discipline of history has been much less readily apparent. This is notwithstanding the obvious, and indeed inherent, 'overlap between legal thought and the practice of history'[73] as legal history itself is now acknowledging. In some quarters, at least, Legal History is now championing law as an 'object of enquiry' and presenting it as one which *inter alia* persists through time (across time and place) and which can be explored 'via multiple temporalities'.[74] Students are introduced to these exciting developments and possible new directions, and the possible implications of them for 'Law and History' as an idea.

For the latter, the module explores the possibility that as Legal History itself evolves, this may render 'Law and History' a temporary 'gateway' analytical label and direction. Indeed, there are promising signs of legal scholarship's recognition of historians' interest in treating a subject as a 'variable over time'.[75] Alongside this, students are encouraged to reflect on the usefulness of 'Law and History' as a label for a particular analytical approach to law. At the very least, it might be able to serve legal scholarship whilst new directions in Legal History are being worked through, especially given that currently, the latter remain undertaken in pockets and being conducted in (largely horizontal) 'whispers'.[76] It is also not clear at present that Legal History will embrace the benefits which could flow from trying to connect law's history with understandings of society and social change across long timeframes as fully and extensively as 'Law and History' does, with Law and History regarding this as its core remit.

VII. Concluding Thoughts: Law and History and Its Popularity as a Subversive Agenda Within Legal Education?

From the remit of the module which has been set out, it should be clear that the Law and History module demands a great deal from students, and students require considerable support for undertaking and successfully completing it. This module is fraught with challenges arising from exposing Law students to a different discipline, albeit one with similarities with as well as differences from their own.[77] Students are encouraged to explore these ideas by directing the set thematic reference points towards their own interests and using these interests to comment on whether lawyers might benefit from adding historical approaches to their analytical toolkit and why this might be the case.[78] Students are supported in this endeavour beyond formal classes through the provision of key resources that are strongly geared towards the assessment, which also requires the students to work with primary historical source material. The support received by students includes a dedicated 'sourcebook' of historical sources and sites which are likely to resonate strongly with law students (e.g. Parliamentary Papers and *Hansard*) alongside conventional ones used by historians (e.g. newspapers and periodicals), and also interactive library use training for historical sources. The module is also supported by the development of an interactive 'Collection of ideas' for assessment focal points, which is generated by students' interests as well as tutor reflections on the formal classes.

In terms of how the students experience the module, feedback is very strong. This is most evidently so at the end of module evaluations conducted by YLS, but it is also readily apparent from ongoing feedback throughout the module. From this, the students clearly enjoy this distinctive module, but more significantly, they consider it an important dimension of their study. Reflections that the module is 'transformative' might sound dramatic, but they are commonplace. Companion perspectives that such approaches are sorely absent from the mainstay of legal studies – and even that such approaches could usefully be introduced sooner in LLB study and should be part of compulsory study – are also perennially evident student reactions. What is perhaps most striking is just how relevant the students consider theorising with 'historical sensitivity' for their studies. As the module progresses, students typically become more curious about studying law in historically enriched ways and more convinced that doing so is far from 'marginal'.

YLS does have a number of non-vocational electives subsisting alongside its many vocationally oriented ones, and thus what makes Law and History subversive isn't perhaps this, albeit that because teaching history does not obviously 'deliver' vocational experiences, its presence within legal education might be considered subversive for this reason alone. What makes Law and History teaching particularly subversive may not even be its very consciously non-vocational aims. What might make it subversive is, perhaps instead, how it encourages students to think about and engage with law holistically, doing so in ways which are not commonplace in legal analysis, let alone in legal education specifically. And perhaps a further face of subversiveness lies in how it champions values which are very consciously *avocational* in such a highly marketised context. The module does look to promote goals for legal education which have been associated with giving meaning to professional and personal lives, and its directions can coincide with ambitions for harnessing its transformative qualities and ability to generate paradigm-shifting thinking. For the latter, there follows a very brief reference to the current place of history in the public sphere. But in a more everyday life sense, surely it is important for *any* Higher Education program to embody values of social cohesion and citizenship, which underpin understandings of societal functionality and the role of individuals within the social fabric, and thus 'the creative development of social practice through time'.[79]

This might be considered subversive, but its imperative value is also strongly self-evident. The twenty-first century does present many grand challenges for settled patterns of life and expectations for many people. Even prior to COVID-19 and long before the current context provided by the terrifying implications of Russia's invasion of Ukraine, the present and future lives of many looked set to be dominated by changing global economics, complex geopolitics, and risks from terror, together with (very likely) enforced adjustments reflecting concerns about environmental fragility and climate change. These are thus times ripe for a core message of Law and History; that there is 'usually more than one way of interpreting a predicament or responding to a situation, and that the choices open to us are often more varied than we might have supposed'.[80] Legal education's currently strong vocational emphasis doesn't obviously lend itself to recognising a world which is in 'constant, accelerating, [and] ubiquitous change' and does not obviously deliver approaches which support the mastering of concepts necessary to survival in a rapidly changing world.[81] An ambitious agenda for reimagining legal education in ways which push against its commodification and narrow 'employment applications' and instead encourages manifesting meaning across 'lives lived' and embraces promoting transformative capabilities – for individuals and for society as a whole – *is* thus a subversive agenda in the current context. Neoliberal values do not simply cascade into key societal institutions. They actually predominate within British society today, fostering and perpetuating high levels of individualism and propositions of a 'marketised society'.[82] Many Higher Education educators are likely to configure attempts to subvert this as important and, indeed, necessary, and thus consider disrupting this as subversiveness which is properly celebrated. Moreover, the current emphasis on 'Covid recovery', as future employment markets look less certain than ever, and a wider social fall-out from COVID-19, which still remains unmapped, could engender a further imperative for conscious foregrounding of avocational values of what amounts to social cohesion, and what being a 'good citizen' might require of us.

It is perhaps particularly subversive to propose a central role for history given legal education's overall strongly 'chronocentric' nature.[83] Indeed, even in the absence of directly vocational emphasis associated with legal education, historians themselves acknowledge that objections to history having any use or even relevance for the present do subsist.[84] However, subversiveness is also complex. Whilst the Law and History module doesn't obviously deliver vocational experiences, and the context of 'Covid recovery' might enable greater foregrounding of avocational values, teaching history in the Law School setting might also sit comfortably with or even serve current broader dominant pro-vocational trends in legal education, whilst also appearing to conflict with them. In the early stages of their Law and History studies, students learn about the current appetite for history in the public sphere. Examples, including ones drawn from the UK and Australia relating to banking sector policy and reform,[85] help the students to understand that even if 'historical sensitivity' is largely absent from their studies, it *is* visible in reflections from those at the forefront of legal change. Moreover, reflections from students who are looking to enter the legal profession and those who already have done so are equally interesting. Through the YLS alumni network, past students who are now practitioners frequently express how impactful the module has been in how they now think about law. And during their studies, or immediately afterwards, students often express views that studying Law and History is likely to give them an 'edge' and serve them well going forward in a highly competitive practitioner market. This suggests that subversiveness embodied in Law and History teaching *is* complex.

From this, it is now proposed that as legal educators, we should remain open to how teaching history within studies of law can be subversive whilst also supporting vocational directions. Perhaps this is best understood as configuring Law and History teaching as generating possibilities for disruptive thinking to 'cascade' within vocational environments which would not otherwise express openness to them. And remaining with proposing what should happen within legal education in a subversive and disruptive way, there is perhaps a more subversive aspect of Law and History teaching still. At the very time that traditional UK Law School undergraduate provision is at considerable risk from a further onslaught of vocational emphasis by the SQE, and when the COVID-19 pandemic might seem likely to accentuate a still further appetite for more employment-oriented directions, Law and History's popularity is holding and has even increased. For the past decade, student feedback has consistently expressed calls for greater emphasis on history throughout their time as undergraduates and from a much earlier stage. This sentiment has continued to remain strong as the module has operated during the COVID-19 pandemic. How this might be achieved must be held over for further consideration, but this feedback from YLS's 'consumers' together with current calls from within Legal History scholarship for greater emphasis of 'historical sensitivity' within legal analysis suggest that this is an exciting time to be reflecting on history's proper place in undergraduate law curricula. It is also thus an exciting time, and an important one, to configure this as a subversive agenda for law teaching.

Notes

1 Neil Postman and Charles Weingartner, *Teaching as a Subversive Activity* (Penguin Education Specials 1971) 4.

2 Eg Russell Sandberg, *Subversive Legal History: A Manifesto for the Future of Legal Education* (Routledge (Transforming Legal Histories) 2021).

3 'York Law School' (*University of York*) <https://www.york.ac.uk/law/>.
4 Raewyn Connell, 'The Neoliberal Cascade and Education: An Essay on the Market Agenda and Its Consequences' (2013) 54(2) Critical Studies in Education 99.
5 Connell (n 4) 99.
6 ibid.
7 Connell (n 4) 105.
8 *Office for Students* <https://www.officeforstudents.org.uk>.
9 The latter, competitive bidding for public support, was until recently administered through the Higher Education Funding Council for England (HEFCE). HEFCE has now been replaced by UK Research and Innovation (UKRI) and which together with the Office for Students, came into existence on 1 April 2018.
10 Connell (n 4) 100.
11 ibid.
12 See 'Solicitors Qualifying Examination (SQE) Route' (*Solicitors Regulation Authority*, September 2021) <https://www.sra.org.uk/become-solicitor/sqe/>.
13 ibid. See also different perspectives from the Solicitors Regulation Authority, 'News from the Board: Reflections on Our July 2020 Board – Anna Bradley' (*Solicitors Regulation Authority*, 20 July 2020) <https://www.sra.org.uk/sra/how-we-work/our-board/news-from-the-board/july-2020/>; and from a law teacher: Doug Morrison, 'The SQE and Creativity: A Race to the Bottom?' (2018) 52(4) The Law Teacher 467. By way of an important update, on 25 August 2022, the SRA published results from the inaugural SQE assessment – see <https://www.sra.org.uk/sra/news/press/sqe2-results-august-2022/>
14 Traditional undergraduate provision has been manifested in the 'qualifying' bachelor's degree in Law, or LLB (see also n 18). Concerns expressed include ones that as the SQE places greater emphasis on skills (not only mooting/debate and negotiation etc. but also form completion and precedent drafting etc.) and knowledge, traditional insignias of undergraduate study – especially critical thinking and exposure to wider ideas and perspectives – will be squeezed out, and this development amounts for some (eg Morrison n 13) to a 'race to the bottom'.
15 Per John Tosh, *The Pursuit of History: Aims, Methods and New Directions in the Study of History* (5th edn, Longman 2010).
16 'York Law School: Problem-based Learning' (*University of York*) <https://www.york.ac.uk/law/undergraduate/pbl/>.
17 YLS opened for its first cohort of undergraduate students in September 2008.
18 So called on account of the 'Foundations' of legal knowledge set out by the legal professions of England and Wales, reflected in Qualifying Law Degree (QLD) requirements for being accredited by the Bar Standards Board and Solicitors Regulation Authority. See further n 24 and text thereto.
19 As discussed below in the main text, principally with reference to the contributions of leading present generation scholars Sir John Baker and David Ibbetson.
20 As discussed below in the main text, principally with reference to the work of WH Sewell Jr and John Tosh.
21 Maksymilian Del Mar, 'Philosophical Analysis and Historical Enquiry: Theorizing Normativity, Law and Legal Thought' in Markus D. Dubber and Christopher Tomlins (eds), *The Oxford Handbook of Legal History* (Oxford University Press 2018) 3; 4.
22 Or more accurately, the profession's regulatory bodies, the Solicitors Regulatory Authority and the Bar Standards Board.
23 Reference in the main text to 'traditional' approaches is quite deliberate, on account of potentially far-reaching changes to pathways to qualifying as a solicitor currently being made by the Solicitors Regulation Authority, as noted on the University of York's webpages: 'LLB(Hons) Law' (*University of York*) <https://www.york.ac.uk/study/undergraduate/courses/llb-law/>.

24 As signposted (above n 18). The 'Foundation' subjects are: Public Law, including Constitutional Law, Administrative Law and Human Rights; Law of the European Union; Criminal Law; Obligations including Contract, Restitution and Tort; Property Law; and Equity and the Law of Trusts, alongside which students are also expected to receive training in legal research. See further: 'Joint Statement on the Academic Stage of Training' (*Solicitors Regulation Authority*, September 2021) <https://www.sra.org.uk/students/academic-stage/academic-stage-joint-statement-bsb-law-society/>.

25 As explained above (n 24) and main text thereto.

26 As assessment guidance given to the students notes, an 'area of law' includes any conventional classifications of law but extends beyond this to spheres of legal policy (such as criminal justice and penal policy) and law-making processes, and where most emphasis is on connections which can be made with learning experiences.

27 As evident in the classic Whig history, Ernest Llewellyn Woodward, *The Age of Reform 1815–1870*: *Oxford History of England* (Clarendon Press, first published 1938).

28 Eg Council of Legal Education (Great Britain), *A Century of Law Reform: Twelve Lectures on the Changes in the Law of England During the Nineteenth Century* (MacMillan 1901).

29 Chantel Stebbings, 'Benefits and Barriers: The making of Victorian Legal History' in Anthony Musson and Chantel Stebbings (eds), *Making Legal History: Approaches and Methodologies* (Cambridge University Press 2012).

30 See 'A Levels' (UCAS (Universities and Colleges Admissions Service)) <https://www.ucas.com/further-education/post-16-qualifications/qualifications-you-can-take/levels>.

31 F.M.L. Thompson, *The Rise of Respectable Society: A Social History of Victorian Britain 1830–1900* (Fontana 1998) 6.

32 David Ibbetson, *A Historical Introduction to the Law of Obligations* (Clarendon Press 1999) v.

33 Tosh (n 15) 40.

34 Ibbetson (n 32) v.

35 John H. Baker, 'Why the History of English Law Has Not Been Finished' (2000) 59(1) Cambridge Law Journal 62, 63.

36 Baker (n 35) 63.

37 ibid.

38 Ibbetson (n 32) v; see also Baker (n 35) 63.

39 Baker (n 35) 62–63.

40 Del Mar (n 21) 4.

41 ibid.

42 Ibbetson (n 32) v.

43 ibid.

44 Baker (n 35) 66, reiterating the views of Maitland.

45 Del Mar (n 21) 4.

46 ibid.

47 ibid.

48 For example, through the longstanding activities of the Australian and New Zealand Law and History Society, and whose origins can be traced at least as far back as 1982: see 'Home' (*Australia and New Zealand Law and History Society*) <https://anzlhs.org>.

49 See reflections on cross-disciplinary engagement in Peter King, 'Locating Histories of Crime: A Bibliographical Study' (1999) 39(1) British Journal of Criminology 161, 161.

50 William R. Cornish and George de N. Clark, *Law and Society in England 1750–1950* (Sweet & Maxwell 1989).

51 Baker (n 35) 63, with Baker explaining how this was a vision for the legal historian Plucknett.

52 Baker (n 35) 63–64.

53 As expressed eloquently by Chris Tomlins. This general reflection on the effects of critical legal studies on legal scholarship is in many ways a truism for legal history's interest in law. See Christopher Tomlins, 'What Is Left of the Law and Society Paradigm after Critique?: Revisiting Gordon's "Critical Legal Histories"' (2012) 37(1) Law & Social Enquiry 155, 157.

54 William H. Sewell, *Logics of History: Social Theory and Social Transformation* (University of Chicago Press 2005), see especially 1 and 6.

55 Sewell (n 54) 6.

56 Tosh (n 15) eg viii, 29.

57 ibid viii.

58 Per Michael Zundel, Robin Holt, and Andrew Popp, 'Using History in the Creation of Organizational Identity' (2016) 11(2) Management & Organizational History 211.

59 Sewell (n 54) 1, 6.

60 Tosh (n 15) 30.

61 ibid 33.

62 ibid 1.

63 ibid 11–12, 40–42.

64 ibid 33–34.

65 So called for insisting on respect for the autonomy of the past, and acknowledging 'gulfs of time' between past and present; Tosh (n 15) 35–36.

66 So called for highlighting the importance of understanding events as they were experienced by those living through them before 'wrenching' ideas from their original setting and examining them through present-day 'lenses'; Tosh (n 15) 36–38.

67 Tosh (n 15) 40–42.

68 See the reflections in Sarah Wilson, 'Law and Equity, and "Law and History" as a Resource of Critique' (2017) 11(1) Pólemos: Journal of Law, Literature and Culture 23.

69 See reflections on this in Roger Cotterrell, 'Power, Property and the Law of Trusts: A Partial Agenda for Critical Legal Scholarship' (1987) 14 Journal of Law & Society 77, 78.

70 An example of reaction against the premises of the doctrinal tradition through contextualism, through acknowledging human influences on law and legal institutions, can be seen in Cornish and Clark (n 50).

71 Critical legal studies (CLS) has generated a rich and voluminous body of critical legal history, see eg Tomlins (n 53). In essence CLS builds on contextualism through challenging key assumptions of inclusiveness, autonomy and individual action etc, (which are built into acknowledging human influences) and in doing so asserts that the law is not neutral and manifests inherent social biases.

72 Eg as embodied in Del Mar (n 21).

73 Del Mar (n 21) 4.

74 ibid 6.

75 ibid.

76 King (n 49) 161.

77 Explored in brief in Wilson (n 68).

78 This also provides the core of post-assessment feedback returned to students.

79 Connell (n 4) 104.

80 Tosh (n 15) 33.

81 Postman and Weingartner (n 1) 5.

82 Eg Rowan Williams, *Faith in the Public Square* (Bloomsbury 2012).

83 Per Paul Rock, 'Chronocentrism and British Criminology' (2005) 56(3) British Journal of Sociology 473.

84 Tosh (n 15) 47–48.

85 Witness eg Report of the Australian Royal Commission into Misconduct in the Banking, Superannuation and Financial Services Industry, *Final Report* (2019) <https://www.royalcommission.gov.au/banking>; and from the UK, Andrew Haldane 'Credit is Trust – Speech at the Association of Corporate Treasurers, Leeds' (*Bank of England*, 14 September 2009) <https://www.bankofengland.co.uk/speech/2009/credit-is-trust>.

10 Education for Citizenship and Social Justice

Students as Co-Creators

Kellie Toole and Peter Burdon

The practice of co-creation, or partnership between students and teaching staff, is an increasingly popular expression of the move away from teacher-centred learning towards students taking greater ownership of their learning experience. The active involvement of students challenges the traditional 'transactional nature' of higher education,[1] where staff within institutions design curriculum for students and deliver it to them. While the practice of co-creation is becoming more common, the rationales for its adoption vary markedly because it is underpinned by diametrically opposed educational philosophies. At one end of the spectrum, co-creation reflects a principle of 'participatory pedagogy',[2] and on the other hand, it reflects a consumer-driven market approach to education.

The Adelaide Law School's Sentencing and Criminal Justice (SCJ) elective invites students to partner with staff as co-creators in the development of curriculum and assessment and the delivery of course content. This article uses SCJ as a case study to demonstrate how co-creation between academics and students can challenge both the neoliberal values that are increasingly entrenched in higher education and some key principles underpinning co-creation that support those neoliberal values. The course embraces co-creation to offer an empowered educational experience so that interested and motivated students can gain preparation for future engagement in participatory democracy. This goal connects directly with theories of democratic citizenship as expressed by writers such as John Dewey, who argued that the ultimate goal of education was to produce a freer society: 'the ultimate aim of production is not the production of goods, but the production of free human beings associated with one another on terms of equality.'[3] A similar sentiment was expressed by Bertrand Russell, who noted that the goal of education is to

> give a sense of the value of things other than domination, to help create wise citizens of a free community, and through the combination of citizenship with liberty in individual creativeness to enable men [sic] to give to human life that splendour which some few have shown that it can achieve.[4]

From this perspective, education is central to the democratic project and a fundamental public good. However, staff are also influenced by neoliberal views and

DOI: 10.4324/9781003175216-13

pressures and were challenged by the tension between the two discourses underpinning co-creation.

This chapter begins by explaining and challenging the prominence of neoliberal values in higher education. It then introduces key opposing strands of scholarship that support co-creation. It situates the teaching of SCJ in the tradition that challenges, rather than adopts and validates, neoliberalism. However, it acknowledges that, in practice, the course sits at the intersection of the philosophical strands of neoliberalism and genuine student-led learning. It then draws on the results of two years of student evaluation to demonstrate that co-creation in higher education courses has the potential to prepare students for active citizenship.

I. Neoliberalism and Education

Over the last decade, there has been a rapid growth in generalist books critiquing the corporatisation of higher education. In Australia, titles like 'Silencing Dissent',[5] 'Whackademia',[6] 'Selling Students Short'[7] and 'The Good University'[8] have become a sub-genre of political analysis. While each text is unique, they each put forward a critique of higher education and its relationship to 'neoliberalism'. Neoliberalism is one of the most used terms in contemporary academic writing, and it is also subject to diverse interpretations. As Elizabeth Humphrys notes, Neoliberalism can be used to describe:

> (1) a doctrine, set of ideas and/or ideology; (2) a set of economic policies, an entire economic regime and/or a distinct phase of capitalism; (3) a political project, form of political rule and/or type of state; (4) a category of denunciation or criticism; and (5) a complex mix of some or all of these elements.[9]

The first two interpretations are most relevant to the analysis in this chapter. While the dominant history of neoliberalism stresses the role of new-right governments[10] and conservative think tanks,[11] in Australia, the shift was ushered in by the Labor Party and the Dawkins reforms, which started in 1987.[12] While not every aspect of these reforms was neoliberal,[13] it was during this period that fields of study were expanded in areas considered vital for economic growth and the cost burden began to shift from the State to individual students. Moreover, Hannah Forsyth argues that during the 1990s, our universities entered into a 'Faustian bargain' which 'explicitly reposition[ed] higher education as an industry, seeing financial reward.'[14]

Changes in funding, combined with the dominance of free market liberalism in public policy, economised the idea of higher education and allowed it to be described in terms of 'individuals exchanging goods and services at prices set by the laws of supply and demand, these prices providing the signals that allowed factors of production to be allocated with maximum efficiency.'[15] In practical terms, this rendered higher education a 'service to the consumer that should be bought and sold like any other commodity'[16] rather than something that could be framed in non-instrumental terms or through alternative values such as educating citizens for robust participation in a democracy.

In Australia, Margaret Thornton's book, *Privatising the Public University,*[17] remains the most sustained and detailed analysis of how neoliberalism has impacted law schools. Thornton theorises neoliberalism primarily as a political theory that promotes the marketisation of public goods and the erosion of state responsibility for producing an 'educated and culturally aware citizenry.'[18] Marketisation, according to Thornton, is a process rather than something that has been fully accomplished. Thus, she argues that while 'there has been a notable shift away from public to private responsibility', we currently operate in a hybrid public/private system.[19]

Thornton's main argument in relation to higher education teaching is that legal education is increasingly concerned with 'what law is, with little regard for critique, reflective analysis or what the law ought to be.'[20] This is a general statement, and practices vary considerably between institutions (and even between courses in a single degree). More directly relevant to our argument is Thornton's discussion of pedagogical practices and her claim that law schools have returned to a 'sage on the stage' model of pedagogy to cope with a massive increase in student numbers without a concomitant increase in resourcing.[21] In approaching this issue, it should first be noted that legal educators have known for a long time that the top-down delivery of information stifles critical thinking and promotes a black/white interpretation of the law. It was on these grounds that, in the 1960s, the Martin Report condemned the form of legal education that developed in Australia in the post-war period:

> most of the instruction in the law provided by busy practitioners was of the dogmatic kind [which] meant little or no teacher/student contact, no supervised work by the student, little or no student work concerned with original materials, and, for the majority of students, a strong temptation to satisfy all requirements by cramming potted information in short periods before examinations. In brief, legal education of that kind was fairly simple and very cheap, but it had very little else to commend it.[22]

Further, it was dissatisfaction with passive pedagogy that led to the creation of law schools at UNSW and Macquarie in the 1970s. The guiding vision for these schools was for teaching to focus less on lectures and move towards small interactive seminars.[23] Marlen Le Brun and Richard Johnstone documented these changes, and by the 1990s, it was commonplace for law schools to develop a 'student-centred, interdisciplinary approach to learning, in which the undergraduate law student assumes an active role in the making of meaning within the discipline of law.'[24]

However, the turn towards student-centred learning was only brief and small group teaching lasted only five years in some law schools.[25] At the same time as legal education was becoming more professional and focused on pedagogy, government policy was moving towards massification to 'augment the supply of new knowledge workers with the aim of ensuring that Nation-states are competitive within the global economy.'[26] This policy decision was not matched by funding, and so law schools have been coerced into the model of the firm – finding money from the private sector, locating efficiencies, and adopting an entrepreneurial posture towards the international student market.[27] These tendencies have only exacerbated following the COVID-19 pandemic and the downturn in international student numbers.[28]

In terms of teaching pedagogy, Thornton argues that Australian law schools have reverted to 'talk and chalk – albeit that the chalk has been replaced with PowerPoint.'[29] An anonymous academic from a sandstone law school expressed the shift as follows:

> In the 1990s, it would have been the standard subjects taught by 2 x 2hr seminars. Then that was compressed to 1 x 3hr seminar and, just in the last year or so, it's 1 x 2hr seminar, with the option of a 1hr lecture.[30]

What is driving this shift is not pedagogy but economics and efficiency. 'It means', Thornton notes, that 'one lecturer can teach, or at least purport to teach, 500 students simultaneously, and possibly many more in distant sites through online transmission and video-link.'[31]

The pressures that coerced law schools to move away from student-centred learning have not gone away. In fact, we find it very difficult to imagine how student participation, small group learning or critical reflection can genuinely occur across all compulsory courses without a significant increase in resourcing. For this reason, our experience of co-creation has not taken place within one of the Priestley 11 subjects but in smaller electives where enrolment is capped at 80 students. Before discussing this experience, we turn now to co-creation to explain its meaning and relationship to neoliberalism in the context of higher education.

II. Co-Creation – Two Traditions

Two distinct educational philosophical traditions underpin the co-creation scholarship. One strand of the scholarship emerges from neoliberalism, and the other is a direct challenge to it.

A. Co-Creation as Support for Neoliberalism

A significant strand of the co-creation scholarship supports the neoliberal values that are increasingly entrenched in higher education through recurrent calls to recognise the university as a 'marketised environment'[32] and the association of co-creation with 'profession-oriented learning'.[33]

Marketised Environment

The periodic substitution of the term co-creation, with 'co-production' betrays the development of the concept in the fields of marketing and consumer behaviour. Business schools that advocate this approach assert that 'theories on customers and enterprises apply to education as well as to any other service or product. The services of universities [are] just one of the many services provided in society.'[34] Theorists who adhere to this view advocate the reform of learning and teaching to 'shift the paradigm away from dictating brand attributes to consumers, to jointly building brand meaning with them.'[35] Co-creation to achieve this aim is intended to provide a 'service orientated relationship'[36] between staff and students where students do, and should, have a 'customer experience', and the role of teaching staff constitutes 'provider participation'.[37] The SCJ model explicitly rejects this view of education and staff and student interaction. It does not encourage students to view their education in a purely instrumental way or as a consumer activity. Similarly, it does not encourage them to conceptualise their relationship with staff, their learning experience, or their higher education institution as one of consumer-provider or to associate the process of co-creation to material 'outcomes' or 'products'.[38] However, as discussed below, it does partially accept that a university education can legitimately and usefully include the development of practical skills that will assist students in securing employment and transitioning successfully into legal practice.

Profession-Oriented Learning

Much of the co-creation literature, like much of the discourse in higher education generally, also considers that the primary purpose of a university degree is to 'foster competences [that] contribute to the employability of workers'.[39] SCJ incorporates teaching and assessment components that assist interested students in developing career readiness skills. The lecture program includes guest lecturers who are chosen to demonstrate the range of career options available in criminal law. They are invited to complement their presentations on the substantive law by providing advice to students on transitioning into criminal practice. A group oral assessment task, worth 30% of the final mark, replicates the work a junior criminal lawyer would undertake when making sentencing submissions on behalf of criminal clients or the Crown. The advocacy is undertaken in the Moot Court and is assessed by a District Court judge to create an authentic courtroom experience and provide student advocates with realistic and honest advice on how their performance compares to the standards required in court. The teaching staff are firm adherents of Margaret Thornton's argument that the neoliberalisation of legal education in Australia has led to the jettisoning of critical material in favour of more practical forms of knowledge.[40] SCJ is, consequently, focused on how the critical skills required for democratic citizenship would be enhanced by understanding and experience of legal practice. The thrust of the more functional career readiness components is that students do not need to mould themselves to the expectations of the workforce but rather can be well informed about diverse pathways and empowered to forge a long-term career that is well-suited to their personal strengths, interests and values. However, the course simultaneously recognises the competitive nature of the legal employment market and the stress about career outcomes that students experience. The actual state of the legal employment market in Australia has been contested for decades and is open to various conflicting interpretations of factors, including the oversupply of legal grades, changing demand for legal services, and graduate interest in entering legal practice.[41] However, there has been persistent media attention on the number of graduates exceeding available legal positions,[42] which spiked in 2018 when then Prime Minister Turnbull publicly claimed that too many students were studying law.[43] Irrespective of their accuracy, media reports about the competitiveness of the legal career market are stressful for students. The SCJ course recognises that the development of practical skills used in the profession can assist students to feel, and actually be, prepared for legal practice and more likely to secure and succeed in employment.

B. Co-Creation as Challenge to Neoliberalism

The philosophy underpinning co-creation in SCJ, however, draws much more strongly on two strands of educational theory that starkly contrast with the 'business school approach' to co-creation. First, it reflects the ideas that Neil Postman and Charles Weingartner put forward 40 years ago, that 'We learn best that which we participate in selecting and planning ourselves', and that '[g]enuine participation . . . intensifies motivation, flexibility, and rate of learning.'[44] Secondly, it further reflects more recent scholarship on participatory pedagogy and educating students on citizenship and social justice.

The co-creation process in SCJ seeks to undermine the neoliberal construction of higher education as 'a private good for individual advancement.'[45] It sought to renew universities' 'historic commitments to the greater public good and more ardently educate their students for democratic citizenship, social responsibility, commitment to social justice, and engagement in their communities'.[46]

In rejecting the key values presented in the business and marketing literature as the goals of co-creation, SCJ embraced co-creation as a 'participatory pedagogy',[47] wherein students are challenged to eschew a passive or consumer approach to education and invited to become more active participants in a communal relationship with academic staff.[48] The co-creation process, and the relationship with staff on which it is based, is designed to encourage students to think about SCJ, and their education generally, as providing opportunities for more than just preparing them for the workforce in the capacity of employee lawyers. The course encourages them to consider challenging power structures within and outside of the university and assist them in developing skills that could empower them to be active, democratic citizens who do not envision their education as just producing them as workers.

III. Democratic Citizenship and SCJ

A major aim of the co-creation process was to create the opportunity for students to envision their education as not producing them as workers but affording them a mindset and a skillset that has the potential to motivate and enable them to be able to be active, democratic citizens. Many law students are regularly and effectively developing knowledge and skills for democratic citizenship within the law school through volunteering for its well-being program and peer mentor schemes; within the university through student politics and ambassador programs; and within the broader community through paid and voluntary work in social justice and other organisations. Adelaide Law School courses foster these commitments through the substantive content, not only in electives like Human Rights and Citizenship but in compulsory courses, such as Criminal Law and Property Law,[49] that deliberately present substantive law content alongside notions of social justice, human rights, equality before the law and First Nations perspectives. However, these critical and ethical skills are rarely developed by including students in the process of the design of courses. This is, in part, due to specific organisational limitations related to timelines for approval of course details. However, the limitation is consistent with other international higher education institutions, as studies have found that university and college students do not, typically, gain through their formal education 'the types of skills, competencies, and mind-sets needed to effectually engage in social change'.[50] This aim of addressing this deficit in SCJ was not explicitly articulated to students.

However, the following section draws on student evaluations from 2018 and 2019 to demonstrate that the co-creation process used in SCJ met with some success in showing students that their educational experience could incubate a commitment and ability to engage in broader social activism and active citizenship. The section is divided into five categories: (1) Achieving Change; (2) Being Heard and Having Experience Valued; (3) Building Community With Peers Through Shared Effort; (4) Working Collaboratively With Staff; and (5) 'Wearing' Consequences of not Getting Involved. The findings in each of these categories indicate that students' reflections on the course suggest that it stimulates students' thinking and enables them to develop skills that are compatible with them translating their experience in the course to a contribution to social justice, not just individual, or even communal, economic or financial achievement.

A. Co-Creation Method

SCJ is an upper-level elective available to law students who have completed the compulsory course of Criminal Law. Students enrolled in the course are invited to participate in creating curriculum and content in the months before the course commences. They are invited to discuss or express their views on topics, teaching style, student participation, and assessment through a pre-semester meeting, online discussion board, email, and a topic checklist/suggestion sheet. The pre-semester student input is used to generate an overview of the course, but the program is fluid throughout so that students can propose topics or guest speakers, request to present their own research, or make suggestions regarding assessment deadlines or content at any time throughout the semester. They were also provided with standard university-wide online evaluations, hard copy surveys specific to the co-creation aspects of the course, and time for discussion in the penultimate seminar to make suggestions for changes for future iterations of the course.

B. Achieving Change

The neoliberal state has created an alienating 'Catch 22' situation for the political involvement of young people. They are criticised for low rates of voter registration and voter turnout in countries with both compulsory and voluntary voting regimes. However, at the same time, neoliberal policies emphasise individualism and reduce welfare support, which diminishes opportunities for electoral participation and citizenship and disenfranchises young people from the political system.[51] The inclusion of co-creation in SJC seeks to enliven students to the possibilities of grassroots activism to make politics meaningful and challenge the common but demotivating view that 'an ordinary person without unusual power, abilities, or wealth, cannot make a difference in this world'.[52]

By participating in the process of co-creation in SCJ, students are able to experience firsthand how active participation and engagement can produce positive changes for themselves and others in an educational setting that is applicable to the broader social context. The 2018 co-creation surveys[53] included frequent positive references to the co-creation process, allowing students to 'have input into the areas that we wanted to learn about' and exert a '[d]irect influence in what we learn'. Students acknowledge that '[s]tudent input is rare at uni, so it was good to get involved in shaping learning'. They identify that as a result of student involvement, the content and assessment of the course is more appropriate to their learning goals as it is 'focused upon areas that the students found interesting' and accommodated 'students suggested activities that were relevant – particularly like the court exercise'. Even more importantly, students do not just recognise that the outcome of the course was more tailored to their interests on account of the co-creation process. They also identify the process as '[e]mpowering for students' and 'engaging and exciting to be able to influence the topics studied.' Co-creation gives students a lived experience of the satisfaction that results from a democratic process that produces tangible benefits for themselves and others. Some students were able to extrapolate the lesson and make the general observation that '[w]hen people make decisions they are more likely to be more involved in implementation',[54] which is a solid basis for engagement and leadership in social activism.

C. Being Heard and Having Experience Valued

The Australian Parliament's 2007 inquiry into Civics and Electoral Education identified the enduring, and indeed almost universal, reality that young people perceive that conventional politics and democratic processes are not directly relevant to their lives and do not take their voices into account.[55] This long-standing situation of disenfranchisement is exacerbated by neoliberal policies wherein '"the mainstream" dominates over the voices of those with particular or special perspectives or needs'.[56]

The SCJ students recognised the inherent value in being listened to, taken seriously, and treated as having a legitimate right to influence experiences that will affect them. Students who gave lecture presentations on their research or practical experiences found it 'good practice', 'enjoyed being able to present my Law Reform research', and 'thought it was good to have the student perspective.' The appreciation of the student's role in delivering content was not, however, expressed only by the students who participated in the lecture program. Other class members recognised that co-creation '[a]llowed students to voice their interests', and through it, 'students were given a voice in how the course was run and particular interests addressed'. Students realised there was profound personal satisfaction in feeling respected enough to be consulted in matters related to their education. One student found that '[t]he co-creation aspect is very cool in that students can basically have a say in what they want in the course and have an input that matters'. Another observed that '[i]t was really good to feel like students' opinions re: time/class structure were valued.' They appreciated the chance to 'have their input considered and have their interests represented through guest lecturers, assessment, and aspects of the course'.

A potentially even greater benefit to the co-creation process was that students recognised, equally, the benefit of listening to other students as well as being heard. Responses acknowledged that it was 'valuable to hear from other students' and '[g]reat to hear a student perspective', which raised 'issues at the forefront of our thoughts'. There was an appreciation that co-creation 'gives a good perspective of the views and perspectives of fellow colleagues' and created a culture that was 'very inclusive and pressure free'.[57] The benefits of hearing from other students also had a practical dimension because the 'experience of my peers was not only informative but made me aware of opportunities I didn't know existed'. The co-creation process showed the value of being listened to in an educational environment where student voices are not always expressly sought or factored into decision-making about course content and delivery and assessment. It concurrently allowed students to appreciate how much they had to learn from peers with different experiences and knowledge than themselves, which was consistent with a study of an American college which found that communication across student groups created a 'narrative community' that required and developed self-reflection, empathy, acknowledgement of personal privilege, understanding of diversity and the recognition of the entitlement of others to speak.[58]

The heightened experiences of listening and being heard reinforce to students that in most settings, different people have different perspectives, and personal dignity and community outcomes will be enhanced where professionals and people in positions of authority seek to understand and include those views.

D. Building Community With Peers Through Shared Effort

Student feedback also demonstrated that working collectively to achieve a common goal with a group whose members have shared interests can yield positive, personal benefits for the individuals involved as well as outcomes that benefit the group overall. Students recognised that the 'Sense of group work' and 'good collaborative relationship'[59] made it 'satisfying getting results' in SCJ. They also appreciated the 'promotion of collaboration and discussions with other students (welcoming environment)' and that the co-creation process 'Helps students feel like they have a say in their learning and instils sense of community in cohort'. There are also some indications that the process allows students to look beyond their own experience and appreciate the opportunity to 'give positive feedback to make it easier for next year's students' and provide feedback that 'benefits future students as well as the course co-ordinator'.[60] For some students, at least, the course highlighted the personal satisfaction and experience of altruism associated with collective effort for a common cause. This outcome is compatible with a study of social workers that found that group work in tertiary education encouraged more empathetic and socially-aware practice and the development of understanding of the need to deal with practical problems more broadly than by simply addressing clients' immediate needs to communicate and build relationships across diverse professional and client groups; facilitate meaningful discussions at a group level in which the client, not the practitioner, is the focus; and build relationships based on deep empathy and genuine listening skills.[61]

E. Working Collaboratively With Staff

In addition to the benefits of working closely with peers, the students clearly appreciated the opportunity to enter a dialogue with staff about course design. The negotiation and engagement with teaching staff through the co-creation process are particularly important in requiring both students and staff to move beyond 'traditional hierarchical models of expertise'.[62] The experience of students being involved in 'changing the traditional power status quo'[63] in the relationship with teaching staff and their own education involves '[r]eflecting on and critically debating . . . power dynamics'.[64] Through the experience in SCJ, some students recognised that '[c]o-creation is great environment for discussion rather than instruction.' They expressed that 'feeling connected to the course and positive relationship with the teacher' 'provides a great opportunity to engage with teaching staff in a positive way'. This communication and relationship 'promoted engagement and also highlights the mutual teacher-student learning experience in the context of adult education', which is equally applicable to other environments. This lends itself, particularly, to future participation in social activism as it helps empower students to both think about challenging power structures outside of the university environment and have some experience in negotiating to be effective in such challenges.

F. 'Wearing' Consequences of not Getting Involved

Finally, while higher education is contingent on students taking responsibility for their own learning, research, and anecdotal evidence suggest that university students, in Australia at least, do not always take such responsibility but rather expect to be 'spoon fed' content.[65] The student expectation of education being 'delivered' to them is highly compatible with the neoliberal consumerisation of higher education. Co-creation does not offer a panacea for this tension in student-teacher expectations, but it does remove focus from perceived deficiencies in 'learner autonomy' and focuses on creating a 'learning situation' that is supportive of 'learners who wish to become responsible'.[66] While most forms of higher education support and encourage learning responsibility, the discussion above demonstrates that co-creation involves a series of tangible markers that unequivocally show students some important, practical implications of personal and educational benefits of taking responsibility. Conversely, co-creation also highlights some clear correlated disadvantages of choosing not to actively engage in the development of curriculum and course content. The student survey responses to the question of 'what are the negative consequences of co-creation?' demonstrated awareness of student responsibility for the success of the course, and that it is detrimental to the class when 'not enough students got involved!', and that on an individual level 'if you didn't participate, you would miss out'. Students were not able only to see the disadvantages to others of choosing not to participate. One found that a negative of the co-creation was '[h]aving topics you are not too interested in', but admitted that to have remedied this situation, 'I could have contributed more to the co-creation process!' The realisation that choosing not to participate in processes and activities where there is potential for engagement that could achieve personal and communal benefits is a powerful motivator for involvement in a range of important community and political activities.

IV. Conclusion

A law degree is a pathway to legal practice. The cohort enrolled in the degree includes students who are passionate about embarking on a career in the profession and graduates who will enter the profession irrespective of their initial motivations for undertaking the law degree. The practical aspects of SCJ curriculum and assessment are designed to assist students and graduates in making this practical transition. In this sense, the course reflects the neoliberal values it purports to reject. However, at a fundamental level, co-creation provides a pathway for academic staff who want to work positively within the current educational system but still resist some of the values that underpin the neoliberal university. The experience in SCJ demonstrates that course design and delivery have the potential for the higher education experience to offer a model for civic engagement that encourages future participation in the community and the polity as well as the economy. Through a constructive but subversive partnership between staff and students, universities can 'serve as examples of a living democratic spirit' by providing 'opportunities for students to see the value of their involvement in communities and political processes [that] encourage students' political and leadership efficacy,'[67] and enable interested and motivated students to gain some preparation for future engagement in participatory democracy. A course structured and assessed without reference to the practical skills needed to secure employment would constitute a more thorough rejection of neoliberal principles. However, the experience in SCJ suggests that a law elective course can both acknowledge economic realities and take a principled stance against neoliberalism.

Notes

1 David William Stoten et al., 'Co-Creation and Online Learning: A Case Study of Online Discussion Boards at an English Business School' (2018) 10(1) Journal of Applied Research in Higher Education 44, 45.
2 Renate Andersen and Marisa Ponti, 'Participatory Pedagogy in an Open Educational Course: Challenges and Opportunities' (2014) 35(2) Distance Education 234–249.
3 John Dewey, *Experience and Education* (Free Press 1999) 34. A more recent articulation of Dewey's ideas can be found in Noam Chomsky, *Chomsky on Democracy and Education* (Routledge 2002).
4 Bertrand Russell, *Power: A New Social Analysis* (Routledge 1938) 251.
5 Clive Hamilton and Sarah Maddison (eds), *Silencing Dissent: How the Australian Government is Controlling Public Opinion and Stifling Debate* (Allen and Unwin 2007).
6 Richard Hil, *Whackademia: An Insider's Account of the Troubled University* (UNSW Press 2012).
7 Richard Hil, *Selling Students Short: Why You Won't Get the University Education You Deserve* (Allen and Unwin 2015).
8 Raewyn Connell, *The Good University: What Universities Actually Do and Why It's Time for Radical Change* (Monash University Publishing 2019).
9 Elizabeth Humphrys, 'The Corporatist Origins of Neoliberalism: Australia's Accord, the Labour Movement and the Neoliberal Project' (PhD Thesis, University of Sydney 2015) 70–71.
10 See David Harvey, *A Brief History of Neoliberalism* (Oxford University Press 2007) 39–63.
11 Philip Mirowski and Dieter Plehwe (eds), *The Road from Mont Pèlerin: The Making of the Neoliberal Thought Collective* (Harvard University Press 2015).
12 Elizabeth Humphrys and Damien Cahill, 'How Labour Made Neoliberalism' (2016) 43(4–5) *Critical Sociology* 669. See also Elizabeth Humphrys, 'Is the Term Neoliberalism Useful?' (*An Integral State*, 12 November 2006) <www.anintegralstate.net/2016/11/12/476/> accessed 19 February 2018. Here, Humphrys argues: 'we argue that the labour movement was not simply an object or victim of neoliberal change but an active constructor of it.'
13 For example, a critical aspect of the Dawkins reforms involved linking funding to a set of national objectives for the economy, society and culture. This goes against the logic of a purely free market as articulated by Milton Friedman. See Milton Friedman, 'The Social Responsibility of Business Is to Increase Its Profits' *The New York Times Magazine* (13 September 1970).
14 Hannah Forsyth, *A History of the Modern Australian University* (UNSW Press 2014) 226.
15 Stuart Macintyre, Andre Brett and Gwilym Croucher, *No End of a Lesson: Australia's Unified National System of Higher Education* (Melbourne University Press 2017) 37.
16 ibid.
17 Margaret Thornton, *Privatising the Public University: The Case of Law* (Routledge 2012).
18 ibid 1. At xiv Thornton captures this shift with reference to a Government report which stated: '[T]he term "public" university now refers more to the historical circumstances at the time of foundation rather than the nature of institutional financing.' See also Department of Education, Employment and Workplace Relations, 'Review of Australian Higher Education, Working Paper, Department of Education, Employment and Workplace Relations' (Canberra, June 2008) 10.
19 Thornton (n 17) 1.
20 ibid 59.
21 ibid 85.

22 Committee on the Future of Tertiary Education in Australia, *Tertiary Education in Australia: Report to the Australian Universities Commission* (Government Printer 1964) vol 2, 57 (Martin Report).
23 Thornton (n 17) 85.
24 Marlen Le Brun and Richard Johnstone, *The Quiet Revolution: Improving Student Learning in Law* (The Law Book Co Ltd 1994) 97. The phrase ‘making of meaning’ derives from Neil Postman and Charles Weingartner, *Teaching as a Subversive Activity* (A Delta Book 1969) 82–97.
25 Thornton (n 17) 90.
26 ibid 13. This goal has only become more overt. See for example Paul Karp, ‘Australian University Fees to Double for Some Arts Courses, but Fall for Stem Subjects’ *The Guardian* (19 June 2020) <www.theguardian.com/australia-news/2020/jun/19/australian-university-fees-arts-stem-science-maths-nursing-teaching-humanities>.
27 Wendy Brown, *Undoing the Demos* (Zone Books 2015) 34.
28 See for example, Naaman Zhou, ‘Monash University Signs Deal with Indonesian Government as Universities Diversify from China’ *The Guardian* (8 April 2021) <//www.theguardian.com/australia-news/2021/apr/08/monash-university-signs-deal-with-indonesian-government-as-solution-to-overreliance-on-china>.
29 Thornton (n 17) 86.
30 ibid.
31 ibid.
32 Stoten (n 1) 45.
33 George Moerkerke, ‘Modern Customers and Open Universities: Can Open Universities Develop a Course Model in which Students Become the Co-Creators of Value?’ (2015) 30(3) Open Learning: The Journal of Open, Distance and e-Learning 235, 249.
34 ibid.
35 Pascale Quester, Kendra Backstrom and Slavka Kovacevic, ‘The University of Adelaide Student Learning Hub: A Case Study of Education Co-Creation’ in Heather Brook et al. (eds), *Foregrounding Social Contexts of Knowledge in the First Year Experience* (Adelaide 2014) 187, 190.
36 Moerkerke (n 33) 235–236.
37 Alison M. Dean et al., ‘Applying Service Logic to Education: The Co-creation Experience and Value Outcomes’ (2016) 224 Procedia – Social and Behavioural Sciences 325, 326–327.
38 The most sustained analysis of neoliberalism and legal education remains Thornton (n 17).
39 Moerkerke (n 33) 249.
40 Thornton (n 17) 59–119.
41 See, for example, Michael McNamara, ‘University Legal Education and the Supply of Law Graduates: A Fresh Look at a Longstanding Issue’ (2018) 20 Flinders Law Journal 223; Naomi Neilson, ‘What the Future of a Soon-to-be Graduate Now Looks Like’ *Lawyer’s Weekly* (20 April 2020) <www.lawyersweekly.com.au/newlaw/28026-what-the-future-of-a-soon-to-be-graduate-now-looks-like>.
42 See, for example, Michael Pelly, ‘Law Firms Reduce Graduate Intake’ *The Australian Financial Review* (21 December 2020) <www.afr.com/companies/professional-services/law-firms-reduce-graduate-intake-20201216-p56nzu>.
43 Louise Yaxley, ‘Don't Study Law Unless You Really Want to Be a Lawyer, Malcom Turnbull Says’ *ABC News* (2 February 2018) <www.abc.net.au/news/2018-02-02/malcolm-turnbull-says-too-many-kids-do-law/9387508>.
44 Postman and Weingartner (n 24).
45 Zak Foste, ‘Engaging Undergraduate Men in Service-Learning: Exploring Motivations to Serve’ in Tania D. Mitchell and Krista M. Soria (eds), *Educating for Citizenship and*

Social Justice Practices for Community Engagement at Research Universities (Palgrave Macmillan 2018) 11, 31.

46 Krista M. Soria, Tania D. Mitchell, Mathew Lauer and Anthony Scali, 'Undergraduates' Development of Citizenship at Public Research Universities: A Data-Driven Imperative for Social Justice' in Tania D. Mitchell and Krista M. Soria (eds), *Educating for Citizenship and Social Justice Practices for Community Engagement at Research Universities* (Palgrave Macmillan 2018) 11. On the erosion of these values under neoliberalism, see Wendy Brown, *Undoing the Demos: Neoliberalism's Stealth Revolution* (Zone Books 2015) 175–200.

47 Andersen and Ponti (n 2) 234–249.

48 Stoten (n 1) 54–55.

49 For a discussion of property law see the chapter by Burdon in this edited collection.

50 Soria, Mitchell, Lauer and Scali (n 46) 29.

51 Kathy Edwards, 'Disenfranchised Not "Deficient": How the (Neoliberal) State Disenfranchises Young People' (2009) 44(1) Australian Journal of Social Issues 23, 24–34.

52 Saul Smilansky, 'Discussion: On the Common Lament, that a Person Cannot Make Much Difference in This World' (2012) 87(1) Philosophy 109.

53 Unless indicated otherwise, the quotations from students are from the 2018 course-specific hard copy survey on the co-creation process (Co-Creation Survey, 2019).

54 Co-Creation Survey, 2019.

55 The Parliament of the Commonwealth of Australia: Joint Standing Committee on Electoral Matters, *Civics and Electoral Education Report* (May 2007) 7–11.

56 Edwards (n 51) 32.

57 Co-Creation Survey, 2019.

58 Susan E. Chase, *Learning to Speak, Learning to Listen: How Diversity Works on Campus* (Cornell University Press 2011) 224–233.

59 Co-Creation Survey, 2019.

60 Co-Creation Survey, 2019.

61 Manohar Pawar et al. (eds), *Empowering Social Workers: Virtuous Practitioners* (Springer 2017) 57, 69, 108, 114.

62 Catherine Bovill, Alison Cook-Sather and Peter Felten, 'Students as Co-Creators of Teaching Approaches, Course Design, and Curricula: Implications for Academic Developers' (2011) 16(2) International Journal for Academic Development 133.

63 Ina Blau and Tamar Shamir-Inbal, 'Re-Designed Flipped Learning Model in an Academic Course: The Role of Co-Creation and Co-Regulation' (2017) 115 Computers & Education 69, 79.

64 Sarah Abboud et al., 'Co-Creation of a Pedagogical Space to Support Qualitative Inquiry: An Advanced Qualitative Collective' (2017) 50 Nurse Education Today 8, 10.

65 Marcia Devlin, 'Taking Responsibility for Learning Isn't Everything: A Case for Developing Tertiary Students' Conceptions of Learning' (2002) 7(2) Teaching in Higher Education 125, 126–127, 135.

66 Soufiane Blidi, *Collaborative Learner Autonomy: A Mode of Learner Autonomy Development* (Springer 2017) xxiv–xxv.

67 Soria, Mitchell, Lauer and Scali (n 46) 31.

11 Unlearning Real Property Law

Nicole Graham and Kate Galloway

'The significance of crises is the indication they provide that an occasion for retooling has arrived'.[1]

I. Introduction

Real Property is predominantly taught in Australian law schools in much the same way as it has been taught for decades, or (probably) longer.[2] 'How much have the basic rules of property that we teach today . . . changed from what we taught forty years ago?'[3] In this paper, we offer the provocation that the approach to teaching the subject focuses on, if not fetishizes, its technical aspects without connecting these to the logic of related private law subjects and without situating property within its economic, environmental, political and legal contexts. We recognise that individual teachers will engage different pedagogical tools and overlay teaching with different curricular goals[4] but observe that this individualized practice (to the extent that it occurs) exists within a broader established discourse of technical and detailed rules that set the benchmark of what must be known.

A critical review of standard Australian property law textbooks reveals a widespread convention in the selection and presentation of topics and key cases in property law education. While legal history is often used in introductory chapters to explain and/or legitimate the status quo, there is insufficient acknowledgement that colonisation in Australia continues. Quarantining historical contexts to introductory chapters can imply an inaccurate perspective about property law in Australia: that it comprises only Anglo-Australian law and that Aboriginal and Torres Strait Islander Australian property regimes do not currently exist, save through the whitefella law of native title.[5]

Occasional attention to the central role of natural resource ownership and use in property law has increased modestly over time in the curriculum, but often without attention to the social and environmental consequences and contexts. Some real property courses present in a critical way largely outdated notions of gender and sexuality in significant case law, but often without attention to their significance as examples of the agency of property law in constructing and reproducing relations of social and economic power.

DOI: 10.4324/9781003175216-14

In this chapter, we contend that the approach to teaching real property law in Australia takes a 'conserving' approach to the law. It represents the tradition of conservatism articulated by Edward Coke—namely that the common law is 'a fixed body of principles dictated by reason.'[6] This 'establishment' position is apparent in real property textbooks and the structure of courses. While courses are necessarily designed to satisfy the prescribed curriculum requirements of accreditation for professional practice, the almost exclusive focus on the content of real property does not prescribe any particular pedagogy and does not foreclose the diverse approaches to delivery and assessment that are available. Reproducing conventional approaches to teaching real property is a commitment to conserving a particular and self-referential view of property law as neutral rather than agential in constructing significant social and environmental relations. The conventional approach to teaching real property limits the capacity of today's law graduates to develop the field and ensure its continuing viability in the 21st century.

The consequence of the conventional approach to teaching real property law is to reproduce the dephysicalised view of land as the foundation for market transactions[7] that is insensitive to, if not indeed instrumental to, the creation of profound social inequality. We propose a different approach. We encourage real property law educators to better equip lawyers, and society, with a suite of tools to subvert that view, redress its consequences and lay the foundations for a more equitable and sustainable property regime. Our approach values the importance of conserving the foundation tenets of law more broadly, such as the rule of law. But our aim is to achieve the law's purpose by subverting the long outdated and dysfunctional property regime operating in Australia. Elkins observes the paradox of subverting through conserving thus:

> When we were secure in the knowledge that we knew what we were doing, law teaching was (and is) an activity of complicity in the denial of law's failure. Law conserves equally our freedom and social injustice. It is only when law and its teaching are both conserving and subversive activities that the world we make in our teaching will be worth living and the professing of faith and truth(s) will once again be possible.[8]

This chapter foregrounds the importance of teaching real property to the ongoing learning and unlearning of the legitimating function of property law in colonial, patriarchal and anthroparchic land distribution; and the facilitative function of property in creating and entrenching everyday economic inequality and environmental degradation. Part II of the chapter identifies the unique importance of real property law as a regulatory field to either reproduce or subvert the conditions and effects of the climate crisis and social inequality. Part III of the chapter reviews the conventional approach to teaching real property law, which is premised on a traditional view of real property as an exclusively private law subject, and argues that legal education can contribute to a different conceptualisation of what real property is and what it is for. Part IV of the chapter considers potential subversions of the conventional approaches to teaching real property law by paying closer attention to and interrogating both the paradigmatic and contextual registers of land. The chapter concludes that the best strategy through which to achieve these potential subversions is 'conserving' the dominant content as the most appropriate and effective objects of critical and contextual pedagogy.

II. Real Property Law, Climate Change and Social Inequality

Land is the condition of life on Earth, and so it is fundamental to questions of ecology, economy, ethics and power. Successful (long-standing) legal regimes that govern the distribution and access to land have recognised the distinctiveness and importance of land through developing regulatory models that are necessarily adapted to local geophysical conditions.[9] For centuries, legal scholars have recognised the distinctiveness of land and accorded to it a cornucopia of theories, taxonomies and treatises. The distinction between interests *in rem* and *in personam* derives from the truism that the only meaningful remedy in a dispute over land is the land itself. There is no substitute. But this materially centred logic of land law gradually gave way to the current dominant idea of property as an abstract legal right with the socio-economic transition from feudalism to capitalism.[10] In property theory, this change is referred to as the dephysicalisation of property.

Dephysicalised property is a model of property in which the legal relationship is not between a person and a physical thing (lands and/or waters) but a relation that is exclusively between human beings. This model of interpersonal relations is articulated in terms of property rights. The model replaces the physical thing that is thought to be owned with an abstract legal right. This model is the dominant model of property law in Anglophonic legal culture. In the early 20th century, American legal scholar Wesley Newcomb Hohfeld lamented society's 'unfortunate tendency to confuse and blend'[11] physical things with abstract legal property rights. The notion that property referred to land or physical things was 'fallacious', he argued, since rights between persons constituted the entire property relation. By the end of the 20th century, one of the leading property lawyers in the common law world, Kevin Gray, wrote that property had become so abstracted and meaningless as a legal category that it might be regarded as 'an illusion.'[12]

The model of dephysicalised property relations, by design, is potentially applicable to any valuable right so that it can facilitate the exchange of capital in whatever form it might take now and into the future. One of the earliest consequences of this versatility was the fragmentation of landscapes into sets of various separable resources. Solid, liquid and gaseous parts of landscapes were mapped, quantified, legally separated from the land and then physically extracted and removed to resource markets. The impact of dephysicalised property is apparent in adverse anthropogenic environmental changes associated, in part, with the fragmentation of landscapes that it has facilitated.[13] These changes remind us that 'dephysicalisation is not just a theory – it is a practice'[14] reshaping physical forms and processes. Analyses of dephysicalised property relations into the 21st century[15] are informed in part by the growing recognition of the agency of law in the conditions of climate change.

The concept of dephysicalised property relations was instrumental to the projects of enclosure and colonisation and continues to be instrumental to the dispossession of human and non-human communities from their lands and habitats. The moral rationale to dispossess people of their lands, often violently, and change long-established legal relations between people and places relied heavily on the notion of the 'improvement' of both.[16] The goal of improvement discourse was the cultivation of 'waste' lands into commercially productive landscapes and the progress of human society itself.[17] Land-taking necessarily involved both law avoidance and law reform. The reconceptualisation of property relations apparent in the 'socioeconomic experimentation' with taking foreign lands and establishing slavery in colonies 'outside the customs and conventions' of Europe is an instance of the former.[18] In England, dephysicalisation involved law reform on a massive scale through enclosure acts of Parliament.[19]

The simplicity of the concept of dephysicalised property masks the complex, dynamic and networked nature of socio-political inequalities because it is premised on a liberalist understanding of people's relations to each other and the means to access the goods of life which are premised on the exercise of autonomous choice. The model begins and ends with the transaction of legal rights regarding land without situating these rights in relation to the economic and psychological interests of non-rights holders whose dispossession and labour are necessary prerequisites to the existence of property rights. Subsequently, the dominant model of property law struggles to recognise and protect 'relations with the land asserted by third parties, particularly those premised on interdependence, reciprocity or responsibility. These "non-owners", who neither own nor control any part of the bundle, are presumed to be peripheral to the central relations of ownership.'[20] The interests of 'non-owners' in land raise important questions about the role of real property law in the ongoing dispossession of First Nations peoples from their traditional lands, homeless encampments and social housing.[21]

Legal research has closely examined the role of property law in producing the conditions of social inequality and climate change.[22] This research suggests that many concepts and doctrines that dominate private law today developed in large part for the purposes of protecting and defending the socio-economic institutions that supported the rise of industrialisation and growth-based economies premised on the philosophies of liberalism and capitalism.[23] The dominant and almost ubiquitous legal model of dephysicalised property is abstract but has material consequences, including environmental and social harms. There is an urgent need to redress the contribution of property law to these problems. The 'legally disruptive nature of climate change'[24] challenges the functionality and viability of existing laws and policies[25] and places pressure on national and international governance structures more broadly.[26]

In May 2020, the International Bar Association published a Climate Crisis Statement in which the Association resolved to 'take a climate conscious approach to problems encountered in daily legal practice' and to 'engage with law students and schools concerning education on legal elements of the climate crisis and its impact on human rights.'[27] Since the ownership and use of land and its resources are critically important to both the numerous and complex problems arising from the climate crisis and to their potential solutions, the way that the laws of land ownership and use are taught and learned by lawyers in the 21st century is necessarily, also, critically important. In the next section, we argue that it is urgently imperative to subvert the teaching of property law by restoring and foregrounding its material foundations in, and impacts upon, the land.

III. Conventional Approaches to Teaching and Learning Property Law

'Lawyers as lawyers are uniquely placed to consider taking active steps to do things about the injustices they see around them.'[28] But whether or not they do is a question veiled by the cloak of professionalism that often assumes an impersonality and impartiality suggestive of the absence of values.[29] Should lawyers hold values, and what should they be? Does real property law contain values? What are they, and how are they taught? When law students learn real property law, do they learn to evaluate the relationship between law and land?

The pedagogy of property law varies significantly across and within Australian universities.[30] This may be attributed to the 'challenging', 'problematic' and 'difficult' nature of legal education which attempts to 'satisfy simultaneously the immediate demands of legal practice and the traditional values associated with the university.'[31] The disparity of purpose apparent in this dual commitment defines the contrast between the two main approaches to legal education: the doctrinal and the critical.[32]

The doctrinal approach emphasises the immediate practical function of legal knowledge through a consideration of the interaction of various rules in real and hypothetical disputes. Here, the law is learned and practised as the administration of rules that pre-exist the specific dispute before the law by reference to statute and the decisions of superior courts. Accordingly, law students are trained to master and engage in the technical craft of statutory interpretation and the analysis of judicial reasoning to resolve disputes.

Critical legal education emphasises the broader contexts of legal doctrines and relates these to disputes. Here, the law is learned as a set of rules determined in part by socio-economic, cultural and historical conditions that are neither fixed nor inevitable. Whether law students become capable of improving society by virtue of their legal education depends to some extent on the pedagogy adopted by their teachers, irrespective of the content of the property curriculum.

A. Real Property Law Is a Hard Subject

Real property law is a 'hard' subject in two different senses. First, the heavily-structured curriculum of property law secures its status as an important, pragmatic, 'hard' subject fulfilling the Uniform Admission requirements. Second, the common method of rote-learning core rules and doctrines can render the subject seemingly incoherent: this is what lecturers and textbooks sometimes refer to as the 'difficulty' of real property law.

The first lecture in real property law often starts with the announcement that property law is in pretty bad shape, a point echoed in several textbook introductions. 'Property law has a reputation for being a difficult subject.'[33] Indeed, a common feature of critiques of legal education is that the law of real property suffers from being 'dauntingly difficult' and intellectually demanding,[34] a 'tortuous and ungodly jumble'[35] of outdated concepts, rules and vocabulary. Why is property law so regarded? And how is it negotiated? Real property is regarded as a difficult or 'mystifying'[36] subject because its 'notorious complexity'[37] is approached via a strategic deployment of history[38] and anachronistic grammar[39] that makes any conceptual framework or meaning 'elusive.'[40]

In the conventional approach to teaching real property law, the statutes and case law are rarely situated within their socio-economic contexts. Such disconnection means that students learn the 'archaic maxims' as though they were 'mathematical formulae' rather than cultural paradigms.[41] The 'training' of law students to apply existing rules and procedures characterises the doctrinal approach.[42] The twin objectives of this approach are to prepare law students for commercial practice and to satisfy Uniform Admission requirements imposed on University law schools. This approach has neither the time nor the reason to invite students to question the function of property law and its agency in shaping our physical, material reality.

Learning property law by rote is a real risk with conventional approaches to legal education. We learn by rote things that are beyond our capacity to prove or disprove. For example, times tables and the alphabet. These things are beyond reason because they are neither true nor false, they just are. But if real property law is learned by rote, students might not learn to question and understand its rules as having normative significance. The changes and development of property law rules are thereby depicted as 'objective and apolitical'[43] rather than logical or meaningful, which then distances and devalues the historical logic and context from contemporary application. The predominant form of assessing property law is a heavily-weighted exam which generally prioritises problem-solving skills.[44] In preparation for exams, students of property law rote learn the principles from superior court decisions.[45]

Learning real property law is hard under the conventional approach in part because it is divorced from contexts: historical, social and economic, that make sense of what may otherwise seem incoherent collections of statutory provisions and case law. It is taught and assessed in ways that reward the mastery of rules irrespective of their continuing relevance and utility under substantially shifting socio-economic contexts.

B. Real Property Is not about Things

Early in the real property law subject, teachers might feel the need to 'disabuse'[46] students of any 'unreflective and naïve'[47] ideas of property, such as those held by 'ordinary non-lawyers,'[48] that property is a 'thing'. To the contrary, students are informed that the fundamental prerequisite to understanding real property law is to 'un-learn previous notions'[49] that property is about physical things such as land. The pedagogy of property law might thus begin with the explicit disregard of its material conditions. American property law professor Greg Alexander argues that 'many property teachers would probably consider one of the principal objectives of their course to be just this transformation of consciousness.'[50]

Property theory confirms that property law is not about things, not about land – it is about persons, and specifically, about interpersonal relations. This dephysicalised conceptualisation of real property law is common to both doctrinal and critical approaches to teaching the subject. The question for educators is whether the pedagogy and curriculum of property law lead or follow the status quo. Who or what is responsible for the development of property law?

Critical legal educators are concerned about avoiding the unreflective reproduction of the status quo. Their students learn to recognise and evaluate the economic and moral choices made and upheld through property rules. Maureen Cain observes that for lawyers, 'changing the law is not just their job but the most prestigious part of their job.'[51] Critical legal educators view law reform as intellectually and practically available and possible.

Critical property lawyers argue that key social inequalities are established and perpetuated by property laws and the relations it facilitates and protects. 'The institution of private property plays a significant part in preserving material inequalities and legitimating the uneven distribution and use of power in contemporary societies.'[52] Critical property lawyers relate the prevalence of homelessness and poverty, the ongoing dispossession of First Nations and the refusal to recognise Indigenous sovereignty to the ideologies and practices of property law. They juxtapose the dephysicalisation and abstractness of real property law to the physical reality of abundant social injustice.

The dephysicalised model of property law taught in law schools depends on the degree to which land is regarded as an object of property relations or otherwise entirely irrelevant. Teaching students that property law regulates relations between persons with respect to a 'thing' rather than relations between persons and things[53] obscures the fact that the dephysicalisation of property is a culturally and historically specific model of legal relations with regard to land. The efficient distribution and use of land solely as a resource for human interests is a value and a choice that is learned by many law students through the successful completion of real property law.

The dephysicalisation of real property law is mirrored in discussions about appropriate titles for the subject. In law schools today, the subject is increasingly taught as Property Law. 'Law schools which offer land law as a separate course constitute a rapidly dwindling minority.'[54] This development is also apparent in legal publishers' textbook titles and introductions, remarking on the importance of the recent shift. It is a shift partly attributed to the *Uniform Admission Rules* that require knowledge of both real and personal property.[55] This 'comprehensive' subject that delivers both property categories in a single course thus meets 'the demands of legal practice'[56] without increasing the number of compulsory or 'core' subjects in the law program. Mugambwa relates the 'advantages' of this 'switch' to the anachronism of the twin categories of real and personal property laws and the increasing similarities between 'real' and 'personal' property relations. 'What are the possible policy or theoretical reasons for treating land and personal property differently? Are the reasons still justified in this day and age?'[57] Mugambwa accepts that the line between the categories of real and personal property is blurred, as fact. Indeed, he argues that by combining the two categories into a single property law course, their diminishing contradistinction can be better understood and theorised.

> Though the concept of property could (indeed should) be covered in land law, the scope for its discussion is likely to be limited to land-related issues. In property law, on the other hand, the scope for discussion of the concept of property is almost limitless.[58]

If property law is a subject not about 'things' and not directly related to land, then what is it about? It is not in any meaningful sense about a relationship of land to people. The introduction of a form of common law and later statutory title based on precisely such a relationship between people and land, native title, demands of Australian land law students the ability to identify and recognise lawful human-place relations. Concepts of land and place are non-existent in property law education, and 'few students have an understanding of Indigenous concepts of property, relationships and "country."'[59]

Native title continues to challenge the teaching and learning of property law because it is based on the idea that land matters and that there can be a legally significant relationship between people, lands and waters. The following section considers this and various other ways through which the teaching and learning of property law can be transformed so that law graduates have the capability to develop real property law to take account of land and its life-giving function, which is inadequately regulated.

IV. Unlearning Real Property Law: Returning Land to the Centre

Neil Postman and Charles Weingartner's classic monograph, *Teaching as a Subversive Activity*,[60] seeks to provide learners with the things that would help them in the world within which they live. In applying these ideas to subverting the teaching and learning of real property, we are informed by Postman's acknowledgement that a subversive pedagogy is also one that conserves.[61] In this section, we propose a subversive approach to teaching real property law through a series of key changes. First, subversion by conserving the original language of law regulating relations between people and land, as land law, and eschewing the relatively recent shift to referring to the field as real property law. Second, allocating equal significance to skills and content, particularly the skills of critical thinking and interrogation – rather than prioritising content over skills. Third, challenging the taxonomic structure in which real property law is situated as a private law subject. Fourth, conserving and foregrounding the context of land law, including the reasons for its amendment and reform over time.

A. Subverting by Conserving the Nomenclature of Land

Unlearning real property law and the dephysicalised model of property that disentangles human and more than human communities from their lands and waters begins with restoring the idea of land to the subject itself. The conceptual shift from land law to property law associated with the dephysicalisation of property is apparent in the corresponding change to curriculum nomenclature. In law schools today, across the Anglophonic world, the core curriculum subject of land law 'constitutes a rapidly dwindling minority'[62] compared with the increasingly prevalent 'Real Property' or simply 'Property Law'. Legal publishers' textbook titles and introductions remarking on the shift also evidence the acceptance and ubiquity of dephysicalised property. One simple step away from conventional approaches to teaching real property law is, therefore, to rename the subject 'land law'. This might help to reset students' expectations about the content and function of this field of law and enable them to connect it to social and environmental justice in relation to lands and waters.

B. Subverting by Conserving Mastery: Assessing Skills of Critical Thinking and Interrogation

Unlearning real property law depends on the extent to which students are capable of interrogating what they have learned. If they have mastered the subject, they should be sufficiently educated in the skills of critical thinking and interrogation (through reading lists, learning activities and assessment tasks) to question the rules, operation and broader functions of the field. Specifically, law students should be able to observe: the tendency of property law to fragment land into component commodities[63] and to transform human interests in land into disembodied (liquid) interests;[64] the discourse of legal education as facilitative of commercial enterprise;[65] and the centrality of real property law in the ongoing dispossession of Aboriginal and Torres Strait Islander Australians from country and masking unceded sovereignty.[66]

Law students are 'embryonic lawyers',[67] and their education is fundamentally important to the development of law. It is for this reason that Ronnie Warrington argues in his article subtitled 'Is There Any Morality in Blackacre?' that real property or 'land law' teachers have a 'moral responsibility':[68]

> If one thinks that the world can and ought to be improved, and that lawyers have a role to play in fostering the necessary climate which might enable change to be made, and if it is possible to argue that lawyers are uniquely placed in society to help develop 'progressive' changes, then it is incumbent on law teachers to recognise that they ought to perform a role in helping students learn to question.[69]

The ability to question is a technique taught by demonstration as much as encouragement. In addition to asking students questions that require an answer, to varying degrees of correctness in relation to the application of rules, teachers could also ask students to ask questions about the rules. When and why were these rules laid down, and by whom? How do these rules support or frustrate certain property relations?

> Although it may be possible to learn the law relating to mortgages as an abstract body of rules, a coherent understanding of the contemporary significance of these rules requires study of the contexts, policies and practices which influence their operation. Thus, an analysis of the property/power relations between mortgagees and mortgagors might draw upon . . . a comparison of different types of housing tenure, the relationship between housing markets and capital finance markets (including the role of lending institutions), the development of housing policies and the ideology of home ownership.[70]

In 2018, legal educators in England considered the importance for students of real property to develop critical thinking skills and the ability to know which questions to ask, having first mastered the rules. Professor Martin George argued that students need

> to develop the intellectual creativity not to simply accept existing judgments – to consider why a court might be wrong. In many ways, these ideas were not so far divorced from Mark's emphasis on the potential of land law to 'change society and help the oppressed, but you can't win the game unless you know all the rules.'[71]

C. Subverting by Conserving Connections

Challenging the position of real property within its taxonomically determined home in private law is important in enabling students to appreciate the fundamental public law foundations and functions of property. This would prevent students from conceptualising property relations, wrongly, as principally or even exclusively the private concerns of autonomous individuals regarding abstract rights with no material manifestation or consequence beyond the parties to the transaction. In particular, this reframing of real property as both private and public allows law students to see the relevance of the field to non-owners, including the public, First Nations, homeless people and the more-than-human world.

Private property rights exist only through their creation by the state and subsequent recognition and protection through state laws and legal procedures, including public courts and tribunals. In Australia, the Torrens system is contingent on the Assurance Fund, which fundamentally establishes a government guarantee of the allocation, transaction and protection of property rights through the government's system of title by registration established under statute. From a broader perspective, although real property law is classified as private law, the legal rights established under this law are valuable only to the extent that the public consents, or at least does not challenge, their existence. 'Modern property scholarship recognises that property rules should be and are collectively designed to serve broad public values, whether those are framed in terms of efficiency and utility maximisation or a more progressive human flourishing ideal.'[72]

Teachers might introduce students to the and/also instead of the OR of the private/public dichotomy by presenting disputes about the development and continuing application of real property law to reject claims of sovereignty from Aboriginal and Torres Strait Islander Australians. Other options include the interaction of private property rights and constitutional law.[73]

D. Subversion through Conserving and Foregrounding Context

Conventional approaches to teaching real property law tend to isolate statutory provisions and the principles for their interpretation arising from decisions of (usually) superior courts from the contexts in which they exist, including, especially, the important functions that those provisions and judicial principles perform. This is problematic because it prohibits law students' contemplation of those contexts and removes the possibility of them formulating questions about the continued viability, probity and effectiveness of the rules generated by them.

This subversive step involves the careful and selective foregrounding of significant contextual information, including case transcripts, second reading speeches or media coverage of particular amendments, bills and court proceedings. This allows students to situate a legal rule within the broader function of law's agency in constructing certain social, economic, political and legal relations. Unsurprisingly, given the dominance of the dephysicalised model of property, some property rights holders conflate their legal interests in land with capital. Real property law is instrumental to the fluidity of capital by providing certainty for investors' transactions of land and natural resources through, for example, mortgages, leases and transfers of title. While the relationship between real property law and the land market is invisible or presumed, it might teach law students that the dephysicalised model of property, and especially the notion of land as a commodity, is normal and unproblematic. It conceals the more complex function of land and real estate in 'regulatory capitalism.'[74] For example, the distribution and transaction of land and real estate underpin social relations (wealth creation, poverty, housing); political relations (sexually-transmitted debt, dispossession, the influence of property developers, the mining and agricultural sectors); and ecological relations (pastoral leases, mining leases, the interaction of planning law with property, conservation covenants).

Foregrounding the economic context of real property law does not subvert either. However, students would be limited in their capacity to critically evaluate various proposals for statutory reform and judicial developments in relation to their fundamental proximity unless they are adequately educated in the origins and consequences of significant relevant contexts. The subversion is to make it possible for students to join the dots between otherwise isolated points of doctrinal content. The content must be conserved for this contextual analysis to be effective and should be equally valued with the skills development of critical thinking and interrogation.

Rather than teaching Torrens title as an object of study, detached from any material conditions and consequences, this subversion situates us all, owners and non-owners, within the property regime rather than outside it. This can overcome perceptions of distance between self and the object of study, which would otherwise generate cognitive dissonance. 'Judges, practitioners, and even jurists grow so accustomed to (law's) rituals that they do not see how deeply weird they are.'[75] It is subversive to provide and foreground context because it makes it possible for us to ask questions that are otherwise prohibited. These questions, in their asking alone, indicate the importance of the role of real property law in regulating interests in land and natural resources held not only by previous, current and prospective rights holders but also those interests not held as legal rights but as broader interests in the material conditions, limits and consequence of the exercise of those rights.

V. Conclusion

Real property law plays a critical role in shaping the world around us: our economy, our social and political relations and our environment. Legal education contributes to the reproduction of property law through the provision of curricula including both content and skills that have not changed very much over time. Today, law graduates work in changing social, political, economic and environmental contexts and need the capability to respond effectively to these changes by adapting existing legal forms and concepts to new challenges. This is particularly obvious with regard to the challenges of climate change. Subverting conventional approaches to teaching real property law is not compulsory, but it is necessary to the extent that 'institutions that are resistant to change or that change in small increments can operate as barriers to adaptation, especially when transformational shifts are required.'[76] In this chapter, we have: considered the role of real property law in perpetuating the conditions of climate change and social inequality; reviewed conventional approaches to teaching this field of law; and suggested ways through which educators might subvert those conventions. 'If the cradle of legal thought and practice is the law school, then the contribution of legal education . . . is clear.' We have a role to play in 'developing the capacity of future lawmakers to connect and review'[77] the interaction of real property law with the world in which it operates and which, ultimately, it is designed to serve.

Notes

1 Thomas Kuhn, *The Structure of Scientific Revolutions* (3rd edn, Chicago University Press 1996) 76.

2 Lynden Griggs and Rick Snell, 'The Curriculum and Teaching of Property Law in Australian Law Schools' (1997) 5 Australian Property Law Journal 213; Penny Carruthers, Natalie Skead and Kate Galloway, 'Teaching Property Law in Australia in the Twenty-First Century: What We Do Now, What Should We Do in the Future?' (2012) 21(1) Australian Property Law Journal 57; Penny Carruthers, Kate Galloway and Natalie Skead, 'Teaching Property Law in a Changing World: A Longitudinal Study 2011–2019' (2020) 28 Australian Property Law Journal 123.

3 Joseph Sax, 'Environmental Law Forty Years Later: Looking Back and Looking Ahead' in Michael Jeffery, J. Firestone and Karen Bubna-Litic (eds), *Biodiversity Conservation, Law and Livelihoods: Bridging the North-South Divide* (Cambridge University Press 2008) 11.

4 See, eg, Kate Galloway, 'Sustainability in the Real Property Curriculum: Why and How' (2015) 8(2) Journal of Learning Design 31; Allan Ardill, 'Critique in Legal Education: Another Journey' (2016) 26 Legal Education Review 137.

5 Nicole Graham and David Pittavino, 'Bauxite and Boundaries: 50 Years Since *Milirrpum v Nabalco* (1971) 17 FLR 141' (2021) 29(3) Australian Property Law Journal 335-351.

6 See, eg, discussion in George P. Fletcher, 'Comparative Law as a Subversive Discipline' (1998) 46(4) American Journal of Comparative Law 683, 683.

7 Nicole Graham, 'This Is Not a Thing: Land, Sustainability and Legal Education' (2014) 26(3) Journal of Environmental Law 395; Nicole Graham, 'Dephysicalised Property and Shadow Places' in Robyn Bartel and Jennifer Carter (eds), *Handbook of Space, Place and Law* (Edward Elgar 2021).

8 James R. Elkins, 'Professing Law: Does Teaching Matter?' (1986) 31(1) Saint Louis University Law Journal 35, 51.

9 Nicole Graham, 'Property and Environment' in Douglas Richardson and others (eds), *The Wiley-AAG International Encyclopedia of Geography: People, the Earth, Environment, and Technology* (Wiley-Blackwell 2017).

10 Graham, 'Dephysicalised Property and Shadow Places' (n 7).

11 Wesley Newcombe Hohfeld, 'Some Fundamental Legal Conceptions as Applied in Legal Reasoning' (1913) 23 Yale Law Journal 16, 20.

12 Kevin Gray, 'Property in Thin Air' (1991) 50 Cambridge Law Journal 252.

13 Craig Anthony Arnold, 'Sustainable Webs of Interests: Property in an Interconnected Environment' in David Grinlinton and Prue Taylor (eds), *Property Rights and Sustainability: The Evolution of Property Rights to Meet Ecological Challenges* (Martinus Nijhoff 2011).

14 Nicole Graham, *Lawscape: Property, Environment, Law* (Taylor and Francis 2011) 160.

15 See for example, David Grinlinton and Prue Taylor (eds), *Property Rights and Sustainability: The Evolution of Property Rights to Meet Ecological Challenges* (Martinus Nijhoff 2011); Penny Carruthers, Sharon Mascher and Natalie Skead (eds), *Property and Sustainability: Selected Essays* (Thomson Reuters 2011).

16 Graham, *Lawscape: Property, Environment, Law* (n 14) 32–34.

17 Andrew McRae, 'Husbandry Manuals and the Language of Agrarian Improvement' in M. Leslie and T. Raylor (eds), *Culture and Cultivation in Early Modern England: Writing the Land* (Leicester University Press 1992).

18 Onur Ulas Ince, 'Primitive Accumulation, New Enclosures, and Global Land Grabs: A Theoretical Intervention' (2014) 79(1) Rural Sociology 104, 112.

19 Graham, *Lawscape: Property, Environment, Law* (n 14) 51; Henry Jones, 'Property, Territory, and Colonisation: An International Legal History of Enclosure' (2019) 39 Legal Studies 187, 201–202.

20 Estair Van Wagner, 'Notes from the Periphery: Finding More Than (Non)Ownership in Property Law?' in Nicole Graham, Margaret Davies and Lee Godden (eds), *Routledge Handbook of Property, Law and Society* (Routledge 2023) 217.

21 ibid; Libby Porter, Wendy Steele and Wendy Stone, 'Housing and Resilience – When, for Whom and for What? A Critical Agenda' (2018) 35(4) Housing, Theory and Society 387.

22 Nicole Graham, 'Learning Sacrifice: Legal Education in the Anthropocene' in Kirsten Anker and others (eds), *From Environmental to Ecological Law* (Routledge 2020).

23 Dan Priel, 'The Political Origins of English Private Law' (2013) 40(4) Journal of Law and Society 481.

24 Elizabeth Fisher, Eloise Scotford and Emily Barritt, 'The Legally Disruptive Nature of Climate Change' (2017) 80(2) MLR 173.
25 Eric Biber, 'Law in the Anthropocene Epoch' (2017) 106(1) Georgetown Law Journal 1; Sally Wheeler, 'The Corporation and the Anthropocene' in Louis J. Kotzé (ed), *Environmental Law and Governance for the Anthropocene* (Bloomsbury 2017) 289.
26 Jason W. Moore, 'The End of Cheap Nature' in Christian Suter and Christian Chase-Dun (eds), *Structures of the World Political Economy and the Future of Global Conflict and Cooperation* (LIT Verlag 2014); Rosemary Rayfuse, 'The Anthropocene, Autopoiesis and the Disingenuousness of the Genuine Link: Addressing Enforcement Gaps in the Legal Regime for Areas Beyond National Jurisdiction' in Erik J. Molenaar and Alex G. Oude Elferink (eds), *The International Legal Regime of Areas Beyond National Jurisdiction: Current and Future Developments* (Martinus Nijhoff 2010); Louis J. Kotzé, 'Rethinking Global Environmental Law and Governance in the Anthropocene' (2014) 32(2) Journal of Energy and Natural Resources Law 121; Tim Stephens, 'Governing Antarctica in the Anthropocene' in Elizabeth Leane and Jeffrey McGee (eds), *Anthropocene Antarctica: Perspectives from the Humanities, Law and Social Sciences* (Routledge 2019) 17.
27 International Bar Association, 'Climate Crisis Statement' (5 May 2020).
28 Ronnie Warrington, 'Land Law and Legal Education: Is There Any Justice or Morality in Blackacre?' (1984) 18 The Law Teacher: Journal of the Association of Law Teachers 77, 84.
29 For an excellent discussion of the impersonality of law as power see Roberto Unger, *Law in Modern Society* (Free Press 1976) 178–181, 192–203.
30 Griggs and Snell (n 2).
31 Margaret Thornton, 'Portia Lost in the Groves of Academe: Wondering What to Do about Legal Education' (Inaugural Lecture, La Trobe University, 1991).
32 The dichotomous distinction between doctrinal and critical legal education is reductionist and non-comprehensive, but is a familiar one sufficient for the purposes of this chapter.
33 Robert Chambers, *An Introduction to Property Law in Australia* (Law Book Company 2001) 4.
34 Melissa Castan and Jennifer Schultz, 'Teaching Native Title' (1997) 8(1) Legal Education Review 75, 78–79.
35 Frank Bates, 'Like an Unwelcomed Guest: The Moral Crisis in Modern Legal Education' (1984) 18 Law Teacher Journal 182.
36 Anthony O'Donnell and Richard Johnstone, *Developing a Cross-Cultural Law Curriculum* (Cavendish Publishing 1997) 65.
37 G. Alexander, 'Critical Land Law' in S. Bright and J. Dewar (eds), *Land Law: Themes and Perspectives* (OUP 1998) 52.
38 Gregory S. Alexander, 'History as Ideology in the Basic Property Course' (1986) 36(3) Journal of Legal Education 381.
39 Warrington (n 28) 80.
40 Gray, 'Property in Thin Air' (n 12).
41 O'Donnell and Johnstone (n 36) 16.
42 See especially Bates (n 35) 190–193.
43 Alexander, 'History as Ideology in the Basic Property Course' (n 38) 382.
44 Penny Carruthers, Natalie Skead and Kate Galloway, 'Assessment, Skills and Outcomes: The Changing Approaches of Australian Property Law Teachers' (2021) 29(3) Australian Property Law Journal (forthcoming).
45 ibid.
46 ibid.
47 K. Gray and S.F. Gray, 'The Idea of Property in Land' in S. Bright and J. Dewar (eds), *Land Law: Themes and Perspectives* (OUP 1998) 15.

48 Alexander, 'History as Ideology in the Basic Property Course' (n 38) 382.
49 Castan and Schultz (n 34) 79.
50 Alexander, 'History as Ideology in the Basic Property Course' (n 38) 382.
51 Maureen Cain, 'The Symbol Traders' in M. Cain and C. Harrington (eds), *Lawyers in a Postmodern World: Translation and Transgression* (Open University Press 1994); David Sugarman, 'Blurred Boundaries: The Overlapping Worlds of Law, Business and Politics' in M. Cain and C. Harrington (eds), *Lawyers in a Postmodern World: Translation and Transgression* (Open University Press 1994) 19.
52 Ian Grigg-Spall and Paddy Ireland, *The Critical Lawyers Handbook* (Pluto Press 1992) 90.
53 See, eg, Harold Demsetz, 'Toward a Theory of Property Rights' (1967) 57 American Economic Review 347.
54 John Mugambwa, 'From Teaching the Law of Real Property to Teaching Property Law in Australasian Law Schools' (1997) 4 James Cook University Law Review 1, 2.
55 ibid.
56 Thornton (n 31).
57 Mugambwa (n 54) 4.
58 ibid 6.
59 Castan and Schultz (n 34) 81.
60 Neil Postman and Charles Weingartner, *Teaching as a Subversive Activity* (Delta 1969).
61 Neil Postman, *Teaching as a Conserving Activity* (Delacorte Press 1979).
62 Mugambwa (n 54) 2.
63 Kate Galloway, 'Landowners' vs Miners' Property Interests: The Unsustainability of Property as Dominion' (2012) 37(2) Alternative Law Journal 77.
64 Sarah Keenan, 'From Historical Chains to Derivative Futures: Title Registries as Time Machines' (2019) 20(3) Social and Cultural Geography 283.
65 Graham, 'Learning Sacrifice: Legal Education in the Anthropocene' (n 22); Graham, 'This Is Not a Thing: Land, Sustainability and Legal Education' (n 7).
66 Nicole Graham, 'Indigenous Property Matters in Real Property Courses at Australian Universities' (2009) 19(1–2) Legal Education Review 289.
67 Warrington (n 28) 86.
68 ibid 87.
69 ibid.
70 Grigg-Spall and Ireland (n 52) 95–96.
71 Emily Carroll, 'Re-Imagining the Teaching of Land Law' (CEPLER Working Paper Series, 03/2018) <http://epapers.bham.ac.uk/3116/>.
72 Nicole Graham and Jessica A Shoemaker, 'Property Rights and Power across Rural Landscapes' in Nicole Graham, Margaret Davies and Lee Godden (eds), *The Routledge Handbook of Property, Law and Society* (Routledge 2023) 428.
73 Nicole Graham, 'The ALRC Freedoms Inquiry, Real Property and Environmental Law' (2017) 31(10) Australian Environment Review 364.
74 John Braithwaite, *Regulatory Capitalism: How It Works, Ideas for Making It Work Better* (Edward Elgar 2008).
75 Bernard Rudden, 'Things as Things and Things as Wealth' (1994) 14(1) Oxford Journal of Legal Studies 81.
76 Jan McDonald, 'Mapping the Legal Landscape of Climate Change Adaptation' in Bonhady, Macintosh and McDonald (eds), *Adaptation to Climate Change: Law and Policy* (Federation Press 2010) 11.
77 Graham, 'This is Not a Thing: Land, Sustainability and Legal Education' (n 7) 422.

12 The Place of Politics in Teaching International Law

Dorothea Anthony

I. Introduction

Law and politics have a particularly close relationship, not least in the field of international law, which concerns standards collectively developed by nations with often contrasting visions for a global order. In consideration of this relationship, educators may wish to assume responsibility for guiding students towards an interpretation of the greater political significance of international law. However, there exists an array of approaches to this task, and some of these approaches, if not the very undertaking of uncovering the true colours of international law, could potentially be characterised as subversive.

When trying to negotiate the vast political context of international law, students can themselves feel a tendency towards subversion. In my experience teaching international law, it is therefore not uncommon for students to seek advice on where the dividing line is between law and politics. Sometimes they are concerned that politics may interfere with their doctrinal discussion of the law, which they prefer to keep neutral. Other times students wish to be aware of their greater responsibility in accounting for the political underpinnings of the law. And occasionally, they are simply trying to understand what to do with their urge to delve deeper into the inviting political side of a problem rather than the apparently more pedestrian legal side. As a student of mine once wrote, in reflecting on his performance in class:

> There is one area I would like to improve on. I sometimes find it difficult in international law to discuss matters by strictly sticking with issues relating to legality rather than politics. I find that I often back up my arguments using historical facts or social policy considerations rather than the relevant international law (e.g. treaties).[1]

Arguably, the best way to respond to such concern is to encourage students to give attention to the political—but also the economic, social, cultural, and historical—dimensions of international law in emphasising that these features are intrinsic to the law. As long as the primary subject matter of their study remains the law, students can be assured that their analysis of this social setting for international

DOI: 10.4324/9781003175216-15

law will give rise to a rich understanding of the law and make a material academic contribution, and perhaps even have a social impact.

Some prominent academics have expressed caution. Jan Klabbers believes that academia on international law is at risk of being subsumed by politics: 'Interdisciplinary scholarship, in a word, is about power, and when it comes to links between international legal scholarship and international relations scholarship, the power balance tilts strongly in favour of the latter.'[2] David Kennedy is concerned that the marriage is hampered by the inherited 'blind spots and biases' that each discipline brings.[3] However, the matter for students need not be one of competition between the disciplines or of what the disciplines do not, rather than do, contribute. It is vital to broaden students' horizons and provide them with more tools, not take them away, so as to set them up for success academically and professionally. As Tanja Aalberts writes, 'reaching beyond one's discipline' is akin to applying '3D glasses' in opening up a whole new perspective.[4]

Students might be instructed that it is not only accepted but also expected that they acknowledge political dimensions in their international legal study and thereby explore the practical implications of legal conclusions. In this regard, they may be advised against adopting a view that they figure is purely legal and self-sufficient and justifiable on its own terms, lest the position has unsavoury political ramifications that they would be unable or unwilling to defend. As a Professor at the University of Indonesia succinctly states, 'international law does not stand alone'; its rule-based teachings should be supplemented with the development of political awareness.[5]

This position brings welcome relief to students interested in being challenged in new ways and who would like the content of their study to be more multi-dimensional and socially meaningful. It can also relieve the conscience of academics—namely, those who feel that we have 'given up too much of ourselves' by adopting a so-called 'strategy of concession' in the classroom, which, in contrast to a 'strategy of challenge', focuses on the minutiae of practical legal issues at the expense of broader issues surrounding the law.[6]

Yet how law teachers might convey a sense of the political context and its interaction with the law is a complex matter, particularly if they are to play an impartial role. Needless to say, they ought not to present a personal political position or concentrate on a particular type of politics as though no others exist. Such an approach could be contrary to professional standards. Instead, from the perspective of a bird's eye, they should carefully explain the different ways in which politics is relevant to the development and operation of a variety of international laws, as well as scholarship on international law.

This chapter presents a framework for such an exercise. It outlines three chief ways in which politics can inform international law and therefore shape one's teaching of the law. One way is at a basic level through the influence of everyday politics. A second way is at a deeper level with the impact of imperialist structures on international law. A third way is at an even more fundamental level involving the manner in which class interests within these structures find expression in the law. In addition, the chapter refers to the compulsory international law subject at the University of New South Wales, 'Law in the Global Context', designed by colleagues who have enlivened international law pedagogy with the first form of politics and inspired me to contemplate the latter two.

II. International Law and Everyday Politics

First, everyday politics plays a particularly visible role in international law. It includes current affairs and the day-to-day activities and pursuits of governments and political parties. It covers high-level political interactions in the form of international relations, as well as politics on the ground in the form of social movements. These various modes of politics find their way into international forums and governing bodies, whose work represents a rich microcosm of the most prominent concerns of the day, albeit not always in proportion to the actual importance of matters.

At this simple level of political influence, there is a direct relationship between, for example, a border war in the news headlines and a territorial dispute on the docket of the International Court of Justice (ICJ), which is the principal court of the United Nations (UN). One can often trace the line of political events that has led to an international legal case and identify points at which legal argumentation in the case amounts to 'political manoeuvring' in support of a State's foreign policy objectives.[7]

Philip Jessup, whose name graces an international law moot court competition, observes that, in contrast to tumultuous political developments, international law is the rational element in providing a framework 'for the orderly management of international relations'.[8] Similarly, AA Fatouros sees politics simply as a governing process for the debate and technical drafting of laws.[9] However, others believe that the politics of everyday life is manifestly intertwined with the law and influences its very framework. Shirley Scott remarks that 'international law is a part of international politics in a way that is not true vice versa', such that there can never be 'an ultimate set of rules appropriate for ever more' that is untouched by dynamic political developments.[10]

As suggested, everyday politics is the most prominent type of politics in Law in the Global Context. This subject is structured around recent international events, including Japanese whaling in the Southern Ocean, newsworthy cases of international parental child abduction, and developments in the plight of controversial figure Julian Assange. The readings include academic texts that draw on such events. Students are encouraged to follow the events in the media as they unfold and to pay attention more generally to what is happening in the world. One student developed such a good habit that within seconds of Assange leaving the Ecuadorian Embassy, where the activist received refuge for almost seven years, the student informed me of the news—several years after attending my class on diplomatic asylum.

A. Everyday Politics and Nations

The political angle of an international law course may be particularly engaging for students where it involves the strategic concerns of their domestic jurisdiction.

Hence, in Law in the Global Context, all the case studies are anchored in some way to Australian law and politics, although students are also encouraged to explore the international legal positions of their other respective countries of origin.

A useful resource for making the connection between everyday Australian politics and international law is the book *Australia as a Good International Citizen* by Alison Pert. In this cleverly conceived book, Pert looks at how changes in the political composition of the federal government over the years have affected Australia's involvement in international law. She documents how Labor governments since World War II have often been keener than Liberal governments to participate in international organisations, subscribe to treaties, implement treaties through the external affairs power of the Constitution, and consent to international adjudication.[11]

A similar trend can be noted in relation to the United States (US), which is another jurisdiction of interest to students. The former Trump administration, with its 'America First' policy, provides a good illustration of how political conservatism can mean more unilateral and less multilateral activity—at least among organisations such as the UN, as opposed to, say, the North Atlantic Treaty Organization (NATO) or International Monetary Fund (IMF).

Under President Trump, a purported 'gravedigger of international law',[12] the US renounced treaties, including the Paris Agreement on climate change, the Iran nuclear deal, the Intermediate-Range Nuclear Forces Treaty, the Treaty on Open Skies, the Universal Postal Treaties, the Trans-Pacific Partnership Agreement, and an Optional Protocol to the Vienna Convention on Diplomatic Relations that provides recourse to the ICJ. It withdrew from international organisations, including the United Nations Educational, Scientific and Cultural Organization; the Human Rights Council; the Universal Postal Union; and the World Health Organization. It obstructed and threatened to leave the World Trade Organization (WTO). It reduced or terminated funding to international organisations, including the Organization of American States and a Palestinian refugee agency, while supporting causes contrary to them, including Israeli occupation. In addition, the former President issued an executive order designating the International Criminal Court (ICC) as a security threat and imposing sanctions on some of its personnel after the ICC initiated an investigation into alleged US war crimes in Afghanistan.

The United Kingdom (UK) serves as a further example, with the conservative Tory government removing the UK from the European Union (EU). At the extreme end, Nazi Germany withdrew from the League of Nations in 1933. This is not to say that reactionary governments will always withdraw their nation from the international stage, especially where participation in a particular alliance serves a purpose, such as reinforcing the State's power.[13] However, as Martti Koskenniemi maintains, they may see involvement in multilateral organisations as a sign of weakness and a legitimisation of the institutions.[14] Thus, the relationship between the everyday politics of the State and its activity (or lack thereof) in the international legal arena is appreciable.

B. Everyday Politics and International Organisations

At the same time, the politics of States that make up an international organisation contributes to the politics of such an organisation. Moreover, the political composition of the international sphere can influence the politics of States. The Soviet Union and other socialist countries came under pressure from the outside world to change their human rights program and, by extension, their economic model and way of life. Their shift to capitalism, in turn, influenced the international organisations of which they were a member.

Indeed, it has been documented that the UN General Assembly and human rights bodies have moved several steps to the right of politics since their reformist period of the 1960s and 1970s and the end of the Cold War.[15] The UN Security Council has no doubt entered more conservative political territory with the demise of socialism that shaped the societies of two of its veto-holders. Perhaps a political pattern on the ICJ can also be identified, or does the interplay of political and legal opinion not always have predictable outcomes in the court?[16]

An ICJ case to ponder in this regard, introduced in Law in the Global Context, is *Questions relating to the Seizure and Detention of Certain Documents and Data*, decided in 2014.[17] It was brought by Timor-Leste (East Timor) against Australia after Australian secret agents seized and detained documents and other property from an office of one of East Timor's lawyers in the Australian Capital Territory. The seized material contained information on the pending international arbitration between the countries concerning the Timor Sea Treaty. This treaty initially gave Australia significantly more than its fair share of lucrative oil and gas reserves in the Timor Sea and was negotiated after Australia planted listening devices in an East Timorese parliamentary office to gain an advantage.

The ICJ ordered Australia to: (1) not use the seized material to the disadvantage of East Timor; (2) keep it under seal; and (3) not interfere in current communications between East Timor and its legal advisers and future negotiations between the States on maritime delimitation or other matters. The ad hoc judge from Australia, Ian Callinan, who was appointed to the ICJ hearing by then-Attorney-General George Brandis, who had authorised the raid on the lawyer's office, dissented on all three points. The judges from New Zealand, the UK, and the US, which are parties to the 'Five Eyes' intelligence alliance of the UK–USA Agreement, dissented on the first two points.

The position of the Anglophone nations was to be expected. But notably, the ICJ majority did not require Australia to return the seized material to East Timor, which had been at the mercy of its powerful neighbour. While the court did not accept Judge Callinan's curious argument that 'free nations' must defend against terrorism,[18] it also could not identify with Judge Cançado Trindade of Brazil, who urged the court to take a more decisive position on the case whose 'factual context . . . may well cross the threshold of human imagination'.[19] So, there is room for debate as to where the case situates the ICJ politically, as well as how Australia's involvement with the ICJ shows the country's political leanings.

C. Further Considerations

Another point of entry for the discussion of everyday politics is diplomatic relations. The US provides stark examples of diplomatic interventions that reveal immediate political motivations. For instance, over the last few years, US authorities have seized a diplomatic bag from a North Korean diplomat attending a UN conference in New York, denied an Iranian Foreign Minister a visa to enter the US to attend a Security Council meeting, and actively encouraged States to withdraw their diplomatic embassies from countries towards which the US is hostile. At the same time, the US has sought to expand its own diplomatic presence by, for example, forming an agreement that would allow McDonald's stores in Austria to provide basic consular assistance, in keeping with efforts by the US to advance its monopolies.

Furthermore, students can learn to appreciate how the political activity of ordinary people or social movements may come to have a place in international law. One moment Greta Thunberg was sitting outside the Swedish parliament in protest against government inaction on climate change, and the next, she was speaking to the UN in an attempt to influence the direction of future environmental rules. She was not the first young person to address the UN on the environment—David Suzuki's daughter led the way some decades earlier. Nonetheless, she demonstrated for us the lively relationship between everyday political actions and international law that one can find many engaging examples of to highlight in the classroom.

III. International Law and the Politics of Imperialism

The second way international law relates to politics is through the general influence of global power structures or imperialist arrangements. Students can appreciate why particular international laws and theories are the way they are at different historical stages through an awareness of these geopolitics.

In her international law textbook, Gillian Triggs, now an Assistant Secretary-General of the UN, writes: 'It is broadly true that traditionally, customary international law was developed by a few Western states with special interests'.[20] We can assume that these States were the European colonisers who established customs for carving up the world and its wealth and managing the disputes that inevitably arose between them. Triggs goes on to say that with developing States now dominating the General Assembly, international law has become 'a more genuinely international' species of law.[21]

This position occupies a middle ground. It sits between a view that modern international law arrived more or less 'fully formed', without representing inherent biases of its colonial past,[22] and a view that the monopolisation by Western States of international law did not end with the decline of the colonial era, but instead persists under current forms of imperialism—that is, forms of domination by stronger States over weaker ones, occurring not simply through physical might but by economic means.[23]

The latter perspective is adopted by various schools of thought, including Third World Approaches to International Law (TWAIL), which maintains that imperialist ideology pervades international law in pervading society more generally. A pioneer of the TWAIL movement, BS Chimni, states, 'capitalism cannot *not* be imperialistic',[24] with people of the Third World fated to have been wronged and alienated by the First World, just as sections of the First World are ineluctably marginalised.[25] Another central figure, Antony Anghie, suggests that international law accordingly 'permits' and even 'endorses and adopts' practices that bear the hallmarks of imperialism.[26] Certainly, while international law may no longer accept as it once did that one country can acquire title to another country's territory through conquest,[27] it allows interventions of various kinds, explicitly and implicitly.

The rationale behind teaching international law in connection with the politics of imperialism is to help students recognise where there may be tendencies in the law that serve to create and maintain an inequitable distribution of power and resources globally. Where students are inclined to question this state of affairs, they may go on to strategise legal responses to such imperialist mechanisms.

Initially, however, this way of seeing international law can be introduced to students with reference to particular countries that are objects or subjects of subjugation, international organisations that are imperialist or anti-imperialist in their orientation, and disciplines of international law that have played a noticeable role in perpetuating imperialist relations. I now provide examples of these three areas.

A. Imperialism and Nations

Regarding imperialist countries, the US, which has extensive ownership of transnational capital, continues to be an exemplar of international domination. Yet commonly, commentators discuss the international legal role of the US merely at the level of everyday politics. They refer to the 'Machiavellian power politics' of the likes of Henry Kissinger in the international halls of power[28] and the history of conservatives on the US Senate blocking the ratification of key treaties such as the UN Convention on the Law of the Sea (UNCLOS)—developments that have supposedly presented an obstacle to multilateralism.[29] They see the conduct of the US on the international stage mainly as a 'result of domestic politics'.[30] However, while these politics are important to consider, students are entitled to a deeper explanation.

General connections can be drawn between the power a country such as the US asserts economically in the world and the power it asserts politically in the international legal context. Power is not in itself problematic if the body in power is virtuous. Therefore, it is necessary to delineate a relationship between the type of economic power and the type of political power in question. If the economic power has been derived by dominant nations at the expense of weaker ones, then it is to be expected that the former States will promote their interests disproportionately in international forums. While the US and the Soviet Union both enjoyed economic strength, it is the US whose economic power has been exploitative and whose political contribution has thus been known to be directed towards self-interest—for example, where it famously opposed the concept of communal ownership under UNCLOS.

There is also the case of Australia. While a keen supporter of US imperialism, it is an imperialist country in its own right, or what some call a sub-imperial power. Australia has a history of imperialist pretensions to neighbouring territories in the Pacific region, including Nauru and New Guinea, which it administered through much of the 1900s. Cait Storr explains that Australia's attempts at empire-building in this part of the world, in fact, motivated its move towards federation and its establishment of an international legal personality.[31] Clinton Fernandes documents ongoing imperialist tendencies in Australia's policies towards its regional neighbours, which he notes are directed at creating favourable conditions for Australian business.[32]

Accordingly, when teaching the abovementioned ICJ case concerning East Timor, the discussion may extend beyond the everyday politics of an Australian government that uses underhanded tactics in its negotiations with an impoverished nation. The educator can invite perspectives from the class on how Australia's conduct in the matter more generally reflects an imperialist posture towards Pacific nations. Similarly, it is worthwhile referring in the lesson to Australia's controversial submissions to the ICJ's advisory proceedings on Palestine and the Chagos Archipelago and whether they reveal support for the masters of these territories—Israel and the UK, respectively—over the oppressed subjects. In this connection, students may wish to consider how it is possible to distinguish between Australia's specific legal argumentation and its broader political purpose.[33]

B. Imperialism and International Organisations

On the question of international organisations, it is useful to consider the extent to which they are being used by imperialist powers to pursue political objectives. Educators can turn their attention to the League of Nations, whose establishment consolidated the achievements of the victorious European powers at the time, much to the chagrin of Germany, and which purportedly used undemocratic methods to expel the major opponent of imperialism, the Soviet Union.

Its successor, the UN, developed into a more politically complex organisation, particularly in accompanying the movement towards decolonisation. However, while Triggs mentions the diversity of the General Assembly, it is clear that Western States have predominated on the Security Council, which decides essential matters of war and peace. Although the UN is officially founded on pacific principles, its Security Council authorised the use of force on North Korea (1950) when the Soviet Union was absent in protest over Taiwan holding China's seat on the Security Council and permitted such war to take place under the command of the US.[34] It authorised the use of force in various territories following the dissolution of the Soviet Union, including Iraq (1990; 2002)[35] and the former Yugoslavia (1992),[36] in which the US and NATO played a major role, and it continues to impose sanctions in line with US policy.

US imperialism conspicuously rears its head among two UN specialised agencies—the IMF and the World Bank—in which the US has the greatest share of voting power and is the only State with veto power. These Bretton Woods institutions, which may perplex students expecting to encounter a more economically agnostic UN, have thus been referred to as 'branches of Wall Street'.[37] While they have made a point of establishing development programs, they commonly impose conditions on developing countries in accordance with market-oriented economic policies, which could be deemed anti-developmental.

The primary forum in which European imperialist interests are satisfied is the EU. Influenced by the mainstream press, students often come to class supportive of the EU and critical of the UK's withdrawal from the Treaty of the European Union. They are aware that the secession of the UK was largely motivated by populist sentiments against immigration and regional cooperation and integration.

Yet it should be questioned, at the level of the politics of imperialism, whether the EU is a genuinely cooperative body that represents the interests of all European States, and not principally the dominant ones, and acts equitably towards States outside the bloc. Students may be directed to the EU's one-sided trade agreements with underdeveloped countries in Africa, the Caribbean, and the Pacific and its migration schemes that drain professional workers from developing regions.[38] Dennis Canterbury has observed in relation to such initiatives: 'There is hardly any territory left for EU bloc imperialism to conquer'.[39] Peo Hansen and Stefan Jonsson similarly report that one reason why the EU's predecessor, the European Economic Community, was founded was to facilitate an orderly sharing of the European management of Africa.[40] Further, when it comes to the treatment of its own people, the EU and its European Central Bank have joined the IMF in imposing austerity measures on European countries in economic distress, which effectively deprives already-deprived people. The EU has been unwilling to entertain an alternative approach that prioritises people's needs over business interests, evidenced by its unequivocal critique of Eastern Europe's socialist past.[41]

But not all international organisations have an imperialist character. It may help students to grasp this point by comparing international organisations that are concerned with the same subject matter but are politically distinct, such as NATO and the World Peace Council. NATO, established in 1949, is a political and military alliance of North American and European countries, which has been involved in various imperialist wars. Its founding treaty permits the use of armed force by any member of the alliance in defence of any other member.[42] In contrast, the World Peace Council, established in 1949–1950 under the auspices of the Soviet Union, is an anti-imperialist international peace organisation. Although less well-known and influential than NATO, it campaigns for global disarmament and calls on NATO and belligerent States to respect the sovereignty of nations and not interfere in their internal affairs.

Another challenge to imperialism is the manifestation of inter-imperialist rivalry between States such as the US and China—with China now inclined to imperialist conduct given its shift towards a capitalist economy in recent decades. UN Secretary-General António Guterres describes these States as 'creating two competing worlds'.[43] Their competition means that they sometimes clash in their drive for markets, as with recent trade disputes and tensions on the major trading route of the South China Sea. With international forums such as the WTO and Permanent Court of Arbitration engaged in resolving such disputes, international law is a significant site of inter-imperialist rivalry.

C. Imperialism and International Legal Disciplines

Educators may explain to students that entire disciplines of international law have developed from this form of rivalry and its consequences and from imperialist subjugation in general, including the international law of war, international humanitarian law, and international refugee law. As colonialists and imperialists extended their rule geographically, international territorial law, international law of the sea, international aviation law, and space law emerged. Even the ostensibly harmless area of international human rights law may be associated with imperialism, where States intervene by force in purportedly illiberal societies in the name of democratic rights or where peoples subjected to such intervention seek to defend their right to self-determination.

International investment law also reflects imperialist interests. Kate Miles explains how it has historically consisted of 'unequal' or 'capitulation' treaties that granted 'nonreciprocal rights' to imperialist powers that defended the terms by force.[44] She notes that while investment treaties are no longer accompanied by the gunboat diplomacy of colonial times, they still have 'systematic "investor bias"' in permitting business enterprise, such as mining operations, of capital-exporting States to have a devastating social and environmental impact on local communities without being properly accountable.[45] The world of international investment, she says, remains 'unresponsive' to negative externalities as companies operate under the aegis of international and national law and have an increasing influence on this legal apparatus through 'commercial diplomacy'.[46]

While international laws concerning business thrive under the banner of free trade, less profitable areas, such as tackling climate change, struggle. The Paris Agreement and related treaties are lauded by some but regarded as weak instruments of temporary compromise by others. Supposedly, not only are their goals timid, they reduce pollution to its atmospheric impact, as distinct from its immediate effect on people's natural environment and health. The only carbon-negative country in the world—Bhutan—still grapples with extensive pollution on the ground. Yet multinational companies such as BHP Group Ltd, which infamously caused severe environmental contamination from mining waste at Ok Tedi in Papua New Guinea under an investment agreement, and States continuing to build up arms, which are undoubtedly destructive to the environment, boast of their achievements in reducing carbon emissions. Regardless of the efforts of young Greta Thunberg in the sphere of everyday politics, imperialist interests appear, in the greater scheme of things, to stifle international progress on the environment.

IV. International Law and the Politics of Class Structure

Finally, there is a third and even more fundamental way in which politics bears influence on international law. Identifying it may be considered subversive by those who believe that it captures social dynamics that are so elemental that a careful rearrangement of it would upend the foundations of international law and, indeed, any social or legal institution. The phenomenon to which I refer is the politics of social class.

The politics of imperialism, while constituting a necessary step in our understanding of international law, has its limits. Although it is instructive to address imperialist struggles between West and East, or North and South, or West and West, and so on, there is also an essential battle *within* the category of West—that of different classes—and now within most countries globally. Indeed, when the West colonised the world, one of the most significant Western traditions that it imported was the division of society into classes.

Students, especially those with Indigenous heritage, can be asked whether Indigenous peoples had a concept of class distinction before the colonisation of Australia. Based on archaeological and anthropological evidence, it appears that in emphasising collective ownership of land and production instead of individual accumulation of property to the detriment of others, Indigenous society did not have relations of domination and subordination.[47] Only when British colonisers arrived did the Indigenous people come to know a class-based method of organising society, having been cast into the lower social strata and often made to work for little or no wage. Their new class status was exacerbated by their new minority status, which was also a product of colonisation.

The concept of class should be explained to students rather than taken as assumed knowledge, as it is a technical area of study within the field of political economy. In simple terms, there are two main classes: the class that owns society's wealth and the class that does not. More specifically, these classes are distinguished in terms of their relationship to production.[48] In capitalism, the owners of production occupy the capitalist class, and the workers, who produce the commodities through labour that is purchased at a profit by the owners, make up the working class. Those who lie between these categories or do not have a direct relationship to production and may express differing sympathies towards the two classes, such as lawyers who act for or against trade unions, tend to constitute the middle class.

This class structure is naturally imbalanced and therefore antagonistic,[49] but it is respected by governments that focus their attention on the owners of production, who are seen as the driving force of the capitalist economy. One example is where the Papua New Guinean government criminalised compensation claims against BHP for its environmental contamination so as not to discourage investment in the country.[50] Another is where Western governments have created legal barriers to their corporations being sued by foreign claimants on Western soil, leaving victims of industrial pollution in a state of legal uncertainty.[51] Thus, the owners of production possess de facto authority and are often referred to as the ruling class. So, when diplomats representing the world's 193 members of the UN converge on this international organisation, they take an implicit class position in embodying select interests to a significant extent.

What does this mean for international law? It means that, give or take differences between the Labor and Liberal parties of the world and their relative forms of influence, international law is heading in a certain direction overall. Pert herself recognises this tendency towards homogeneity in which 'the foreign policies of the parties (at least until Howard) have had more similarities than distinctions'.[52] For instance, both the Labor and Liberal parties refused for a time to abrogate the maritime delimitation treaty with East Timor that Australia allegedly negotiated in bad faith. While governments change and the dynamic between the classes in society shifts, the ruling class stays the same and continues to exert significant influence on government and its construction of the law in one way or another. Hence, it may be useful to conceive of national and international law through the ages 'as an instrument of the state, and the state as an instrument of a dominant economic class'.[53]

A. Some Historical Appreciation of Class

The world's first socialist society, which came to be called the Soviet Union, perceived international law as an instrument of the capitalist State and its dominant capitalist class.[54] It entered the post-war phases of international law cautiously, as it saw that this domain of law was already formed in the image of the West by the time of the advent of socialism and then the victory over fascism. The Soviet Union approached international law as an outsider, at least in the beginning. It won some favour but eventually succumbed to pressure to relinquish its class position.

China has shown a similar pattern of broadening its class outlook. In his paper expressing a Chinese perspective, penned in the 1980s, shortly after China started experimenting with a market economy, Chen Tiqiang argues that while national laws represent State and hence class interests, international laws have a less clear class basis.[55] He contends that because different capitalist classes of different States can compete with one another, they too may be at odds on basic questions of law; that socialist States often found points of coincidence with capitalist States of the Third World; and that certain rules originating in a bourgeois context could serve working-class interests in another context.[56]

However, while the writer has an optimistic view of the capacity for international law to attend to the concerns of multiple types of societies and classes, he acknowledges obstacles. One is that the class interests of capitalist countries often give rise to nationalist sentiments, which are antithetical to international objectives. Tiqiang notes that, in contradistinction, working-class morality aligns with 'proletarian internationalism', which looks to advance the interests of the working class across the world.[57] He suggests that States should therefore be selective with international laws that do not represent appropriate values. As such, internationalist-leaning countries in a capitalist-oriented world may ironically have become some of the more outspoken proponents of national sovereignty in guarding their progressive outlook.[58]

As with a number of States, China has perceived human rights as a particularly ideologically laden area of international law that can serve as a pretext for intervention in its affairs.[59] Purportedly, human rights are used to criticise even those societies that have liberated workers from exploitation under capitalism and serfs from the former system of feudalism, as with China's efforts regarding over one million Tibetans in 1959.[60] In other words, human rights can be deployed to undermine social systems that do away with classes, while legitimising Western societies that deliberately maintain class distinctions. This viewpoint turns human rights on its head, which can be a revelation to students who have become accustomed to using human rights as their main language of social justice across their law subjects, particularly where they have not been taught other methods, including class analysis.

B. Increased Inattention to Class

Representations of human rights that reinforce class-based society appear to be increasingly conspicuous in international law and discourse. Even where the rhetoric of the indivisibility or equal significance of different rights is employed, the human rights that tend to be most celebrated are those that have the most affinity with the owners of wealth—that is, civil and political rights, including the right to the ownership and protection of private property.[61] In former times when there was an Eastern bloc, which eschewed classes, more emphasis was placed on economic, social, and cultural rights. These rights were of greater relevance to socialist society, which sought to liberate people from their economic shackles. However, even they have been framed in a manner convenient to the West and so cannot necessarily be said to have had a dramatic impact on the situation of underprivileged people in the class system.

Where rights other than civil and political rights *are* celebrated today, there is often an emphasis on commercial interests attached to them. One commonly hears business cases put forward to justify the provision of workers' rights and environmental rights. For instance, there is the case that responding to modern slavery is good for business because it improves brand reputation, leading to increased sales and profit. Another case is that combatting climate change is good for business because it creates opportunities to invest in green energy and engage in emissions trading; in other words, it generates new avenues for profit, enabling the expansion of capitalist enterprise.

Therefore, the interests of workers in not being exploited or enjoying a healthy environment is not always the most prominent message because it is business that is at the helm of a class-based economy. Supposedly, we should aim to satisfy the interests of every class, not least the one that is causing the problem, even though this position is counter-intuitive and appears to take the human element out of human rights. International laws and policies, such as the United Nations Global Compact for corporate participants, are increasingly designed to get businesses voluntarily on board the human rights train rather than respond singularly and directly and necessarily to the needs of the people. Thus, these legal developments are not typically game-changing.

C. A Case for More Class Awareness

The advantages of an approach that is instead centred on the working class and popular strata are enumerated at the conclusion of Chimni's article 'Prolegomena to a Class Approach to International Law'.[62] Chimni writes that this approach enables international lawyers to understand international laws and institutions within their historical and societal context, helps the legal profession identify who the 'principal beneficiaries' of 'international legal regimes' are, 'clarifies the limits of international human rights law', explains how oppressed people may be estranged from international law, showcases their 'narratives of resistance', provides a nuanced picture of the role of social movements and civil society organisations, and encourages us to rethink liberal conceptions underpinning international law.[63]

One may add that a class approach consists of a compassionate methodology for studying the law, as it directs students to the needs and interests of the lower echelons of society. Further, it may inspire students to seek higher standards for disadvantaged people than those traditionally found in international law. Proponents of class analysis would be expected to discountenance, for instance, the international goal of achieving 'core minimum levels' of human rights, as this initiative does not seek to lift the position of oppressed people beyond the class structure. According to a class perspective, people deserve more than the bare minimum, particularly where some enjoy virtually no limits.[64]

The reader may see that employing the concept of class in relation to international law is challenging for students and teachers alike who are unfamiliar with its intellectual history and usage. But not acknowledging it does not mean that it will cease to exist. Class distinctions will continue to affect the ability of international law to make progress and deliver concrete outcomes. Students will remain frustrated by an international legal regime that reproduces hollow aspirations such as the Sustainable Development Goals, which are a rebranding of the failed Millennium Development Goals and have limited connection to the tangible, class-based issues of people's lived experience. An awareness of these issues can help provide a realistic perspective on the law. And just maybe, rather than learning to accept 'the unsettling facts of international life'[65] and patterns of regression in international law,[66] students can begin to look forward to a more prosperous international law of a time when there is movement beyond a class-divided world.

V. Conclusion

In conclusion, in order to enrich the pedagogy of international law, students may be directed to the basic interconnections between law and politics. Different types of politics can be entertained in the international law classroom, from everyday politics to the politics of imperialism to the politics of class. They co-exist and overlap. More essentially, they ascend in complexity—not simply the type of intellectual complexity found in Bloom's taxonomy of learning,[67] but ideological complexity with the politics of class at the pinnacle. Although seldom addressed in international legal scholarship and teaching and wanting in explication as a teaching tool, class illuminates international legal analysis in epitomising relations between people.

Teaching the three forms of politics should complement rather than overshadow the law. The political perspectives can be raised at the stage of introducing international laws to students, when the educator is framing the laws within a historical and political context, and at any stage thereafter, when preparing students to analyse the broader significance of the laws. They should be broached intentionally, keeping in mind Chimni's observation that 'critical approaches' are often a mere add-on in international law courses that focus on 'mainstream discourse',[68] although the educator ought to strive to be an impartial conduit of critical ideas as opposed to a critic per se. In any event, once seeds of thought are planted in the minds of students, it is the case that every now and then those seeds will start to grow on their own.

Finally, it is hoped that by being exposed to ideas from this chapter, students will develop a materialist understanding of the international legal order and global governance. They should come to the realisation that international law is not an ideal haven from all bad things in society; it is part of the real world. If there is imperialism and a class structure in the world, international law will probably reflect and defend this state of affairs. If there is a movement against imperialism and class division, international law will likewise hold up a mirror to this reality.

International law is not a 'self-contained', 'static', 'comprehensive', 'neutral', 'objective', and 'universal' set of principles.[69] One might therefore advise students not to look to it for all the solutions but rather to see it as a crystallisation of where the world sits on the political spectrum at any point in time.[70] International law and not least international human rights law make many grand statements about being above politics.[71] Law teachers can potentially bring balance to this discussion.

Notes

1 The quotation is extracted, with the permission of the student author, from a self-reflection undertaken for the subject Law in the Global Context at the Faculty of Law, University of NSW (2018).
2 Jan Klabbers, 'The Bridge Crack'd: A Critical Look at Interdisciplinary Relations' (2009) 23(1) International Relations 119, 120.
3 David Kennedy, 'The Disciplines of International Law and Policy' (1999) 12(1) Leiden Journal of International Law 9, 9 ff.
4 Tanja E. Aalberts, 'The Politics of International Law and the Perils and Promises of Interdisciplinarity' (2013) 26(3) Leiden Journal of International Law 503, 508.
5 Hikmahanto Juwana, 'Teaching International Law in Indonesia' (2001) 5(2) Singapore Journal of International and Comparative Law 412, 418.
6 Jay Feinman and Marc Feldman, 'Pedagogy and Politics' (1985) 73(3) Georgetown Law Journal 875, 930.

7 Shirley V. Scott, *International Law in World Politics: An Introduction* (3rd edn, Lynne Rienner Publishers 2017) ch 7.
8 Philip C. Jessup, *A Modern Law of Nations: An Introduction* (Macmillan 1948) 16. See also Stephen C. Neff, *Justice among Nations: A History of International Law* (Harvard University Press 2014) 483.
9 A.A. Fatouros, 'International Law and the Third World' (1964) 50(5) Virginia Law Review 783, 785.
10 Shirley V. Scott, 'International Law as Ideology: Theorizing the Relationship between International Law and International Politics' (1994) 5(3) European Journal of International Law 313, 317, 321.
11 Alison Pert, *Australia as a Good International Citizen* (Federation Press 2014) 216–217.
12 Stefan Talmon, 'The United States under President Trump: Gravedigger of International Law' (2019) 18(3) Chinese Journal of International Law 645, Title.
13 Allen Weiner, interview in José Alvarez, Curtis Bradley, Allen Weiner and Sarah Cleveland, 'The Politics of Teaching International Law' (9–12 April 2008) 102 Proceedings of the Annual Meeting (American Society of International Law) 305, 308.
14 Martti Koskenniemi, *International Law and the Far Right: Reflections on Law and Cynicism* (TMC Asser Press 2019) 26.
15 See, eg, Dorothea Anthony, 'The World Conference on Human Rights: Still a Guiding Light a Quarter of a Century Later' (2019) 25(3) Australian Journal of Human Rights 411, 421–423.
16 See Henry Burmester, 'Australia's Experience in International Litigation' in Natalie Klein (ed), *Litigating International Law Disputes: Weighing the Options* (Cambridge University Press 2014) 61, 73.
17 *Questions relating to the Seizure and Detention of Certain Documents and Data (Timor-Leste v Australia)*, Order on Provisional Measures, ICJ, 3 March 2014.
18 Dissenting Opinion of Judge ad hoc Callinan, *Questions relating to the Seizure and Detention of Certain Documents and Data (Timor-Leste v Australia)*, Order on Provisional Measures, ICJ, 3 March 2014, para 33.
19 Separate Opinion of Judge Cançado Trindade, *Questions Relating to the Seizure and Detention of Certain Documents and Data (Timor-Leste v Australia)*, Order on Provisional Measures, ICJ, 3 March 2014, para 1.
20 Gillian D. Triggs, *International Law: Contemporary Principles and Practices* (LexisNexis Butterworths 2006) 60.
21 ibid.
22 Antony Anghie, *Imperialism, Sovereignty and the Making of International Law* (Cambridge University Press 2004) 4.
23 Callinicos 1994, cited in China Miéville, *Between Equal Rights: A Marxist Theory of International Law* (Brill 2004) 226.
24 B.S. Chimni, interview in Silvia Steininger and Tom Sparks, 'On History, Geography, and Radical Change in International Law: An Interview with BS Chimni' *Völkerrechtsblog* (2 May 2018) <https://voelkerrechtsblog.org/de/on-history-geography-and-radical-change-in-international-law/> italics added.
25 ibid; B.S. Chimni, 'The Past, Present and Future of International Law: A Critical Third World Approach' (2007) 8(2) Melbourne Journal of International Law 499, 500.
26 Anghie (n 22) 274.
27 Surya Prakash Sharma, *Territorial Acquisition, Disputes and International Law* (Martinus Nijhoff Publishers 1997) 143.
28 Francis Anthony Boyle, *World Politics and International Law* (Duke University Press 1985) 293.
29 Daniel Bodansky, 'International Law in Black and White' (2006) 34(2) Georgia Journal of International and Comparative Law 285, 301.
30 ibid.

31 Cait Storr, 'Imperium in Imperio: Sub-Imperialism and the Formation of Australia as a Subject of International Law' (2018) 19(1) Melbourne Journal of International Law 335, 367.
32 Clinton Fernandes, *Island off the Coast of Asia: Instruments of Statecraft in Australian Foreign Policy* (Monash University Publishing 2018) 126, 176.
33 Written Statement of Australia, ICJ Advisory Proceedings on the Legal Consequences of the Construction of a Wall in the Occupied Palestinian Territory (29 January 2004); Written Statement of Australia, ICJ Advisory Proceedings on the Legal Consequences of the Separation of the Chagos Archipelago from Mauritius in 1965 (28 February 2018).
34 UN Security Council resolution 83, S/1511, 474th meeting (27 June 1950); UN Security Council resolution 84, S/1588, 476th meeting (7 July 1950).
35 UN Security Council resolution 665, 2938th meeting (25 August 1990); UN Security Council resolution 678, 2963rd meeting (29 November 1990); UN Security Council resolution 1441, 4644th meeting (8 November 2002). Note that it is open to debate whether the latter resolution authorises the use of force on Iraq.
36 UN Security Council resolution 770, 3106th meeting (13 August 1992).
37 A.J.M. van de Laar, *The World Bank and the Poor* (Martinus Nijhoff Publishing 1980) 12.
38 Dennis C. Canterbury, 'European Bloc Imperialism' (2009) 35(6) Critical Sociology 801, 804–805.
39 ibid 805.
40 Peo Hansen and Stefan Jonsson, 'Eurafrica: History of European Integration, "Compromise" of Decolonization' *EuropeNow* (1 March 2018) <https://www.europenowjournal.org/2018/02/28/eurafrica-history-of-european-integration-compromise-of-decolonization/>.
41 European Parliament of the European Union, 'European Parliament Resolution of 2 April 2009 on European Conscience and Totalitarianism' (2 April 2009).
42 North Atlantic Treaty (4 April 1949) art 5.
43 'Warning Against "Great Fracture", Secretary-General Opens Annual General Assembly Debate with Call to Avoid Zero-Sum Politics, Revive United Nations Values' *United Nations Meetings Coverage and Press Releases* (31 January 2020) <https://www.un.org/press/en/2019/ga12183.doc.htm>.
44 Kate Miles, 'International Investment Law: Origins, Imperialism and Conceptualizing the Environment' (2010) 21(1) Colorado Journal of International Environmental Law and Policy 1, 6–9.
45 ibid 19–20, 25.
46 ibid 34, 38.
47 Antonina Yermakova and Valentin Ratnikov, *What Are Classes and the Class Struggle?* (Progress Publishers 1986) 38.
48 L. Harry Gould, *Marxist Glossary and Philosophical Dictionary* (4th rev edn, Current Book Distributors 1967) 19.
49 Boris Putrin, Valentin Kochetkov (trs) and Selena Kotlobai (trs), *Political Terms: A Short Guide* (Novosti Press Agency Publishing House 1982) 11.
50 Miles (n 44) 29.
51 ibid 34–37; Dorothea Anthony, 'Resolving UN Torts in US Courts: Georges v United Nations' (2018) 19(2) Melbourne Journal of International Law 462, 474–475.
52 Pert (n 11) 217.
53 John N. Hazard, 'Soviet Union and International Law' (1948–1949) 43(5) Illinois Law Review 591, 606.
54 ibid.
55 Chen Tiqiang, 'The People's Republic of China and Public International Law' (1984) 8(1) Dalhousie Law Journal 3, 17.
56 ibid 18–19.

57 ibid 20.
58 Anthony (n 15) 420.
59 Athanassios Vamvoukos, 'Chinese and Soviet Attitudes toward International Law: A Comparative Approach' (1979) 5(2) Review of Socialist Law 131, 148.
60 ibid.
61 Anthony (n 15) 415.
62 B.S. Chimni, 'Prolegomena to a Class Approach to International Law' (2010) 21(1) European Journal of International Law 57, 82.
63 ibid.
64 Dorothea Anthony 'The Problematic Use of Human Rights Discourse in the Greek Crisis Debate' (2016) 5(2) ESIL Reflections <https://esil-sedi.eu/post_name-125/>.
65 Andreas F. Lowenfeld, 'On Teaching International Law' (1968) 1(1) New York University Journal of International Law and Politics 61, 64.
66 Neff (n 8) 481.
67 Benjamin S. Bloom, *Taxonomy of Educational Objectives: The Classification of Education Goals — Handbook 1: Cognitive Domain* (Longmans 1956).
68 Chimni (n 24).
69 Shirley Scott, 'Beyond Compliance: Reconceiving the International Law-Foreign Policy Dynamic' (1998) 19 Australian Year Book of International Law 35, 44–45.
70 See also Umut Ozsu, 'The Question of Form: Methodological Notes on Dialectics and International Law' (2010) 23(3) Leiden Journal of International Law 687, 697ff.
71 Dorothea Anthony, 'The Human Rights Principle of Indivisibility and Its Ideological Significance in the Contemporary Age' (PhD dissertation 2018) ch 2: Indivisibility as a Doctrine of Neutrality.

Part IV

Subverting Pathways to the Profession

13 Challenging BigLaw

Questioning the Dominant Discourse in Law Student Employment Aspirations

Nick James and Kana Nakano

I. Introduction

Claims by legal practitioners and media commentators that there are too many law schools graduating too many law students[1] are sometimes difficult to reconcile with the inability by many members of the community to readily access legal assistance.[2] Such claims are also difficult to reconcile with the demand for more legal practitioners in certain geographic regions[3] or with expertise in certain areas.[4] But what if the problem is not that there are too many law graduates competing for a dwindling number of jobs but that too many law graduates aspire to positions within a narrow band of the wide range of career options and employment opportunities available to them?[5]

This paper is an investigation into Australian law student career aspirations using discourse analysis, with a focus on the apparent assumption by many students that the best possible outcome of legal education is securing employment with a large law firm (the 'BigLaw narrative'). The paper is presented in five parts. In Part II, we explain and justify the use of discourse analysis to investigate the issue. In Part III, we describe and contrast two discourses relating to law student career aspirations: the BigLaw narrative and the alternative, pluralistic narrative. In Part IV, we consider the evidence in support of the dominance of the BigLaw narrative and identify the historical, social, and political contingencies that contribute to that dominance. In Part V, we evaluate the consequences of that dominance, both positive and negative. And finally, in Part VI, we propose some strategies for challenging and subverting the dominance of the BigLaw narrative.

We begin with an important clarification. This paper is not intended as a criticism of the decision to pursue employment with a large law firm. Such a decision has many potentially positive outcomes. Large law firms can be excellent places to develop a law graduate's expertise.[6] They have the potential to open doors to other career opportunities. Working for a large law firm can provide access to training and mentoring by highly experienced, highly accomplished practitioners.[7] The desire to secure a job with BigLaw is certainly understandable. But defining law school success in terms of one or more successful applications to a large law firm is something that many law students – and law schools – have been accepting without question for a long time, despite several harmful consequences. In this

DOI: 10.4324/9781003175216-17

paper, we investigate the role that law schools have played in perpetuating the BigLaw narrative and suggest some ways in which legal educators can subvert the dominance of BigLaw.

II. Discourse Analysis

The methodology used in this paper is discourse analysis with a Foucauldian flavour. Rather than seeking to identify the truth regarding law student career destinations, the focus is on the competition among different discourses about those destinations.[8]

A discourse is a coherent series of statements about a topic or theme dispersed across space and time. The statements may be written, oral, official, unofficial, informed, uninformed, serious, or humorous. They take the form of texts, images, conversations, behaviours, and practices. They are made by a variety of speakers, but they are united in their faith in certain fundamental 'truths'.[9]

Legal education itself is a nexus of competing discourses, each with its own set of fundamental beliefs about the purpose of law school. 'Doctrinal discourse' privileges legal doctrine by locating it at the core of the legal curriculum and by emphasising its intellectual rigour, academic value, and social importance. 'Vocationalism' claims that the content of the curriculum must be governed by its occupational utility. A 'liberal' approach to teaching and learning about law is one that insists that the law curriculum include not only the learning of rules and the development of legal skills but also exposure to the history, philosophy, politics, and culture of law. 'Corporatism' is a legal education discourse that is characterised by an emphasis on the accountability of academics, the efficiency of the teaching process, and the marketability of the university. These and other discourses compete to establish the 'truth' of legal education.[10]

The career destination discourses that are the subject of investigation in this paper sit within the broader legal education discourse of *vocationalism*. In many common law jurisdictions, including Australia, the earliest forms of University legal education were primarily vocational: the first law teachers were usually practitioners appointed to the university on a part-time basis, and lectures were generally given in the evenings to students who were studying part-time while completing articles of clerkship.[11] More recently, vocational discourse has had something of a resurgence, and the dominance of vocationalism within contemporary legal education – and within higher education generally – is readily apparent.[12] Governments frequently emphasise the importance of universities contributing to graduate employability and producing graduates capable of making substantial contributions to national productivity. Universities and law schools promote themselves to prospective students by emphasising their employability rates and the starting salaries of their graduates. Scholarship about curriculum reform frequently emphasises the importance of embedding practical skills within the law curriculum to ensure law students are adequately prepared for legal practice. Legal education scholarship abounds with examples of ways the law curriculum can be made more practical, clinical, and authentic, and law student employability can be enhanced. The vocational approach to teaching law is so widely advocated today that it appears to be taken for granted by many participants within the legal education enterprise that law schools exist primarily to educate the next generation of lawyers.[13]

The focus of this paper is upon the way the dualistic ('BigLaw v alternatives') and pluralistic narratives regarding law student career destinations co-exist and compete within the broader discourse of vocationalism. As a method for analysis of a phenomenon, discourse analysis is well suited to our post-modern era. Rather than assume a single, consistent, shared view of the world, it acknowledges the co-existence of multiple perspectives and explores the relationships between them without having to identify the 'correct' perspective.

Foucault reminds us that each discourse is much more than an expression of knowledge. It is also an expression of power: discourses shape our beliefs and, through our beliefs, our behaviours, and, ultimately, our subjective realities.[14] A discourse that aligns 'success versus failure' with 'a career with a large law firm versus other careers' is more than an abstract notion; it colours how law students see themselves and the world around them and influences many of the choices they make as they progress through life.

Foucault also reminds us of the value and importance of challenging dominant discourses.[15] As an expression of power, discourses often marginalize and subdue competing discourses,[16] and the more dominant a discourse, the more likely it is that subjects will limit themselves to a singular perspective and a singular truth. In an aspirationally pluralistic community, we have an obligation to question and challenge dominant discourses, identify marginalized discourses, and allow their stories to be heard. The status quo should always be challenged. The injustices and inequities that arise as a consequence of the dominance of a particular discourse – whether it be vocationalism, capitalism, neo-liberalism, feminism, or socialism – are perpetuated when that dominance is unchallenged. Those in the academy are often privileged to be able to critique discourses and other social phenomena from a secure position, and they have an obligation to question the dominant discourses that others may take for granted.[17]

III. The BigLaw Narrative

According to the pluralistic narrative, there are many career options available to law graduates upon the completion of their law degree, and arguably even more for those completing a double degree in law. For those seeking to become solicitors and practise law, the options include working for a top-tier law firm, a mid-tier law firm, a small law firm or a NewLaw firm, in the government sector, in the community sector, or for medium to large organisations as in-house counsel. They might choose to be a general practitioner or to specialise in a particular area of law such as commercial law, conveyancing, personal injury, criminal law, family law, or intellectual property law. They might pursue a career as a barrister, judge's associate, law clerk, or registrar. Graduates might seek employment in academia, legal publishing or politics or start their own business. Of course, there are also many options outside of legal practice where a law degree would also be beneficial.[18]

However, it seems to be the case that for many law students, the plurality of career destinations is presented and discussed as a simple duality: a position with a large law firm or 'something else', with the second option positioned as the less desirable outcome. We refer to this dualistic discourse in this paper as 'the BigLaw narrative'. It looks something like this:

> The best possible outcome of my time at law school is securing employment with an elite law firm. If I am good enough, if I work hard, get the best grades, participate in the right extra-curricular activities, and get good references from my law teachers, I will secure a position with one of the best law firms, and that will mean I have succeeded. If I can't get a position with a large law firm, or if I choose not to even try, I can probably find employment elsewhere, but it will mean I wasn't good enough for BigLaw, and that I have in some sense 'failed' law school.

Accepting the BigLaw narrative informs important career choices by law students. Even if they choose not to pursue a career with BigLaw, it informs how they feel about their career choices and career outcomes. It is potentially carried long into their careers, impacting their overall wellbeing. (It may even contribute to the 'cultural cringe' in the academy and the frequent deference by law schools to the profession generally and large law firms in particular.)

The BigLaw narrative and the dualism between a career in BigLaw and 'settling' for an alternative have been apparent within Australian law schools for a very long time. Consider the experiences of the two authors of this paper.

Nick graduated from law school in 1991. He had decided to study law because he received good grades in high school, he was encouraged to enrol in either medicine or law (because he could), and he did not want to be a doctor. He enrolled at a large public university. At the time, law schools in Australia focused almost entirely on teaching legal doctrine and did very little to prepare law students for legal practice. Support with the transition between law school and legal employment was limited to a noticeboard advertising various placement positions. On the basis of what he was told by other law students and by his academic instructors, Nick understood that he was supposed to apply for as many clerkships as possible, and success would be determined by the size of the firm that accepted his application. This notion was largely unquestioned by Nick and his fellow students, and Nick did not start to question it until he had been practising as a commercial lawyer for several years.

Kana graduated from law school in 2018. She had decided to study law to follow in her late father's footsteps. He would often express his passion to 'fight for the little guy', and this inspired Kana's interest in criminal and social justice issues and her desire to become a lawyer. With 'fighting for the little guy' in the back of her mind, areas of law such as intellectual property and media law initially piqued her interest. She eventually participated in an IP moot which led to other important and valuable learning experiences in other moot competitions. But at the same time, she began to feel the pull of BigLaw. Competitive mooting attracts some of the brightest law students in the cohort, and these students often aspire for a career with a top-tier law firm. Kana felt pressured to mimic their aspirations and applied for several clerkships. After completing the clerkships, Kana realised that a career with a top-tier firm was not for her, but she nevertheless felt crushed and ashamed when she did not receive any graduate offers from these firms.

The authors' personal stories appear to be consistent with the experiences of many law students, then and now. There is an abundance of anecdotal evidence that a large number of law graduates apply for a small number of graduate positions with large law firms every year,[19] and significant numbers of law students are, like Kana, 'crushed and ashamed' about the outcome of their efforts to secure employment with these firms.

Beyond the anecdotal, what evidence do we have of the prominence of the BigLaw narrative and the binary conception of law student career options? Unfortunately, no national graduation destination research has been done since Christopher Roper's work more than 20 years ago.[20] Roper's 1995 study challenged the view that the vast majority of law students intend to become lawyers: he found that only 35.8% of first-year law students and 48.2% of final-year law students aspired to become lawyers.[21] Roper also challenged the myth that law students only study law to earn a high income, as only 5% of first-year students and 4% of final-year students chose 'high income' as a reason to study law.[22] A subsequent study by Roper published in 2000, however, found that 'starting salary' and 'status of jobs' were considered very important by just over and just under 20% of law students, respectively, and that this proportion appeared to be increasing over time.[23] It also found that the majority of law graduates end up in the private legal profession, with substantially less in the public sector or in other roles in the private sector.[24]

Since Roper's work, there has been no comprehensive national study of law student career aspirations or destinations. There has been a handful of relevant state-level studies, but nothing conclusive. The Law Society of New South Wales (NSW) is tracking the career aspirations and destinations of law students in NSW and Australian Capital Territory, but no reports or conclusions have been published yet.[25] Monash University conducted a graduate destination survey in 2018, but no conclusions have been published, and there appears to have been no specific focus on law students.[26] While there are other university-specific data available,[27] studies attempted to be conducted,[28] and other types of data collected,[29] the results are not specific enough to make any meaningful conclusions about law student preferences and intentions.[30]

Where the dominance of the BigLaw narrative and the dualistic conception of law student career options is readily apparent is in the weight of demand by law students for a relatively small number of positions with large law firms. Media outlets such as *Lawyers Weekly* frequently publish stories about (and critical of) the high demand for graduate positions with large law firms.[31] According to the 2016 FLIP Report published by the NSW Law Society, 11,688 applications were received for the 2016 NSW Law Society summer clerkship program, and only 375 were accepted;[32] in the same year, 2,732 applications were received for the graduate employment program, with 46 acceptances.[33] While other states receive fewer applications than NSW, the discrepancy between the number of applicants and available positions is likely to be similar.

Given the breadth of options available to law graduates, why do so many aspire to one particular career pathway?

IV. Explaining the Dominance of BigLaw

In this section, we consider the range of possible explanations for the dominance of the BigLaw narrative. It is our contention that the BigLaw narrative's dominance is not the consequence of a single cause. Rather, it is the outcome of a range of historical and social contingencies consistent with that dominance.

We begin by positing that it must be more than mere ignorance by law students of the career options available to them. Contemporary law schools and organisations like GradAustralia go to considerable lengths to promote the pluralistic narrative and emphasise the wide range of job opportunities available to law graduates.[34] What, then, are the social and historical contingencies that facilitate the dominance of the BigLaw narrative?

One of these contingencies is the tendency of law students to be guided by extrinsic rather than intrinsic motivations, as documented in the wellness literature.[35] Law students often value money, status, and prestige over more intrinsic motivations such as wellbeing, satisfaction, and joy. This is reinforced by the rational desire to pay off student loans and recoup the substantial investment of time and money in their legal studies. According to the Australian Taxation Office, legal professionals are among the top 10 salary earners in Australia, and according to sites such as *Lexology*, while 'the average Corporate Lawyer salary in Australia will depend on their level of experience', an experienced corporate lawyer can earn an annual salary of over $200,000.[36] The widespread perception that a position with a large law firm is relatively lucrative is a significant factor in explaining the dominance of the BigLaw narrative.

There is the inherent competitiveness of law students and the desire to 'win' law school. This inherent competitiveness may stem from the fact that most law students were high-achievers in school and had to work even harder in law school to compete against other high-achievers.[37] For many, 'winning' law school equates to securing the best positions with the largest, most prestigious law firms. As one law student explained: 'One of my lecturers describes law school as being like the Hunger Games. . . . It can be quite cut-throat with everyone fighting for the same jobs at top law firms.'[38]

There is the impact of 'groupthink' and the herd mentality. Law schools in Australia appear to have a career funnelling effect, similar to that identified at Harvard and Stanford.[39] According to Barnes, one of the top reasons law students prefer large law firms is the fact that '[l]aw students and attorneys are risk averse and tend to follow the crowd – both this year's crowd and the shadow cast by earlier generations'.[40]

When students first enter law school, they are often unaware of the practicalities of legal practice and of the career options open to them upon graduation, leaving them open to be influenced by the assumptions of older students and the existing biases amongst the law school cohort. Students end up internalising this process of aiming for the few available top-tier jobs, reinforcing it to others, and distinguishing between 'worthy' and 'ordinary' careers. It is well established that prevailing social norms have a significant impact on human behaviour,[41] and the fact that the BigLaw narrative has been present in law schools for so long, and carries the weight of tradition, makes it difficult to ignore.

There is also an emphasis on larger law firms in legal media. Generally, high-profile cases which tend to concern larger companies will involve top-tier firms as their representatives. As a result, lawyer news is more likely to focus on news about top-tier firms rather than boutique firms.[42] Large law firm profiles and recruitment campaigns are also more prominent on social media.

Career advice for law students provided by law student associations and others often focuses upon 'the clerkship process', emphasises the prestige of a placement with a large law firm, and equates such a placement with law school success.[43] Even when a wider range of careers is presented to law students, the top-tier firms are often placed up front as the main or default option, with other careers described or subtly portrayed as 'alternative' careers.[44] Large law firms have the staff and resources that make it possible for them to send recruiters into law schools and advertise prominently in law careers guides, whereas smaller firms and other legal employers do not, thus ensuring those large law firms are more visible and more likely to be front-of-mind for law students. And when confronted by the potentially overwhelming range of career possibilities or by the challenge of learning more about less obvious career pathways, it is perhaps understandable that many law students favour the easier, more obvious option of applying for positions with large law firms.

There are other, more subtle ways in which the BigLaw narrative is reinforced. These subtle factors can still have a significant impact on law student perceptions, particularly on those law students who are the first in a family to attend law school or who are otherwise unfamiliar with the realities of legal practice and being a legal professional. Regardless of their level of awareness of legal practice, many students come to law school without a strong idea of what they want to do after graduation (including whether or not they even want to practise law), and their job preferences are consequently unstable and open to external influence.[45]

There is the subtle reinforcement that occurs in the ways academics design curriculum and assessment. Consider the ways in which lawyers are often portrayed in tutorial problems and exam questions. Consider the almost inevitable emphasis in the curriculum and assessment upon the decisions of appellate courts and other 'big cases' and the fact that they typically involve large law firms.[46]

There is the way law's 'signature pedagogies' – i.e. the manner in which law is typically taught and assessed – train law students to disassociate from their personal values and focus upon abstract legal rules.[47] It is this gradual disassociation from their personal values that facilitates the well-known phenomenon of law students entering law school intending to pursue a career working to achieve social justice and then graduating and seeking a position with a large law firm.[48]

There is subtle reinforcement in the marketing and promotional materials produced by law schools and universities, with their portrayal of legal academics, law students and law graduates in corporate attire and corporate contexts.[49] Similarly, portrayals of successful lawyers in popular culture – movies and television – often associate 'success' with being a corporate lawyer working for a large law firm. This is both fed by and reinforces the widespread public perception of lawyers and the definition of a 'successful' career in law.[50] This public perception influences the expectations of, and pressures exerted by, law students' families, and friends.[51]

Insidiously, the BigLaw narrative serves and reinforces the political status quo within the discipline and profession of law. The portrayal of employment with BigLaw as the epitome of law school success has obvious status advantages for those who are already employed by BigLaw, and BigLaw benefits from a state of affairs that sees the highest performing students competing for employment with large law firms. It is inevitable that BigLaw itself will use its influence over law school culture and curricula to maintain the dominance of the BigLaw narrative. Critical legal scholars were writing about this issue decades ago. Duncan Kennedy, for example, provocatively described legal education as training for hierarchy more than 30 years ago: 'Legal education structures the pool of prospective lawyers so that their hierarchical organisation seems inevitable, and trains them in detail to look and think and act just like all the other lawyers in the system'.[52]

Finally, and perhaps most insidiously, the dominance of the BigLaw narrative is strengthened by its consistency with neoliberal values generally. Neoliberalism is the dominant discourse of our time. The core values of neoliberalism include individualism and wealth maximisation.[53] The notion that law school success equates to securing the most well-paid employment (rather than personal well-being, social justice or contributions to the public good) is consistent with the neoliberal narrative.

V. Evaluating BigLaw's Dominance

The social and historical contingencies identified in the previous section explain BigLaw's dominance as a career destination for law graduates and the marginalisation of the pluralistic narrative by the BigLaw narrative. They do not, however, justify it. In this section, we critically evaluate that dominance, identifying both the positive implications and the negative.

Beginning with the positive, the BigLaw narrative does offer certain fairly obvious benefits and advantages. It is consistent with the notion of 'just desserts': those who work the hardest at law school become eligible for the greatest rewards (if one accepts that rewards are best defined in terms of income).

The BigLaw narrative also has a positive impact on law student motivation. The intense competition for a limited number of places with large law firms may motivate law students to work harder.[54] If they are then successful in securing a position with a top-tier firm, it will prepare them for what is likely to be a competitive working environment.[55]

The BigLaw narrative may even contribute to law students receiving a broader education. The competition for places with large law firms motivates law students to do what those employers appear to value, which today includes engaging in extra-curricular activities and developing their interpersonal skills.[56] (On the other hand, there is a likely divergence between what law firms want and what law students think law firms want.)[57]

There are benefits for the clients of the large law firms. They are usually obliged to pay the highest rates for the legal services they receive, and the BigLaw narrative's dominance usually ensures the lawyers in those firms are the law graduates with the highest grades (if one accepts that higher grades equate to a capacity to deliver higher quality legal services).

On the other hand, there are many reasons why the dominance of the BigLaw narrative is problematic. Firstly, it creates unrealistic expectations for law students regarding the outcome of their studies. The dominance of a career with BigLaw in law school teaching materials, marketing materials, the media, and popular culture creates an impression that many, perhaps most, law students can secure such a career and, as we have seen, that is not the case. The BigLaw narrative's dominance contributes to feelings of disappointment, dissatisfaction, and disillusionment on the part of those law graduates who find themselves in other types of employment.[58]

There is an impact on individual law student wellness. We have already touched upon the links between the BigLaw narrative and student wellness, including the stress of the competition for limited places and the impact of the loss of ideals and intrinsic motivation. There is also the stress and anxiety experienced by those who actually join a large law firm.[59] There is evidence that lawyers earning the highest salaries, typically in large law firms, are the most dissatisfied with their profession, while lawyers working for government agencies, public interest organisations, and educational institutions are among the most satisfied.[60]

There are then potential broader impacts that the focus on BigLaw has upon the profession and the wider community. The focus on securing employment with a large law firm distracts many law students from exploring other, equally if not more worthwhile and more satisfying, career options. Highly capable law students, who may have been able to have a significantly positive impact upon the community sector, working in remote communities, working in the public sector or specialising in non-corporate specialisations are lost to the large law firms, and if working for those firms does not work out, possibly lost to the profession entirely.[61] As one young corporate lawyer in the first three years of their career explained, while he was prepared to 'work hard' for a career in BigLaw, he felt exploited and '[t]hat's why you see a lot of junior lawyers resign after two or three years. They've seen how the system works . . . and they leave'.[62]

Finally, there is the potential for the dominance of the dualistic discourse to validate and reinforce base motivations like greed, selfishness, vanity, aggression, unhealthy competition, and narcissism. We have already referred to the alignment between the BigLaw narrative and the neoliberal emphasis on individualism and wealth maximisation. Widespread acceptance of the BigLaw narrative has the potential to reinforce those values for the wider cohort of law students, even those who do not end up working for a large law firm. Competition is more highly regarded than cooperation, and a large salary is more highly regarded than working selflessly to help others.[63]

VI. Challenging BigLaw

Given the dominance of the BigLaw narrative has both positive and negative implications, not everyone will be inclined to challenge it. But for those who are so inclined, what can be done? We conclude this chapter by briefly considering how the BigLaw narrative might be challenged and subverted to create a space for alternative, marginalized discourses to emerge.

What seems clear is that the dominance of the BigLaw narrative is unlikely to be subverted by simply telling those who subscribe to the dominant discourse that they are misguided. Telling law students that they are wrong to aspire to a position with a large law firm, or at least wrong to think that that is the definition of law school success, is unlikely to persuade law students to alter their beliefs or their career aspirations. As Foucault reminds us, power always provokes resistance, and such an explicit effort to change students' beliefs will provoke explicit resistance.[64]

There are some less explicit but nevertheless obvious strategies likely to be more successful, such as reconsidering the emphasis placed upon careers with large law firms in careers guides, at careers workshops and conferences, and in employer presentations. Although this can be challenging if the large law firms are the sponsors of these guides, workshops and conferences, we are already seeing a greater willingness on the part of career advisors and others to reposition BigLaw in relation to other career possibilities.[65]

There are also subtler strategies. Direct criticisms of aspirations for large salaries[66] or careers with large law firms are unlikely to be effective, particularly from those disinclined to question neoliberal values. An alternative approach to subversion is to emphasise and empower the competing discourses, including those that emphasise the plurality of employment options, intellectual gratification, intrinsic motivations, wellness and satisfaction, and contribution to the public good.[67]

The subtler strategies include reviewing the way legal careers and lawyers are portrayed in teaching and assessment. Not every tutorial problem, exam problem or moot scenario needs to involve lawyers from large law firms. We could endeavour to balance these traditional types of problems with problems that use scenarios involving sole practitioners, boutique firms, government lawyers, legal app developers and others.

Subtler strategies also include reviewing the way law students and lawyers are portrayed in law school promotional materials. We could challenge the stereotypical portrayal of law students and law graduates and supplement the usual images of corporate lawyer types with less traditional images of other types of legal professionals – or even law graduates who are using their expertise in entirely different fields and industries.

The challenge is considerable. Discourses do not surrender their dominance easily, and as we have seen, there are many contingencies that support the BigLaw narrative's dominance. There are many law students, legal academics and legal practitioners who will question, challenge and even oppose efforts to decentre BigLaw. But at a time when the notions that universities exist solely to produce employable graduates[68] and that employment success equates to the level of salary[69] are so prominent as to be taken for granted by so many, it is crucial that we remind our law students that there are other ways of seeing themselves and their futures. We should strive to reassure law students that not every graduate needs to work for BigLaw . . . or even needs to become a lawyer. We also need to remind them that a professional aspires to serve the public good, and a university education is about much more than securing well-remunerated employment. We need to redefine law school success, not necessarily by replacing the existing definition with a new one, but by creating space for law students to define it for themselves.

Notes

1 See eg Tom McIlroy, '"Too Many Kids Are Doing Law": Malcolm Turnbull Warns Against Law Degrees' *The Australian Financial Review* (Australia, 2 February 2018) <https://www.afr.com/politics/too-many-kids-are-doing-law-malcolm-turnbull-warns-against-law-degrees-20180202-h0sc6h> accessed 2 June 2021; Emma Ryan, 'Universities Must Be "Held Accountable" for Law Grad Oversupply' *Lawyers Weekly* (Australia, 13 February 2018) <https://www.lawyersweekly.com.au/sme-law/22737-universities-must-be-held-accountable-for-law-grad-oversupply> accessed 2 June 2021; Emma Ryan, 'Frustration Grows Over Unis "Cashing In" on Law Grad Oversupply' *Lawyers Weekly* (Australia, 19 February 2018) <https://www.lawyersweekly.com.au/sme-law/22768-frustration-grows-over-unis-cashing-in-on-law-grad-oversupply> accessed 2 June 2021. See also, Francine Ryan, 'Too Many Law Students Not Enough Jobs: How to Stand Out' *Lawyer Monthly* (26 June 2018) <https://www.lawyer-monthly.com/2018/06/too-many-law-students-not-enough-jobs-how-to-stand-out/> accessed 2 June 2021; Steven J. Harper, 'Too Many Law Students, Too Few Legal Jobs' *New York Times* (New York, 25 August 2015) <https://www.nytimes.com/2015/08/25/opinion/too-many-law-students-too-few-legal-jobs.html> accessed 2 June 2021.

2 For Australian claims see Michael McNamara, 'University Legal Education and the Supply of Law Graduates: A Fresh Look at a Longstanding Issue' (2018) 20 Flinders Law Journal 223; Fiona McLeod, '160,000 People Turned Away: How the Justice System is Failing Vulnerable Australians' *ABC News* (Australia, 3 August 2017) <https://www.abc.net.au/news/2017-08-03/how-the-justice-system-is-failling-vulnerable-australians/8770292> accessed 2 June 2021. For examples of similar claims made elsewhere, the International Journal of the Legal Profession dedicated a special issue to the topic of 'Too Many Lawyers' in 2012; see also, Fatos Selita, 'Improving Access to Justice: Community-based Solutions' (2019) 6 Asian Journal of Legal Education 83; Ling Yee Wong, 'Is This the Paradox of Access to Civil Justice? Too Many Lawyers, But Too Few in Civil Courts?' *University of Auckland* (19 November 2020) <https://www.thebigq.org/2020/11/19/is-this-the-paradox-of-access-to-civil-justice-too-many-lawyers-but-too-few-in-civil-courts/> accessed 2 June 2021; Ruth Green, 'Access Denied: Britain's Broken Justice System' *International Bar Association* (13 February 2020)

<https://www.ibanet.org/article/0AE14E9C-A4D7-49D1-B482-0808A4B6AF6A> accessed 2 June 2021; Debora L. Rhode, Kevin Eaton and Anna Porto, 'Access to Justice Through Limited Legal Assistance' (2018) 16 Northwestern Journal of Human Rights, Art 1, 2.

3 Simon Rice, 'Access to a Lawyer in Rural Australia: Thoughts on the Evidence We Need' (2011) 16(1) Deakin Law Review 13; Lisa R. Pruitt and others, 'Legal Deserts: A Multi-State Perspective on Rural Access to Justice' (2018) 13 Harvard Law & Policy Review 15, 120; Raymond H. Brescia, 'Using Technology to Improve Rural Access to Justice' (2018) 17 Government Law & Policy Journal; Robin Runge, 'Addressing the Access to Justice Crisis in Rural America' 40(3) Human Rights Magazine 15.

4 Emma Ryan, 'Talent Shortage in Aussie Law Firms "As Acute As Ever"' *Lawyers Weekly* (Australia, 28 August 2018) <https://www.lawyersweekly.com.au/biglaw/23921-talent-shortage-in-aussie-law-firms-as-acute-as-ever> accessed 2 June 2021.

5 McNamara suggests that this is as a result of the 'legal profession's inability to efficiently accommodate higher number of aspiring new entrants' See McNamara (n 2) 230.

6 'Large vs Small Law Firms – What's Right for Your Legal Career' *College of Law* (6 February 2014) <https://www.collaw.edu.au/news/2016/11/14/large-vs-small-law-firms-whats-right-for-your-legal-career> accessed 2 June 2021.

7 Naomi Neilson, '"Top of Their Game": What It's Like to Work as a BigLaw Graduate' *Lawyers Weekly* (Australia, 11 January 2021) <https://www.lawyersweekly.com.au/biglaw/30394-top-of-their-game-what-it-s-like-to-work-as-a-biglaw-graduate> accessed 2 June 2021.

8 Rabinow explains Foucault's approach as follows: 'During most of the 1960s, Foucault sought, in a variety of ways, to isolate and analyse the structures of the human sciences treated as discursive systems. It is important to stress that Foucault did not see himself as a practitioner of these human sciences. They were his object of study. Foucault never took these discourses from the inside. That is, he never posed the question of the truth or falsity of the specific claims made in any particular discipline. Although he traced with great patience the discursive systems of the sciences of life, language and labour, his aim was not to unveil the truths they had discovered or the falsities they had propounded. Rather, once again, it was the effective operation of these disciplines – how and around what concepts they formed, how they were used, where they developed – that was Foucault's prey. The problem became how to analyse the statements of the social sciences without judging their "progress" or lack of it, and without reducing their relative discursive and conceptual autonomy to something else seen to be more basic.' Paul Rabinow, 'Introduction' in Paul Rabinow (ed), *The Foucault Reader* (1st edn, Pantheon Books 1986) 6.

9 Gavin Kendall and Gary Wickham, *Using Foucault's Methods* (1st edn, Sage 1999) 42; see also Alan Hunt and Gary Wickham, *Foucault and Law: Towards a Sociology of Law as Governance* (1st edn, Pluto Press 1994).

10 This is a perspective on legal education explained in more detail in Nickolas James, 'Australian Legal Education and the Instability of Critique' (2004) 28 Melbourne University Law Review 1.

11 Dennis Pearce and others, *Australian Law Schools: A Discipline Assessment for the Commonwealth Tertiary Education Committee* (Commonwealth Tertiary Education Committee, 1987) 3–4.

12 Nick James, 'Why Has Vocationalism Propagated So Successfully in Australian Law Schools?' (2004) 6 University of Notre Dame Australia Law Review 41.

13 Nick James, 'More than Merely Work-ready: Vocationalism Versus Professionalism in Legal Education' (2017) 40 University of New South Wales Law Journal 186.

14 Michel Foucault, *The Will to Knowledge: The History of Sexuality 1* (1st edn, Penguin Press 1998) 101. Foucault insisted that discourses are more than the expression of

particular truths, discourses actually produce those truths; they are 'practices that systematically form the objects of which they speak.' Michel Foucault, *The Archaeology of Knowledge* (2nd edn, Routledge 2002) 54.

15 Keith Hoskin, 'Foucault under Examination: The Crypto-Educationalist Unmasked' in Stephen J. Ball (ed), *Foucault and Education: Disciplines and Knowledge* (1st edn, Routledge 1990) 29. Foucault believed that 'the real political task in a society such as ours is to criticise the working of institutions which appear to be both neutral and independent; to criticise them in such a manner that the political violence which has always exercised itself obscurely through them will be unmasked, so that one can fight fear.' Quoted in Paul Rabinow (n 8) 6.

16 Alan Hunt and Gary Wickham (n 9) 9.

17 For a more comprehensive examination of the subversive potential of teaching and the obligations of educators, see Neil Postman and Charles Weingartner, *Teaching as a Subversive Activity* (1st edn, Doubleday & Co 1969).

18 For examples of texts consistent with the pluralistic narrative, see *Beyond Law* <https://beyondlaw.com.au/>; Naomi Nelson, 'Graduate to Employee: The Law Student's Guide to Securing a Legal Career' *Lawyers Weekly* (Australia, 24 August 2020) <https://www.lawyersweekly.com.au/newlaw/29256-graduate-to-employee-the-law-student-s-guide-to-securing-a-legal-career> accessed 2 June 2021; 'Career Options for Lawyers' *College of Law* (2021) <https://www.collaw.edu.au/your-career/career-options-for-lawyers> accessed 2 June 2021; Kate Allman, '10 Jobs You Can Do With a Law Degree' *Law Society of New South Wales* (2021) <https://www.lawsociety.com.au/resources/resources/career-hub/10-jobs-you-can-do-law-degree> accessed 2 June 2021.

19 See eg, Law Society of New South Wales, *Future Prospects of Law Graduates: Report and Recommendations* (Report, 2015) ('*Future Prospects of Law Grads Report*') <https://www.lawsociety.com.au/legal-communities/law-students/law-graduates-report> accessed 2 June 2021, 10–14.

20 See Christopher Roper, *Career Intentions of Australian Law Students* (Report, Centre for Legal Education April 1995); Maria Karras and Christopher Roper, *The Career Destinations of Australian Law Graduates: First Report of a Five-year Study* (University of Newcastle 2000); Sumitra Vignaendra, *Australian Law Graduates Career Destinations* (Report, Commonwealth of Australia 1998).

21 Roper (n 21) 75–77.

22 Roper also warned of drawing any conclusions from this because people tend to give more altruistic reasons than real reasons. See ibid 51.

23 Karras and Roper (n 21) 35.

24 ibid 63.

25 Law Society of New South Wales, *Future Prospects of Law Grads Report* (n 19); Law Society of New South Wales, *Annual Report 2018* (Report 2018) <https://www.lawsociety.com.au/sites/default/files/2018-12/Annual%20Report%202018.pdf> accessed 2 June 2021, 15–17.

26 See <https://www.monash.edu/law/news-and-events/events/past-events/2018/2018-employability-and-graduate-destination-survey> accessed 26 November 2019.

27 See Australian National University, *2016 Graduate Outcomes Survey (GOS): ANU College of Law* (Report 2016) <https://unistats.anu.edu.au/surveys/GOS/COL_2016_GOS_Results_Employment_Outcomes_with_Appendix.pdf> accessed 2 June 2021; Australian National University, *Graduate Destination Report 2015: ANU College of Law* (Report 2015); Melissa Castan and others, 'Early Optimism – First Year Law Students' Work Expectations and Aspirations' (2010) 20 Legal Education Review 1.

28 M.J. Le Brun, Julie McMillan and Gary Tamsitt, 'Bringing Knowledge About the Career Destinations of Law Graduates into 21st Century Law Schools in Australia: A Summary of What is Proposed' (Australian Law Teachers' Association Conference, Sydney, 2009) 1.

29 *Queensland Law Society Annual Report 2017–18* (Report, 7 September 2018) <https://www.qls.com.au/About_QLS/Queensland_Law_Society/Resources_publications/Corporate_documents/Annual_Reports> accessed 2 June 2021; 'Our Members', (*Queensland Law Society*) <https://www.qls.com.au/About_QLS/Queensland_Law_Society/Our_members> accessed 2 June 2021; Graduate Careers Australia, *GradStats: Employment and Salary Outcomes of Higher Education Graduates from 2017* (Report, February 2018) <http://www.graduatecareers.com.au/wp-content/uploads/2018/01/GradStats-2017-3.pdf> accessed 2 June 2021; Quality Indicators for Learning and Teaching, *2018 Graduate Outcomes Survey: National Report* (Report, January 2019) <https://www.qilt.edu.au/docs/default-source/default-document-library/qilt-gos-national-report-2018.pdf?sfvrsn=23f7ec3c_0> accessed 2 June 2021.

30 A 2018 New Zealand study conducted at four different universities over the span of the law students' degree concluded that there was an identifiable, albeit small, decline in interest in careers in private practice and an increase in interest in other career options such as in-house and government roles. Lynne Taylor and others, *The Making of Lawyers: Expectations and Experiences of Fourth Year New Zealand Law Students* (Report, March 2018) <https://ako.ac.nz/assets/Knowledge-centre/RHPF-s1607-Developing-a-law-student-profile/4593e48e35/RESEARCH-REPORT-The-Making-of-Lawyers-Expectations-and-Experiences-of-Fourth-Year-New-Zealand-Law-Students.pdf> accessed 2 June 2021.

31 See eg McIlroy (n 1); Ryan, 'Universities Must be "Held Accountable" for Law Grad Oversupply' (n 1); Ryan, 'Frustration Grows Over Unis 'Cashing In' on Law Grad Oversupply' (n 1).

32 Law Society of New South Wales, *Future Prospects of Law Grads Report* (n 20) 10–11.

33 ibid 10, 13.

34 See eg 'Career Pathways' (*University of Melbourne*, 2021) <https://law.unimelb.edu.au/students/career-services/career-pathways> accessed 2 June 2021; GradAustralia, *The Law Careers Handbook 2020–2021* (vol 4, May 2020) <https://gradaustralia.com.au/library/2020/sector-guide-law> accessed 2 June 2021.

35 Kennon M. Sheldon and Lawrence S. Krieger, 'Does Legal Education Have Undermining Effects on Law Students? Evaluating Changes in Motivation, Values and Well-Being' (2004) 22 Behavioural Sciences and the Law 261; Kennon M. Sheldon and Lawrence S. Krieger, 'Understanding the Negative Effects of Legal Education on Law Students: A Longitudinal Test of Self-Determination Theory' (2007) 33 Personality and Social Psychology Bulletin 883.

36 Astor Legal, 'Lawyer Salary Australia – How Much Do Lawyers Make in Australia?' (*Lexology*) <https://www.lexology.com/library/detail.aspx?g=2b078407-0194-48cb-b6ed-db13e818935c> accessed 11 June 2021.

37 Gerald F. Hess, 'Heads and Hearts: The Teaching and Learning Environment in Law School' (2002) 52 Journal of Legal Education 75, 78.

38 Quoted in Matthew Jenkin, 'Legally Drained: Why Are Stress Levels Rising Among Law Students?' *The Guardian* (19 November 2019) <https://www.theguardian.com/law/2019/nov/19/legally-drained-why-are-stress-levels-rising-among-law-students> accessed 21 June 2021.

39 Amy J. Binder, Daniel B. Davis and Nick Bloom, 'Career Funnelling: How Elite Students Learn to Define and Desire "Prestigious" Jobs' (2016) 89 Sociology of Education 20–39.

40 Harrison Barnes, 'Top 10 Reasons Most Law Students and Lawyers Prefer Large, Famous Firms' *(BCG Attorney)* <https://www.bcgsearch.com/article/900043069/Top-10-Reasons-Most-Law-Students-and-Lawyers-Prefer-Large-Famous-Firms/> accessed 2 June 2021.

41 Uri Gneezy and Aldo Rustichini, 'A Fine is a Price' (2000) 29 The Journal of Legal Studies 1.

42 See eg Naomi Nelson, 'The Top Law Firms Graduates Want to Work With' *Lawyers Weekly* (Australia, 24 February 2020) <https://www.lawyersweekly.com.au/biglaw/27542-the-top-law-firms-students-want-to-work-with> accessed 2 June 2021; Ynah Edillor, 'Here Are the Top Six Australian Law Firms Based on Revenue' (*Australasian Lawyer*, 10 March 2020) <https://www.thelawyermag.com/au/practice-areas/corporate-and-ma/here-are-the-top-six-australian-law-firms-based-on-revenue/216328> accessed 2 June 2021.

43 See eg University of the Sunshine Coast Law Students Association, 'Careers Guide' (2019) <https://static1.squarespace.com/static/55ca7217e4b0077057183ae4/t/5cb2da9bc830257d56386198/1555225364812/LSA+Career+Guide.pdf> accessed 2 June 2021 (note in particular the advertisement on page 6); 'Careers' (*University of Queensland Law Society Inc*, 2021) <https://www.uqls.com/careers> accessed 2 June 2021.

44 Note the emphasis upon BigLaw in the ordering of the chapters in GradAustralia, *The Law Careers Handbook 2020–2021* (n 35).

45 Aaron Haas, 'The Rationality of Law Students' Career Choices' (2006) 10 Richmond Journal of Law and the Public Interest 54, 58.

46 Assessment activities such as negotiations and moots also have the potential to increase competitiveness among law students, contributing to the competitive need to strive for the best or most prestigious job. Helen Stallman, 'A Qualitative Evaluation of Perceptions of the Role of Competition in the Success and Distress of Law Students' (2012) 31 Higher Education Research & Development 891, 892.

47 Hess (n 38) 77.

48 Matthew Ball, 'The Construction of the Legal Identity: "Governmentality" in Australian Legal Education' (2007) 7 Queensland University of Technology Law and Justice Journal 444.

49 See eg, UQ People, 'UQ Master of Laws – A Postgraduate Program Custom-Built to You' (*University of Queensland*, 30 October 2020) <https://future-students.uq.edu.au/stories/uq-master-laws-postgraduate-program-custom-built-you> accessed 2 June 2021.

50 Victoria S. Salzmann and Philip T. Dunwoody, 'Prime-Time Lies: Do Portrayals of Lawyers Influence How People Think about the Legal Profession' (2005) 58 Southern Methodist University Law Review 411.

51 Haas (n 46) 60.

52 Duncan Kennedy, 'Legal Education as Training for Hierarchy' in David Kairys (ed), *The Politics of Law: A Progressive Critique* (Pantheon Books 1990) 72.

53 Nick James, 'Distracting the Masses: Corporate Convictions and the Legitimisation of Neo-liberalism' (2008) 8 Macquarie Law Journal 179.

54 Kennon M. Sheldon and Lawrence S. Krieger (n 36) 261.

55 Abby Young-Powell, '"Toxic, Cut-Throat": The Work Culture Awaiting Junior Lawyers' *The Guardian* (London, 14 December 2018) <https://www.theguardian.com/law/2018/dec/13/toxic-vile-cut-throat-the-work-culture-awaiting-junior-lawyers> accessed 2 June 2021.

56 Ynah Edillor, 'What Are the Soft Skills Needed by Top Lawyers?' *Australasian Lawyer* (22 February 2020) <https://www.thelawyermag.com/au/practice-areas/workplace-relations-and-health-and-safety/what-are-the-soft-skills-needed-by-top-lawyers/214603> accessed 2 June 2021; Nicholas Waight, 'Advice for New Law Students from a Recent Graduate' *Lawyers Weekly* (Australia, 28 February 2019) <https://www.lawyersweekly.com.au/careers/25130-advice-for-new-law-students-from-a-recent-graduate> accessed 2 June 2021.

57 See eg, Mita Gulati and David B. Wilkins, 'What Law Students Think They Know About Elite Law Firms: Preliminary Results of a Survey of Third Year Law Students' (2001) 69 University of Cincinnati Law Review 1213.

58 Jane Lee, 'Graduates Shun Legal Profession' *The Age* (Melbourne, 20 May 2012) <https://www.theage.com.au/national/victoria/graduates-shun-legal-profession-20120519-1yxt0.html> accessed 2 June 2021.

59 See eg Hannah Wootton, 'Law Students Push Back on "Torture" of Long Hours Culture' *The Australian Financial Review* (Australia, 25 November 2019) <https://www.afr.com/companies/professional-services/law-students-push-back-on-torture-of-long-hours-culture-20191121-p53cur> accessed 2 June 2021; Jerome Doraisamy, 'Why Do Firms Continue to Treat Applicants Like Dirt?' *Lawyers Weekly* (Australia, 3 November 2019) <https://www.lawyersweekly.com.au/biglaw/26832-why-do-firms-continue-to-treat-applicants-like-dirt> accessed 2 June 2021.

60 Haas (n 46) 54, citing Ken Dau-Schmidt and Kaushik Mukhopadhaya, 'The Fruits of Our Labors: An Empirical Study of the Distribution of Income and Job Satisfaction Over the Legal Profession' (1999) 49 Journal of Legal Education 342.

61 Quoted in Lee (n 59).

62 Natasha Gillezeau and Elouise Fowler, 'What It's Like Working as a Young Corporate Lawyer at a Top Tier Firm' *The Australian Financial Review* (25 January 2019) <https://www.afr.com/work-and-careers/workplace/what-it-is-like-working-as-a-young-corporate-lawyer-at-a-top-tier-firm-20181212-h190vt> accessed 2 June 2021.

63 Lawrence S. Krieger, 'What We're Not Telling Law Students – and Lawyers – That They Really Need to Know: Some Thoughts-In-Action Toward Revitalizing the Profession from its Roots' (1998–99) 13 Journal of Law and Health 1; D. Paulhus, 'The Dark Triad of Personality: Narcissism, Machiavellianism, and Psychopathy' (2002) 36 Journal of Research in Personality 556; Thomas Connelly, 'Research: Law Students Are Sociable But Selfish' (*Legal Cheek*, 28 January 2016) <https://www.legalcheek.com/2016/01/research-students-studying-law-are-more-likely-to-be-selfish/> accessed 2 June 2021.

64 Foucault wrote: 'Where there is power there is resistance, and yet, or rather consequently, this resistance is never in a position of exteriority in relation to power. . . . These points of resistance are present everywhere in the power network.' Michel Foucault, 'The Order of the Discourse' in Robert Young (ed), *Untying the Text: A Post-Structuralist Reader* (Routledge & Kegan Paul 1981) 48, 96. See also Michel Foucault, 'Power and Strategies' in Colin Gordon (ed), *Power/Knowledge: Selected Interviews and Other Writings 1972–1977* (Pantheon Books 1980) 134, 142.

65 For example, see the balanced representation of careers in GradAustralia, *The 2019–20 Law Guide: Your Complete Guide to Careers with a Law Degree* (Guide, 2019) <https://gradaustralia.com.au/library/2019/sector-guide-law> accessed 2 June 2021; Australian National University Law Students' Society, *Career Guide 2020* (Guide, 19 March 2020) <https://issuu.com/anulss/docs/careers_guide_draft_15> accessed 2 June 2021.

66 In any event, there are many careers outside of BigLaw that remunerate graduates as well as, if not better than, large law firms.

67 See eg 'Finding Work' (*Social Justice Opportunities*) <https://www.sjopps.net.au/looking-for-a-job/> accessed 2 June 2021; Nick Chowdrey, 'I'm Studying Law – But I Don't Want to Be a Lawyer' *The Guardian* (30 May 2014) <https://www.theguardian.com/law/2014/may/30/students-alternative-careers-law-degree> accessed 2 June 2021; Lisa Gazis, 'Those Who Can, Leave' *Lawyers Weekly* (Australia, 4 March 2013) <https://www.lawyersweekly.com.au/news/12223-those-who-can-leave> accessed 2 June 2021.

68 See eg Andrew Trounson, 'Grim Jobs Outlook for New Graduates' *The Australian* (Australia, 24 July 2015) <http://www.theaustralian.com.au/higher-education/grim-jobs-outlook-for-new-graduates/news-story/3d6a774ebb995dc9ba3f178c721d50d5>

accessed 2 June 2021; Hamish Coates, 'Employability: Time for Higher Education Sector to Step Up' *The Australian* (Australia, 25 November 2015) <http://www.theaustralian.com.au/higher-education/opinion/employability-time-for-higher-education-sector-to-step-up/news-story/bf2846cd3079752a796fc5981f9a239c> accessed 2 June 2021. Cf Zena Hitz, 'Why Rebranding Higher Education as "Job Training" is an Offence to Humanism' (*New Statesman*, 21 August 2020) <https://www.newstatesman.com/politics/education/2020/08/why-rebranding-higher-education-job-training-offence-humanism> accessed 2 June 2021.

69 'Graduate Employment' (*Quality Indicators for Learning and Teaching*) <https://www.qilt.edu.au/qilt-surveys/graduate-employment> accessed 2 June 2021. See also Margaret Thornton and Lucinda Shannon, '"Selling the Dream": Law School Branding and the Illusion of Choice' (2013) 23 Legal Education Review 249, 257–265.

Index

Note: Page numbers in *italic* indicate a figure and page numbers in **bold** indicate a table on the corresponding page.